Cookies
biscuits, bars
and brownies

Cookies
biscuits, bars
and brownies

The complete guide to making, baking
and decorating cookies and bars,
with over 150 delicious recipes

Catherine Atkinson
with recipes by Valerie Barrett
and Joanna Farrow

LORENZ BOOKS

This edition is published by Lorenz Books

Lorenz Books is an imprint of Anness Publishing Ltd
Hermes House, 88–89 Blackfriars Road, London SE1 8HA
tel. 020 7401 2077; fax 020 7633 9499
www.lorenzbooks.com; info@anness.com

© Anness Publishing Ltd 2003

This edition distributed in the UK by The Manning Partnership Ltd, 6 The Old Dairy,
Melcombe Road, Bath BA2 3LR; tel. 01225 478 444; fax 01225 478 440
sales@manning-partnership.co.uk

This edition distributed in the USA and Canada by National Book Network,
4720 Boston Way, Lanham, MD 20706; tel. 301 459 3366; fax 301 459 1705
www.nbnbooks.com

This edition distributed in Australia by Pan Macmillan Australia, Level 18,
St Martins Tower, 31 Market St, Sydney, NSW 2000; tel. 1300 135 113
fax 1300 135 103; customer.service@macmillan.com.au

This edition distributed in New Zealand by David Bateman Ltd, 30 Tarndale Grove,
Off Bush Road, Albany, Auckland; tel. (09) 415 7664; fax (09) 415 8892

A CIP catalogue record for this book is available from the British Library.

Publisher: Joanna Lorenz
Managing Editor: Linda Fraser
Senior Editor: Susannah Blake
Editorial Reader: Jay Thundercliffe
Production Controller: Steve Lang
Photographers: Frank Adam and Craig Robertson
Home Economists: Angela Boggiano, Silvana Franco and Jenny White
Stylist: Helen Trent
Designer: Paul Oakley

10 9 8 7 6 5 4 3 2 1

NOTES

Bracketed terms are intended for American readers.

For all recipes, quantities are given in both metric and imperial measures and, where
appropriate, measures are also given in standard cups and spoons. Follow one set, but not
a mixture, because they are not interchangeable.

Standard spoon and cup measures are level.
1 tsp = 5ml, 1 tbsp = 15ml, 1 cup = 250ml/8fl oz

Australian standard tablespoons are 20ml. Australian readers should use 3 tsp in place of
1 tbsp for measuring small quantities of gelatine, flour, salt, etc.

Medium (US large) eggs are used unless otherwise stated.

Contents

The Cookie-making Tradition   6

The Art of Cookie Making   8

Cookie Ingredients   10

Equipment   18

Methods of Making Cookies   24

Drop Cookies   28

Rolled Cookies   31

Piped Cookies   34

Pressed Cookies   37

Bar Cookies   40

Short-cut Cookies   44

Baking Cookies   48

Cookie Decoration   50

Cookie Fillings   58

Storing Cookies   60

Presentation and Packaging   62

Teatime Treats   66

Cookies for Kids   82

Kids' Party Pieces   98

Celebration Cookies   114

Wholesome Bites   130

Chocolate Heaven   144

Ultimate Indulgence   162

Dessert Cookies   176

Brownies and Bars   192

No-bake Cookies   210

Cookies for Special Diets   224

Savoury Crackers   236

Index   252

The Cookie-making Tradition

Left: *There is little so wonderful as sitting down to a cup of tea and a plate of freshly baked cookies.*

No matter what age you are, there's little so enjoyable as a freshly baked cookie. They always feel like the ultimate treat, despite the fact that they're so simple to make. Cookies, in one form or another, have been around for centuries and some of the most popular cookies today derive from these original treats.

AN AMERICAN INVENTION

The term cookie was first used in the United States when early Dutch settlers brought their *koekje* (little cakes) to New York. At about the same time, wood-burning and coal-fired ovens were introduced, which made baking more reliable and the popularity of cookies and cookie-making soon spread.

Eastern European, Scandinavian and British immigrants who settled in the United States all made great contributions to the cookie-making tradition. For example, refrigerator cookies originated from German Heidesand cookies, which are made by shaping the dough into long, sausage-shaped rolls, cutting them into thin, round slices and then baking them.

In other parts of the world, the word for (and meaning of) cookie varies. In Scotland, a cookie is a sweetened bread bun that is either filled with whipped cream or thickly iced. In Britain and France, cookies are known as biscuits, while in the United States, the term biscuit is used to describe a large, soft scone.

EARLY COOKIES

There are differences in opinion about the origins of the word biscuit, but whether it is derived from the French *cuit* or from the Latin *biscoctus*, all agree that it means twice-cooked.

Originally, cookies were double-baked. They were browned for a few minutes when the oven was at its hottest, then removed and returned to finish baking when the oven was cooling down. This time-consuming process dried out the cookies so that they kept well – essential in the days before airtight containers were available. At this time, not all cookie batters were baked; some were fried into wafers.

Rusks and ship's biscuits, which needed to keep for several months, were also baked in this way. The dough was first baked, then cooled, sliced, and dried in a gentle heat until crisp; Italian *biscotti* are still made in this way.

During the Middle Ages, improvements were made. Sugar and spices were added to biscuits, to make them more palatable and, in the late Middle Ages, it was discovered that adding beaten egg to biscuit dough made the finished cookie lighter and that ground nuts could be used instead of flour. This led to the creation of meringue, sponge and macaroon cookies.

Cookie mixtures changed significantly in the 18th and 19th centuries. The tradition of baking rusks and frying cookies virtually disappeared – although in parts of Europe, India and the Middle East some cookies are still fried today – and enriched short cakes became very popular. These rich, buttery doughs still form the basis of many modern cookies.

Although savoury cheese biscuits (crackers) have their origins in medieval times, plain, savoury biscuits were not created until the 18th century. These later developed into salted crackers and cocktail savouries for nibbling with drinks.

During the 19th century, with the availability of cheap sugar and flour and chemical raising agents such as bicarbonate of soda (baking soda), cookie factories were able to open up. As the quality of factory-made cookies improved, more and more people began to buy rather than make their own cookies.

COOKIE-MAKING TODAY

In more recent years, consumers have started to turn away from foods containing artificial additives. Commercial cookies have become less popular and there has been a resurgence in home-baking.

Time-saving kitchen devices such as food mixers have helped to speed up cookie-making, and the widely available range of more unusual ingredients has opened up the possibilities for the modern cook who can make just about any cookie they want.

With the help of this book, you can learn everything you will ever need to know about cookie-making – from the basic techniques to the perfect cookie to serve with coffee, put in a lunchbox or offer as a gift.

CLASSIC COOKIES

Anzac A crunchy cookie from New Zealand, named after the Australia and New Zealand Army Corps (ANZAC). It is made with butter, golden (light corn) syrup, rolled oats and coconut.

Bath Oliver A hard, crisp savoury cracker created as a health product by Dr W. Oliver of Bath, England, in 1730.

Digestive/Graham cracker Also known as sweetmeal or wheatmeal, this moderately sweet cookie is made with brown flour. Despite its name, it has no special digestive properties.

Maria Popular in Spain, this thin, plain crisp cookie was created in England to celebrate the wedding of the Grand Duchess Maria of Austria to the Duke of Edinburgh.

Fortune Cookie During the Ming Dynasty, political resisters baked cookies containing messages detailing secret meetings and plans. The idea was revived in San Francisco in the 19th century.

Below: Modern fortune cookies contain predictions of the future.

Above: Maryland cookies are one of the most popular and well-known types of chocolate chip cookie.

Jumble Well-known as early as the 17th century, this cookie was originally flavoured with rose water, aniseed or caraway seeds and tied into knots. The mixture is now made into S-shapes.

Petit Beurre This plain, crisp French cookie has been made in Nantes since the 1880s. It was created by Louis Lefevre-Utile and is also known as LU or *P'tit lu*.

Shortbread Scottish shortbread evolved from 16th-century short cakes. The main ingredients are usually flour, sugar and butter. Petticoat tails are shortbread baked in a round, named after the shape of an outspread petticoat.

Snickerdoodle A Pennsylvanian Dutch speciality, this spicy cookie contains nutmeg, nuts and raisins.

Chocolate Chip Cookies These are absolute classics; two of the best-known being Toll House cookies and chocolate chip Maryland cookies.

The Art of Making and Baking Cookies

Cookies are simple to make but there is some basic know-how that will make cookie-making even easier. This chapter explains everything you will ever need to know – from basic equipment and ingredients to making, shaping and baking different types of cookie dough; decorating and storing cookies; and making pretty cookie gifts for friends and family.

Cookie Ingredients

Most cookies are made from a few basic ingredients – butter, sugar, flour and sometimes eggs and other ingredients and flavourings. To make the best cookies, always use really fresh, good quality ingredients.

BUTTER

Unsalted (sweet) butter is best for making cookies; it has a sweet, slightly nutty taste and a firm texture, which is particularly well-suited to cookies made using the the rubbed-in method.

The temperature of butter is important. For rubbed-in cookies butter should be cold and firm but not too hard; take it out of the refrigerator 5 minutes before using. To cream butter, it should be at room temperature. This is very important if you are beating by hand. If you forget to take butter out of the refrigerator in advance, soften it in the microwave on low power for 10–15 seconds.

If you need to melt butter, dice it so that it melts more quickly and evenly. Melt the butter over a very low heat to prevent it burning

and remove it from the heat when it has almost melted; the residual heat will complete the job. If you need to brush baking tins (pans) or sheets with melted butter, use unsalted butter rather than salted, which tends to burn and stick.

STORING BUTTER

Butter should be stored in the refrigerator or freezer. It can absorb other flavours easily so protect it from strong-smelling ingredients by wrapping tightly in greaseproof (waxed) paper or foil. If possible, store in a separate compartment.

Salted butter can be stored in the refrigerator for about a month but unsalted butter should be used within 2 weeks. Alternatively, you can store unsalted butter in the freezer and transfer it to the refrigerator 1–2 days before you need it. All butter can be frozen for up to 6 months.

Left: Unsalted butter produces cookies with a wonderfully rich flavour and warm golden colour.

Above: White vegetable fat (left) and block margarine (right) work well in some cookie recipes.

OTHER FATS

Margarine This won't produce the same flavour as butter but it is usually less expensive and can be used in the same way. Block margarines are better for cookie-making, although soft margarine may be used for creaming.

White cooking fats Made from blended vegetable oils or a mixture of vegetable and animal or fish oils, white fats are flavourless and create light, short-textured cookies. They work well in highly flavoured cookies, in which you wouldn't taste the butter. Lard is an opaque white fat made from rendered pork fat and features in some traditional cookie recipes.

Oil This may sometimes be used instead of solid fat. Sunflower and safflower oils are preferable as they are light in colour with a mild taste. Olive oil has a distinctive flavour but may be added to savoury crackers.

SUGAR

There are many different types of sugar, all of which add their own distinctive character to cookies.

REFINED SUGARS

Produced from sugar cane and sugar beet, refined white sugar is 99.9 per cent pure sucrose.

Granulated sugar This has large granules and can be used in rubbed-in mixtures or to make a crunchy cookie topping.

Caster/superfine sugar This is the most frequently used sugar for cookie-making. It has a fine grain so is ideal for creaming with butter. It is also used for melted mixtures, meringue toppings and sprinkling over freshly baked cookies.

Icing/confectioners' sugar
This fine, powdery sugar is used to make smooth icings and fillings and for dusting cookies. It may also be added to some piped mixtures.

Soft brown sugar This is refined white sugar that has been tossed in molasses or syrup to colour and flavour it; the darker the colour, the more intense the flavour. It makes moister cookies than white sugar, so never substitute one for the other.

UNREFINED SUGARS

Derived from raw sugar cane, these retain some molasses. They often have a more intense flavour but tend to be less sweet than refined sugars.

Golden caster/superfine sugar and granulated sugar These are pale gold and are used in the same way as their white counterparts.

Demerara/raw sugar This rich golden sugar has a slight toffee flavour. The grains are large so it is only used in cookie doughs if a crunchy texture is required. It is good for sprinkling over cookies before they are baked.

Above: *(Left to right) Soft brown sugar and demerara (raw) sugar give cookies a slightly caramel taste.*

Muscovado/molasses sugar
This fine-textured, moist soft brown sugar may has a treacly flavour.

STORING SUGAR

Sugar should always be stored in an airtight container. If white sugar forms clumps, break it up with your fingers. If brown sugar dries out and hardens, warm it in the microwave for about 1 minute.

OTHER SWEETENERS

There are many other ingredients that can be used as sweeteners.

Golden/light corn syrup Slightly less sweet than sugar, this produces moist, sticky cookies and is often used in no-bake recipes.

Maple syrup Thinner than golden syrup, this has a distinctive flavour.

Honey Use blended honey in cookie doughs as the flavour of milder honeys will be lost.

Malt extract This concentrated extract made from barley has a distinctive flavour, thick consistency and dark, almost black colour.

Molasses A by-product of sugar refining, molasses looks like malt extract but has a slightly bitter taste.

Above:
Coarse-grained granular sugar is good for sprinkling.

Left: *Fine-grained caster sugar is widely used in cookie doughs.*

FLOUR

Most cookie recipes use plain (all-purpose) flour as it has a low gluten content, resulting in a crumbly texture. The grains are processed then treated with chlorine to make the flour whiter. You can also buy unbleached flour, which has a greyish colour. Some flour is pre-sifted but you should sift it anyway as the contents tend to settle during storage. Flour, even the same type and brand, may vary slightly, so always hold a few drops of liquid back in case they aren't needed.

SELF-RAISING FLOUR

Known as self-rising flour in the United States, this flour contains raising agents that make cookies spread and rise, giving them a lighter texture. If you run out of self-raising flour, you can substitute plain flour, adding 5ml/1 tsp baking powder to each 115g/4oz/1 cup. Self-raising flour should not be kept for longer than 3 months because raising agents gradually deteriorate.

WHOLEMEAL FLOUR

Also known as whole-wheat flour, this is milled from the entire wheat kernel and contains all the nutrients and flavour of wheat. It is coarser than white flour, giving a heavier result. It absorbs more liquid than white flour so recipes should be adjusted if wholemeal flour is used.

Brown (wheatmeal) flour, contains only 80–90 per cent of the bran and wheat germ and has a finer texture and milder taste.

Above: Rice flour is often added to shortbread to give a crumbly texture.

Left: Cornmeal produces cookies with a golden colour, delicious flavour and distinctive texture.

Left: Wholemeal (whole-wheat) flour gives cookies a lovely taste.

NON-WHEAT FLOURS

These can be great for cookie making, although some should be combined with wheat flour.

Potato flour This fine powder is made from potato starch and can be mixed with wheat flour to give a lighter texture to cookies.

Chestnut flour This light brown, nutty flavoured flour is made from ground chestnuts and is often sold in Italian delicatessens.

Cornmeal Also known as polenta or maizemeal, this is bright yellow and coarse or medium ground.

Cornflour/cornstarch This fine white powder is made from the middle of the maize kernel. It is often used in piped cookie mixtures to give a smooth texture.

Soya flour Made from soya beans, this has a distinctive nutty flavour. It has a high protein content. Medium- and low-fat varieties are available.

Rice flour This is made by finely grinding polished white rice and is used in many cookie recipes, to give a short, slightly crumbly texture.

GLUTEN-FREE BAKING

Some people are allergic or intolerant to the protein gluten, which is found in both wheat and rye. Specially produced gluten-free and wheat-free flour mixtures can be used for baking, as can any of the naturally gluten-free flours such as cornmeal, potato flour, rice flour and soya flour.

Above:
Bicarbonate of soda (baking soda) and baking powder give cookies a lighter texture.

RAISING AGENTS

Although cookies are usually made with plain (all-purpose) flour, raising agents may be added to give them a lighter texture. Raising agents make cookies spread more, so space them well apart for baking.

Raising agents react when they come in contact with water and produce carbon dioxide bubbles that make the cookie rise during baking. Cookie doughs containing raising agents must therefore be shaped and baked as soon as liquid is added. Store raising agents in a dry place and use within their use-by date because they deteriorate with age, becoming less effective.

Baking powder This is a mixture of alkaline bicarbonate of soda (baking soda) and an acid such as cream of tartar.

Bicarbonate of soda/ baking soda This can be added to a cookie mixture that contains an acidic ingredient.

Right: *Eggs are widely used in cookie-making and can help to produce rich, golden cookies with a great flavour.*

EGGS

These are used to enrich cookie doughs and bind dry ingredients. They are often included in rolled doughs because they prevent the mixture from spreading too much during baking. If a recipe does not specify the size of an egg, use a medium (US large) one.

For baking, eggs should be at room temperature; cold egg yolks may curdle and cold egg whites will produce less volume when whisked. Add eggs to a creamed mixture a little at a time, beating after each addition and adding 15ml/1 tbsp sifted flour if the mixture starts to curdle. Whisk egg whites in a very clean bowl and use straight away.

BUYING AND STORING EGGS

Always check the use-by date on eggs and never buy cracked, damaged or dirty eggs. A fresh egg will have a round, plump yolk and a thick white that clings closely to the yolk. Store eggs in the refrigerator, pointed-end down. Do not store near strong-smelling foods or possible contaminants such as raw meat; their shells are porous and can absorb odours and bacteria.

SEPARATING EGGS

Some recipes require only an egg yolk or an egg white. Egg separating devices are available from kitchenware stores but it is easy to separate eggs by hand.

1 Tap the middle of the egg sharply against the rim of a bowl, then, holding the egg over the bowl, prise the shell apart with the tips of your thumbs.

2 Gently tip the white into the bowl, retaining the yolk in the shell. Tip the yolk into the other half-shell, letting any remaining white fall into the bowl.

Cook's Tip
You can also separate the yolk from the white by tipping the whole egg into the palm of your hand and letting the white drain into a bowl through your fingers.

FRUIT, NUTS AND SEEDS

Dried, candied and crystallized fruit, nuts and seeds can be added to cookie doughs to add flavour, colour and texture, or to decorate.

DRIED FRUIT

The drying process intensifies the flavour and sweetness of the fruit. Adding dried fruit does not affect the moisture of the dough so you can usually subsitute one type of dried fruit for another in a recipe.

Vine fruit These include sultanas (golden raisins), raisins and currants. Buy seedless fruit, choosing a reliable brand or go for fruit in clear bags so that you can check its softness and colour. As dried fruit ages, a white coating may develop; it is still usable, but you should never buy it in this condition. It can be kept in an airtight container for up to a year, but is best used within 6 months. Some brands are lightly tossed in oil before packing to keep the fruits separate; uncoated vine fruits may stick together and should be pulled apart before adding to cookies.

Apricots These are produced in California and other parts of the American Pacific coast, Australia, South Africa, Turkey and Iran. Some are very dry and need to be soaked in a little liquid before using; others, usually labelled ready-to-eat, have a softer texture and sweeter flavour and are generally better for cookie-making. After picking and stoning (pitting), the fruits may be treated with sulphur dioxide to retain their colour and prevent mould growing.

Unsulphured apricots, which are darker in colour and very sticky, are also available; they should be stored in the refrigerator.

Apples and pears Dried in rings or as halved fruit, these have a chewy texture. They are best used finely chopped and added to drop cookie mixtures.

Tropical fruits Exotic fruits such as papaya and mango are available dried and have an intense flavour and vibrant colour. They are often sold in strips, which can be easily chopped with a sharp knife or snipped into small pieces with a pair of scissors. Dried pineapple and dried banana are also available and make a tasty addition to cookies.

Left: Dried fruit such as apricots and pears make a delicious, healthy addition to cookies.

Above: *Crystallized fruit such as glacé cherries and angelica can be used both as ingredients to flavour cookies and as decorations.*

Cranberries and sour cherries These are brightly coloured and add a wonderful sweet-and-sour flavour to cookies. They make a very good addition to festive cookies.

Candied and crystallized fruit Fresh fruits such as whole pitted cherries and apricots or pieces of kiwi and pineapple are steeped in sugar. The process retains the original bright colour of the fruit. Angelica, the bright green stem of the herb, is candied in this way. Because of their pretty colour, candied and crystallized fruit are usually used to decorate cookies rather than in the dough.

Crystallizing fruit takes a long time, making the fruit expensive. Candied citrus peel is cheaper and can be bought ready-chopped. However, make sure that chopped candied peel is still soft and moist as it can dry out quickly; it is better to buy whole pieces of candied peel and chop or slice it as required.

NUTS

These can be added to cookie mixtures or chopped and sprinkled over unbaked cookies. Always buy really fresh nuts in small quantities, then chop as necessary. Store in an airtight container, ideally in the refrigerator or freezer.

Almonds Sweet almonds are available ready-blanched, chopped, split, flaked (sliced) and ground.

Brazil nuts These wedge-shaped nuts are actually a seed. Their creamy white flesh has a sweet milky taste and a high fat content. Store carefully and use within a few months. They can be grated.

Cashew nuts These kidney-shaped nuts are always sold shelled and dried. They have a sweet flavour and almost crumbly texture.

Coconut White, dense coconut flesh is made into desiccated (dry unsweetened shredded) coconut and flakes. It is also possible to find sweetened shredded coconut, which is good for decorating cookies.

Below: Hazelnuts have a lovely nutty taste and can be used whole or chopped into small pieces.

Hazelnuts These are particularly good chopped and toasted, as this brings out their flavour.

Macadamia nuts Also known as Queensland nuts, these round, white, buttery nuts are native to Australia but are now also grown in California and South America.

Peanuts Strictly speaking, these are a legume not a nut, as they grow underground. Peanuts may be used raw or roasted, but do not use salted nuts unless specified.

Pecan nuts These are rather like elongated walnuts in appearance, but with a milder, sweeter flavour.

Pine nuts These are the fruits of the stone pine, which grows in the Mediterranean. Small and creamy coloured, they have an almost oily texture and aromatic flavour.

Pistachio nuts Bright green in colour, these are often used for decorating cookies.

Walnuts These are well flavoured with a crunchy texture. In the United States there are several types: white walnuts or butternuts, the large pale-shelled variety called English or Californian, and strong-flavoured, black-shelled walnuts.

SKINNING NUTS

To make skinning easier, either roast or blanch the nuts first.

To roast nuts, spread them out in a single layer on a baking sheet and roast at 180°C/350°F/ Gas 4 for 10–12 minutes, until the skins split and the nuts are golden. Tip the nuts on to a clean dishtowel and rub gently to loosen and remove the skins.

To blanch nuts, place in a bowl, pour over boiling water and leave for 5 minutes. Drain, then slip them out of their skins.

SEEDS

These are a popular ingredient in wholesome cookies and savoury crackers. They can be added to cookie doughs to give a crunchy texture or sprinkled over the tops of cookies before they are baked to give an attractive finish. Sesame and poppy seeds work particularly well because of their small size. However, larger seeds such as sunflower seeds work just as well.

Left: Sunflower and pumpkin seeds can be added to cookie doughs or sprinkled over unbaked cookies.

COOKIE FLAVOURINGS

There are many flavourings that can be added to cookies. They may add a subtle or strong taste, and some can also add texture.

CHOCOLATE

From cocoa-flavoured drop cookies to chocolate chip and chocolate-coated varieties, chocolate is the most popular cookie flavouring.

Dark/bittersweet chocolate

This has a bitter flavour and is the most popular chocolate for cookie-making. The degree of bitterness depends on the percentage of cocoa solids. Continental dark chocolate contains a minimum of 70 per cent cocoa solids so it is ideal for very sweet, sugar-laden cookies. Plain (semisweet) chocolate contains at least 50 per cent cocoa solids; the eating variety may contain as little as 25 per cent. It can be chopped and added to cookie doughs, but does not melt well.

Milk chocolate This contains milk powder and a higher percentage of sugar than plain chocolate. It is more difficult to melt.

White chocolate This contains no cocoa solids, only cocoa butter, milk solids and sugar. Some cheaper brands use flavourings and vegetable oil in place of cocoa butter. Brands that contain more cocoa butter are best for baking and melting. White chocolate may caramelize during baking due to its high sugar content.

Couverture This fine-quality plain, milk or white chocolate is used by professional cooks, and can be bought from specialist stores and by mail order. It melts beautifully and makes glossy cookie coatings.

Chocolate chips or dots These tiny chocolate pieces melt well and are easy to work with. The milk and white versions are more stable than bars of milk and white chocolate.

Chocolate cake covering This usually contains little real chocolate and is flavoured with cocoa powder. It melts well and is good for coating cookies, but has a poor flavour.

Unsweetened cocoa powder

This bitter, dark powder can be added to cookie mixtures or dusted over the tops. (Drinking chocolate contains about 25 per cent cocoa powder and 75 per cent sugar. It is not suitable for baking.)

Complementary flavours

Chocolate can be combined with many other flavourings. The most subtle is vanilla, which often goes unnoticed, yet greatly enhances the taste and aroma of chocolate. The bitterness of coffee can offset

Above: Chocolate – in its many forms – is a popular cookie ingredient.

the sweetness of chocolate, and caramel works well, especially if the sugar is cooked until it is dark, as this helps to reduce some of its sweetness. Both mint and orange add a subtle tang to chocolate cookies, and are especially good for fillings, frostings and icings; nuts are a classic addition.

STORING CHOCOLATE

Chocolate should always be wrapped in foil and kept in a dry, cool place. In hot weather, chocolate can be kept in the refrigerator but it may develop a whitish bloom; this is the cocoa butter rising to the surface. The chocolate will still be safe to use and won't alter the flavour of cookies but it can affect the final texture of the cookies.

SPICES AND HERBS

Adding spices to cookies is a great way to add flavour. Warm spices such as cinnamon, ginger and nutmeg are mainly used in sweet cookies, while whole spice seeds such as cumin and fennel and ground ones such as coriander and chilli are great in crackers.

Vanilla is perhaps the spice most frequently added to sweet cookies, providing a fragrant, delicate flavour. Vanilla sugar is one of the easiest ways to add the flavouring. Pure vanilla essence (extract), which is distilled from vanilla pods (beans), is also a good way to add the flavour. Vanilla flavouring is a synthetic product and may not actually contain any real vanilla.

Fresh or dried herbs can be added to savoury cookie doughs or sprinkled on top before baking.

Above: *Grated citrus rind can be added to cookie doughs to give them a lovely zesty citrus taste.*

Some, such as rosemary, are highly pungent and should be used sparingly. Milder herbs such as mint are good in fillings, and mint essence (extract) can be added to doughs.

Above: *Fresh mint can be added to delicately flavoured cookies and fillings to give them a fresh, aromatic flavour.*

OTHER FLAVOURINGS

There are also a great many cookie flavourings that do not fit into a particular category. These include grated lemon, lime or orange rind, the juice of citrus fruits, rose water, orange flower water and almond essence (extract),

ALCOHOL

Spirits, sherry and liqueurs can be added to cookie mixtures instead of liquid such as milk. They can also be used to soak dried fruit. During baking the alcohol will evaporate, leaving a subtle flavour. They can also be used in glacé icings.

SALT

This helps to bring out the flavour in both sweet cookies and crackers, but add only the tiniest pinch, especially if using salted butter. Coarse crystals of sea salt can be used to sprinkle over savoury cookies to decorate.

Equipment

Most cookies can be made with nothing more sophisticated than weighing scales or calibrated measuring cups, a mixing bowl, fine sieve, rolling pin, wooden spoon, baking sheet and a wire rack. However, there are a few pieces of equipment that can make cookie-making even easier.

Electric gadgets can really speed up the whole cookie-making process and more specialist equipment such as cookie presses, shortbread moulds and piping bags can produce really professional-looking cookies.

BOWLS

Large bowls are good for mixing doughs, while medium and small heatproof bowls are good for melting butter or chocolate and beating eggs. Small and medium bowls are also useful if you need to measure out ingredients beforehand. Some people may argue that a copper or steel bowl is desirable for whisking egg whites to their maximum volume but, for cookie-making, this really is not necessary.

Left: *An electric food mixer takes the hard work out of cookie-making and can be a real time saver.*

Above: *A set of different sized, heatproof bowls for mixing, beating and melting ingredients is invaluable when making cookies.*

ELECTRICAL APPLIANCES

Food mixers and processors are great for creaming together butter and sugar and for beating in eggs. However, if these machines are used, dry ingredients should always be folded in by hand as it is very easy to over-mix cookie dough, which will spoil the final texture.

A food processor is particularly useful for chopping and grinding large quantities of nuts and some come with a mini bowl specifically made for such tasks.

A hand-held electric whisk can be used for beating eggs, whisking egg whites and beating together butter and sugar and it has the advantage that it can be used in a pan over heat. Choose one with three speeds and beaters that can be removed for easy cleaning.

Above: *Flexible palette knives and spatulas make cookie-making easier.*

MEASURING SPOONS, JUGS AND CUPS

A set of accurate measuring spoons is essential. Ordinary spoons vary in size so invest in a commercially produced set. For measuring larger volumes of dry ingredients and liquids, you will need a clearly calibrated measuring jug (cup). They are available in glass, plastic and stainless steel. Use a glass measuring jug for hot liquids; plastic may soften and stainless steel conducts heat.

Below: *A set of special measuring spoons and jugs or measuring cups are essential for successful baking.*

SIEVES

You should invest in a set of strong, fine sieves in at least two sizes; a large one for sifting dry ingredients such as flour, and a smaller one for dusting icing (confectioners') sugar or (unsweetened) cocoa powder over baked cookies. You can also buy dredgers with a very fine mesh or tiny holes in the top for dusting with icing sugar or cocoa powder but a sieve works just as well.

Below: *A set of strong, fine-wire sieves will prove invaluable for cookie-making and last a lifetime.*

SPATULAS

A flexible rubber or plastic spatula can be used to scrape every last morsel of cookie dough from the mixing bowl. They are also very useful for folding dry ingredients such as flour into a creamed or whisked mixture.

PALETTE KNIVES AND METAL SPATULAS

Wide and round-bladed palette knives and metal spatulas are essential for lifting cookies from baking sheets and can also be used for mixing liquid into cookie doughs and mixtures. Small ones are very useful for spreading cookie fillings and icing on to cookies.

WHISKS

A wire balloon whisk or hand-held rotary whisk are useful for whisking egg whites for cookies such as macaroons and for whipping cream to use in fillings. They are also good for removing lumps in icing.

Below: *The flexible wires of a balloon whisk will incorporate air into everything from eggs to cream.*

ROLLING PINS

These come in all shapes and sizes, some with handles and some without. Rolling pins are usually made of wood but they are also available in marble. Mini rolling pins are sometimes available, which are perfect for small children who want to help out in the kitchen. Hollow plastic rolling pins, designed to be filled with iced water, are also available. These have no special advantage over ordinary rolling pins, providing the cookie dough is sufficiently chilled before rolling out.

PASTRY BOARDS

These flat, smooth boards are good for rolling cookie dough out to an even thickness. They are made from many different materials including wood, toughened glass and marble, which remains cool to the touch however warm the weather.

Smooth, laminated plastic kitchen surfaces provide a good alternative to a separate pastry board but take care not to scratch the surface when using cookie cutters and sharp knives.

BAKING SHEETS

These are either entirely flat or have a lip along the length of one side; baking trays have a lip all around the edges. Baking sheets are preferable as they allow better air movement around the cookies, but be careful when removing cookies from the oven because they can slip off easily.

Always measure your oven before buying baking sheets to make sure they will fit. Large sheets will allow you to bake more cookies in each batch but there needs to be a small gap at either side and at the back of the baking sheet so that heat can circulate. Although

non-stick varieties may save greasing or lining with greaseproof (waxed) paper, crisp cookies may not crisp quite so well on them and soft ones may spread out too much.

When buying baking sheets, always choose good-quality, heavy ones; they won't buckle in high temperatures, distort the shape of your cookies or develop hot-spots, which might cause burning. A good baking sheet can last you a lifetime. Avoid baking sheets that are very dark as they absorb more heat, which means cookies burn more easily. Dark baking sheets are intended for other kinds of baking such as bread-baking.

Below: Wooden rolling pins are efficient, inexpensive and very easy to clean.

Left: Baking sheets can vary greatly in size, colour and quality.

TINS/PANS

These are available in many shapes and sizes from round, square and rectangular to petal-shaped. They are used for baking cookie doughs such as shortbread and bar and brownie mixtures. The cookies should be marked into squares, bars or wedges while warm, then cut and removed from the tin when cool. If possible, use tins with a dull finish rather than shiny aluminium ones, as they will give your cookies a crispier texture.

To bake bar cookies, use a rectangular tin measuring 28 × 18cm/ 11 × 7in or a square tin measuring 20 × 20cm/8 × 8in. (If you do not have a tin, you can use an ovenproof glass dish. However, this will not produce such good results and the oven temperature will need to be reduced slightly because glass takes longer than metal to heat up, but retains more heat when removed from the oven.

Below: Wire racks are available in all shapes and sizes.

WIRE RACKS

After baking, most cookies should be transferred to a wire rack to cool. The rack allows air to circulate, preventing trapped warmth turning into moisture and making the cookies soggy. Some cookies should be left on the baking sheet for a few minutes to firm up before transferring to a wire rack.

TIMERS

These are absolutely essential for baking. Even an extra 1 or 2 minutes in the oven can result in overbaked or burnt cookies. Many modern ovens are already fitted with a timer, but if you do not have an oven with a timer, it is well worth investing in one. The simplest timers have a rotating dial that registers any time up to 60 minutes. They are fairly accurate and are perfectly suitable for baking cookies. Modern, digital timers are very useful and accurate and will help ensure that your cookies are removed from the oven at exactly the right time. These small timers also have the advantage that you can take them with you if you need to go into another room while your cookies bake.

Above: Cookie dough can be pressed into tins to make squares and bars.

Above: Digital timers are inexpensive and help to ensure perfect baking.

COOKIE CUTTERS

These come in many different shapes and sizes from the simplest plain or fluted round cutters to people-, animal-, heart- and flower-shaped ones. You will also find tiny cutters that can be used for *petits fours* and savoury cocktail snacks, and multi-sided cutters that have six different shapes arranged around a cube.

For the best results, cutters should be sharp enough to give a clear, precise outline. The top side of the cutter will usually have a smooth, rounded finish for pressing down on.
More intricate cutters will retain their shape better if they have a handle on them as this helps to keep the cutter rigid.

Below: Metal cutters are better for cookie-making than plastic ones, which can compress the cut edges.

Below:
Pretty shortbread moulds are usually carved from sycamore wood, which gives a sharp outline.

SHORTBREAD MOULDS

You can buy shortbread moulds that are decorated with intricate patterns. These are perfect if you are making shortbread for a special occasion or if you are making shortbread to offer as a gift. The moulds are usually made of wood. The classic shortbread mould is traditionally engraved with a Scottish thistle motif and is usually about 18cm/7in in diameter.

They are simple to use; all you need to do is press the dough into the mould with the tips of your fingers, level off the surface with a palette knife and then turn out on to a baking sheet for baking.

Above: An aluminium cookie press comes with a choice of patterned discs to create different shapes.

COOKIE PRESSES

Soft cookie dough can be shaped using a cookie press. The presses look like an icing syringe and work in a similar way. The dough is forced through a disc, which shapes the dough into a pretty cookie.

Right: *Piping (pastry) bags can be filled with dough and used to make cookie shapes, or filled with icing and used to decorate baked cookies.*

PIPING/PASTRY BAGS AND NOZZLES

A medium to large piping bag and a selection of both plain and fluted nozzles is useful for piping uncooked cookie dough. Smaller piping bags are extremely good for decorating baked cookies with icing or buttercream.

Originally, piping bags were made of water-proofed canvas but these tended to weep and were difficult to wash; now piping bags are made of nylon. Look for bags that are double stitched along the seams as well as glued to avoid leakage or splitting. You can also buy disposable piping bags, which are ideal for piping fine lines of melted chocolate or icing as decoration. (A small plastic bag with the corner snipped off makes a good substitute if you don't have a piping bag.)

PASTRY BRUSHES

These brushes are used for glazing unbaked cookies with milk or beaten egg, or baked cookies with a thin sugar glaze. They can also be used for brushing surplus flour from rolled cookie dough and for greasing baking sheets with oil.

The best pastry brushes have natural bristles fixed in a wooden handle, although nylon bristles are

sometimes considered more hygienic. Brushes that have been used for egg glazing should be rinsed in cold water before washing in hot soapy water. Flick them dry and leave to air before using again.

Below: *A pastry brush is very useful for brushing unbaked cookies with a milk or beaten egg glaze.*

PASTRY WHEELS

These make quick work of cutting rolled dough into squares, rectangles or diamonds, although some skill is needed to create even-sized cookies. They are particularly good for young children who want to help with cutting out cookie shapes. They are easy to use and do not have a sharp blade. They are available from kitchenware stores and are either made from wood or stainless steel, and have a plain or fluted blade. (A pizza cutter can be used in the same way.)

Below: *A fluted pastry wheel gives a pretty zigzag edge to rectangular, square and diamond-shaped cookies.*

Methods of Making Cookies

There are many different ways of making cookie dough. Depending on the type of cookie you are baking, the method will vary, so it is useful to know all the techniques.

THE CREAMING METHOD

A wide variety of cookies are made using the creaming method. These include plain Shrewsbury cookies, French sablés, fork cookies, melting moments, snickerdoodles and Swiss butter cookies. The fat and sugar are creamed – or beaten – together either until just blended or, more usually, until they are well-aerated and have a light and fluffy texture. Eggs and dry ingredients are then added a little bit at a time.

The fat should be soft enough to beat easily, so remember to remove it from the refrigerator at least 30 minutes before you start mixing. Unsalted (sweet) butter is the best choice, but if you are going to use margarine, use the firm block type rather than softer margarine that is sold in tubs.

The eggs should also be at room temperature or they may curdle the creamed mixture when they are added. It is not essential to use an electric mixer or food processor for the creaming method – a wooden spoon does a perfectly good job – but it definitely makes the process easier and quicker.

Cook's Tip
Creamed mixtures have a tendency to curdle when the eggs are added. To avoid this, add the eggs a little at a time and beat well after each addition. If the mixture does curdle, beat in 15ml/1 tbsp of the flour before adding more egg.

SWISS BUTTER COOKIES

These crisp cookies are very easy to make and delicious to eat.

Makes 24
115g/4oz/½ cup unsalted (sweet) butter, softened
50g/2oz/¼ cup caster (superfine) sugar
1 egg
200g/7oz/1¾ cups plain (all-purpose) flour
30ml/2 tbsp cornflour (cornstarch)
15ml/1 tbsp ground almonds

1 Put the butter in a large mixing bowl and beat with an electric mixer or a wooden spoon until it is softened and creamy. Add the sugar and beat in until it is completely incorporated. Continue beating until the mixture is light, fluffy and much paler in colour.

2 Beat the egg lightly with a fork. Add the egg to the butter mixture, a little at a time, beating well after each addition.

3 Sift the flour and cornflour over the creamed ingredients. This will remove any lumps and incorporate air, making your cookies lighter. Add the ground almonds and stir together to make a soft dough.

4 Shape the dough into a ball, then flatten it slightly into a round – this makes it easier to roll out. Wrap the dough tightly in clear film (plastic wrap) and chill for about 30 minutes, or until the dough is fairly firm. Meanwhile, preheat the oven to 180°C/350°F/Gas 4. Lightly grease two baking sheets or line them with baking parchment.

5 Roll out the dough on a lightly floured surface to 3mm/⅛in thick. Cut the dough into rounds with a 7.5cm/3in plain cutter and place on the baking sheets. Bake for about 15 minutes until golden. Leave on the baking sheets for 5 minutes, then transfer to a wire rack to cool.

THE RUBBING-IN METHOD

Many traditional cookies, such as shortbread and digestives (Graham crackers) are made by rubbing the fat, which can be butter, margarine, white vegetable fat or lard, into the flour. The fat should be firm and cool but not straight from the refrigerator, so leave the fat at room temperature before using. Beaten eggs, milk or water may be added to bind the mixture.

CLASSIC SHORTBREAD

These buttery cookies are cooked in a round, then cut into wedges.

Makes 8 wedges

175g/6oz/1½ cups plain
* (all-purpose) flour*
115g/4oz/½ cup butter, diced
* and chilled*
50g/2oz/¼ cup caster (superfine) sugar,
* plus extra for sprinkling*

1 Preheat the oven to 160°C/325°F/ Gas 3. Grease a baking sheet or line it with baking parchment. Sift the flour and salt into a large bowl. Use a palette knife (metal spatula) to stir in the diced butter until the pieces are coated with flour. Rub them between your fingertips, lifting the mixture and then letting it drop until it looks like fine breadcrumbs. Stir in the sugar.

2 Holding the bowl firmly, gather the dough into a ball – the warmth of your hand will help bring the dough together.

3 Gently knead the dough on a lightly floured surface for about 30 seconds until it is smooth.

4 Roll out the dough into a round about 15cm/6in in diameter and 1cm/½in thick. Transfer to the prepared baking sheet. Score the top deeply into eight sections, then prick a pattern with a fork. This will allow steam to escape during cooking and prevent the shortbread from rising in the middle. Chill the shortbread for 1 hour.

5 Sprinkle the top lightly and evenly with a little extra caster sugar. Bake the shortbread for 35 minutes, or until it is a pale, golden straw colour. Leave to cool on the baking sheet for 5 minutes, then transfer to a wire rack to cool.

MAKING RUBBED-IN COOKIES IN A FOOD PROCESSOR

This method of making cookies is especially useful where the cookie mixture contains a high proportion of fat.

1 Put the sifted flour and other dry ingredients, such as salt, into the food processor. Process for 4–5 seconds.

2 Sprinkle in the diced, chilled fat. Process for 10 seconds, or until the mixture resembles fine breadcrumbs.

3 Sprinkle any liquid, such as beaten egg, milk or water, over the mixture and, using the pulse button, process for just a few seconds until the mixture starts to hold together. Do not allow the cookie dough to form a ball in the food processor.

4 Remove the mixture from the food processor and form into a ball with your hands. Gently knead the dough on a lightly floured surface for a few seconds until smooth. Wrap the dough in clear film (plastic wrap) and then chill until fairly firm.

THE MELTED METHOD

Cookies, such as flapjacks and gingernuts (gingersnaps) are made by first melting the fat and sugar or syrup together. The dry ingredients are then stirred in to make a soft dough that firms as it cools. The baked cookies become crisp as they cool, so should be quickly shaped, or left on the baking sheets for a few minutes to firm up before transferring to a wire rack.

GINGERNUTS

When baked, these spiced cookies are slightly cracked on the top.

Makes 24

50g/2oz/¼ cup butter, diced
50g/2oz/¼ cup golden (light corn) syrup
40g/1½oz/3 tbsp granulated sugar
115g/4oz/1 cup self-raising (self-rising) flour
5ml/1 tsp ground ginger
5ml/1 tsp bicarbonate of soda (baking soda)

1 Preheat the oven to 180°C/350°F/ Gas 4. Lightly grease two large baking sheets. Put the butter, syrup and sugar in a heavy pan and heat gently until just melted, stirring occasionally until the ingredients are blended. Do not let the mixture boil or some of the liquid will evaporate, altering the proportions.

2 Remove the pan from the heat and leave the mixture to cool for a few minutes. (This is particularly important if you are adding eggs, as they will cook and curdle if the mixture is too hot.) Sift the flour, ginger and bicarbonate of soda over the mixture. Stir until the mixture has blended and is smooth. The raising agents will start to work straight away, so shape the cookie dough and bake as soon as possible.

3 Place small spoonfuls of the mixture on to the prepared baking sheets, spacing the mounds of cookie dough well apart to allow room for the cookies to spread.

4 Bake the gingernuts for about 10 minutes, or until they are golden brown and the top surfaces are crazed. Leave the cookies on the baking sheets for 2 minutes to firm up, then transfer them to a wire rack to cool and crisp.

THE WHISKED METHOD

Airy cookies or crisp, delicate cookies, such as tuiles, macaroons and *langues de chat* are made by folding the dry ingredients into a whisked mixture of eggs and sugar, or into a meringue (whisked egg whites and sugar) mixture.

TUILES

These delicate cookies are named after the French curved roof tiles, which they closely resemble if they are shaped into curls while still hot.

Makes 12

1 egg white
50g/2oz/¼ cup caster (superfine) sugar
25g/1oz/2 tbsp butter, melted and cooled
25g/1oz/¼ cup plain (all-purpose) flour, sifted
flaked (sliced) almonds, for sprinkling (optional)

1 Preheat the oven to 190°C/375°F/ Gas 5. Lightly grease two or three baking sheets or line them with sheets of baking parchment.

2 Put the egg whites in a large, clean, grease-free mixing bowl and whisk until stiff peaks form. Gently fold in the caster sugar to make a stiff and glossy mixture. (It should resemble a meringue mixture.)

3 Trickle about a third of the melted butter down the side of the bowl and fold in with the same quantity of flour. Repeat until all the butter and flour are incorporated.

4 Place small spoonfuls of the mixture, at least 13cm/5in apart, on the prepared baking sheets, then spread out into thin rounds using the back of a spoon. Sprinkle flaked almonds over each round, if using.

5 Bake the tuiles for 6–7 minutes, or until the biscuits are pale beige in the middle and brown at the edges. Leave to cool on the baking sheets for a few seconds, then lift off carefully with a palette knife or metal spatula and cool on a wire rack. (If you want to curl the tuiles, do this while they are still hot.)

THE ALL-IN-ONE METHOD

Some cookies are made by simply placing all the ingredients in a bowl and beating them together. Drop cookies are usually made this way. This easy method can be made even faster by using a food processor, although chunky ingredients such as dried fruit and nuts may have to be stirred in after mixing the cookie dough. It is essential that the fat is soft enough to blend easily.

RAISIN COOKIES

The natural sweetness of raisins gives these cookies extra flavour and a chewy bite.

Makes 24

150g/5oz/1¼ cups plain (all-purpose) flour
2.5ml/½ tsp baking powder
pinch of salt
115g/4oz/generous ½ cup caster (superfine) sugar
115g/4oz/½ cup soft margarine
1 egg, lightly beaten
2.5ml/½ tsp vanilla essence (extract)
150g/5oz/1 cup seedless raisins

1 Preheat the oven to 190°C/375°F/Gas 5. Lightly grease three baking sheets or line them with baking parchment. Sift together the flour, baking powder and salt into a mixing bowl or the bowl of a food processor. Add the sugar, margarine, egg and vanilla essence.

2 Beat with a wooden spoon or blend in a food processor until combined. Stir in the raisins.

3 Drop heaped dessertspoonfuls of the mixture about 5cm/2in apart on to the baking sheets. Bake the cookies for 15 minutes or until golden brown. Leave on the baking sheets for a few minutes then transfer to wire racks to cool.

MEASURING INGREDIENTS

Dry ingredients by weight
Whether you measure in imperial or metric, electronic and balance scales generally give more accurate readings than spring scales. Spoon or pour the dry ingredients into the bowl or tray on the scales and check the reading or dial carefully.

Dry ingredients in measuring cups or spoons
To measure a dry ingredient in a spoon, scoop it up in the spoon, then level the surface using the straight edge of a knife. If you are using measuring cups, make sure you have ¼, ⅓, ½, ⅔, ¾ and 1 cup sizes. Where a recipe calls for a scant cup, fill the cup with the dry ingredient, level with the back of a knife, then scoop out about 15ml/1 tbsp. Where a generous cup is called for, level with a knife then add about 15ml/1 tbsp.

Liquids in litres, pints or cups
Use a clear glass or plastic jug (cup) with calibrations in litres, pints or cups. Put it on a flat surface, pour in the liquid and check the markings by bending down and looking at eye level.

Liquids in spoons
Use proper measuring spoons and carefully pour in the liquid, filling it to the brim then pouring it into the mixing bowl. Do not hold the spoon over the bowl.

Drop Cookies

These are probably the simplest cookies to make. They are called drop cookies because the dough is soft enough to drop off the spoon and on to the baking sheet. The basic mixture is often made by the creaming method where butter and sugar are beaten together until light and fluffy. Eggs are then beaten in, followed by flour, raising agents and any flavourings.

CHOCOLATE CHIP COOKIES

Created in the 1930s, these were originally called Toll House cookies.

Makes 12
115g/4oz/½ cup butter, softened
115g/4oz/generous ½ cup caster
  (superfine) sugar
1 egg, lightly beaten
5ml/1 tsp vanilla essence (extract)
175g/6oz/1½ cups plain (all-purpose) flour
175g/6oz/1 cup plain (semisweet)
  chocolate chips

1 Preheat the oven to 180°C/350°F/ Gas 4. Lightly grease two or three large baking sheets or line them with baking parchment. Cream the butter and sugar together in a bowl with a wooden spoon or an electric mixer until pale and fluffy. Beat in the egg and vanilla essence. Sift the flour over the butter mixture and fold in with the chocolate chips.

2 Drop tablespoonfuls of the mixture on to the prepared baking sheets. (It should fall off the spoon quite easily with a sharp jerk; if not, use another spoon to scoop it off.) Leave plenty of space between the cookies to allow for spreading.

3 Flatten each cookie slightly with the back of a fork, keeping the shape as even as possible. For dropped cookies that have a soft or cakey texture when cooked, the mixture should be left well mounded on the baking sheet and not flattened; very stiff mixtures should be more widely spread. The recipe instructions should indicate this – if you are unsure, test how much the mixture spreads by baking a single cookie.

4 Bake the cookies for about 10 minutes, or until golden. Using a palette knife or metal spatula, transfer to a wire rack to cool.

As long as you follow the basic recipe and techniques, you can make a huge variety of drop cookies. Remember, though, that some added ingredients may alter the consistency of the dough – chopped fresh fruit, for example, may make the mixture too wet, whereas rolled oats will soak up moisture, making the cookies dry and crumbly.

Chocolate Substitute 15ml/1 tbsp (unsweetened) cocoa powder for the same quantity of flour. For a chunkier texture, use coarsely chopped chocolate instead of chocolate chips. You can use milk chocolate or chocolate chips instead of the plain (semisweet) chocolate chips in the recipe on this page.

Mocha Use coffee essence (extract) instead of vanilla essence (extract).

Macadamia nut or hazelnut Add whole or coarsely chopped nuts instead of the chocolate chips. Alternatively, as nuts and chocolate are a classic combination, use 75g/3oz/½ cup of each.

Dried fruit In place of the chocolate chips, add chopped dried fruit, such as raisins, sultanas (golden raisins), apricots, glacé (candied) cherries, or a mixture of candied tropical fruit, such as pineapple, mango and papaya. Add fruit juice or milk instead of vanilla essence.

MELTED DROP COOKIES

Thin, crisp cookies, such as tuiles, florentines and brandy snaps, require the butter and sugar or syrup to be melted together first to start the caramelization process prior to baking. Such cookies usually contain little flour, which helps them spread on the baking sheet – so make sure they have plenty of room.

BRANDY SNAPS

These classic melted drop cookies have a wonderful brittle texture. They melt in the mouth to release a sweet, almost caramelized flavour.

Makes 12–14

75g/3oz/6 tbsp butter, diced
75g/3oz/scant ½ cup caster
   (superfine) sugar
45ml/3 tbsp golden (light corn) syrup
75g/3oz/⅓ cup plain
   (all-purpose) flour
5ml/1 tsp ground ginger
30ml/2 tbsp brandy
15ml/1 tbsp lemon juice

1 Preheat the oven to 190°C/375°F/ Gas 5. Lightly grease several baking sheets or line them with baking parchment. Put the butter, sugar and syrup in a heavy pan. Heat gently over a low heat, stirring occasionally until the mixture has melted and becomes smooth.

2 Remove the pan from the heat. Leave the mixture to cool for a few minutes or the flour will start to cook when it is added.

3 Sift together the flour and ginger and stir into the butter mixture with the brandy and lemon juice. Leave for a further 1–2 minutes to allow the flour to absorb some of the moisture.

4 Drop teaspoonfuls of the mixture at 4cm/1½in intervals on to the baking sheets. Do not attempt to cook any more than three or four on each sheet as they will need plenty of room to spread.

5 Bake, one sheet at a time, for about 8–10 minutes, or until the cookies turn bubbly, lacy in texture and golden brown. Remove the brandy snaps from the oven and leave for about 15 seconds to firm up slightly before attempting to move them.

6 Loosen the brandy snaps from the baking sheet one at a time using a palette knife or metal spatula, and shape before cooling on a wire rack.

SHAPING UP

Some melted drop cookies need to be reshaped or neatened before, part-way through or after cooking.
Tuiles Named after the curved roof tiles in France, these may be round but are usually slightly elongated. Drop heaped teaspoonfuls of the mixture on greased or lined baking sheets then spread each into an oval, measuring 10 x 5cm/4 x 2in.
Florentines The mixture often spreads out further than the fruit and nuts. Remove from the oven 2 minutes before the end of cooking time and press back the edges into a neat shape with a palette knife to create perfect rounds, then return to the oven.
Glass cookies After baking, trim these thin, delicate cookies into shape by pressing a round metal biscuit cutter, slightly smaller than the baked cookie, into each, then pull away or break off the excess.

SHAPING MELTED DROP COOKIES

Melted drop cookies are pliable enough to be shaped into curls, rolls or baskets when they are warm. As they cool, the cookies become crisp and hard, retaining their shape.

MAKING CURLS

Tuiles are usually curled after baking. They make a pretty accompaniment to serve with desserts. Remove the cookies from the oven, lift off the baking sheet and drape over a lightly oiled rolling pin, gently curling them around. Leave them to cool and crisp before removing.

MAKING ROLLS

These tightly rolled, wand-shaped cookies are great for serving as an accompaniment to any dessert. Cigarette Russes are a classic example of a rolled cookie.

1 Shape small spoonfuls of tuile mixture into 7.5 x 5cm/3 x 2in rectangles on greased or lined baking sheets, spacing them well apart, and bake at 190°C/375°F/ Gas 5 for 6–7 minutes.

2 Carefully lift off the cookies and place upside down on a flat surface. Wind each cookie tightly around a greased wooden spoon handle.

3 Cool slightly until firm, then ease the cookies off the handles and place them on a wire rack to cool completely. Brandy snaps can be shaped in the same way, but do not turn upside-down before rolling them up.

MAKING BASKETS

You can use either large brandy snaps or tuiles to make little bowl-shaped containers for desserts such as ice cream, sorbet, fresh fruit or mousse.

1 Bake heaped tablespoonfuls of brandy snap mixture or spread heaped teaspoonfuls of tuile mixture into 12cm/4½in rounds on a large baking sheet.

2 Once cooked, leave the cookies to cool for a few seconds, then lift from the baking sheet. Mould over lightly greased, upturned ramekin dishes, pressing the edges into soft folds with your fingers.

3 If you do not have suitable ramekins, then small bowls, cups or even small oranges can be used to produce a similar effect. If you use oranges to create the basic basket shape, then remember to pat the base flat before the cookie sets so that the baskets will be stable and stand upright. Lift off once set.

Variation
To make chocolate brandy snaps, use 65g/2½oz/9 tbsp plain (all-purpose) flour and 30ml/2 tbsp (unsweetened) cocoa powder. You can always omit the ground ginger, if you prefer.

FORTUNE COOKIES

Originally forming part of an ancient Chinese tradition, these are little folded cookies made from tuile mixture. They contain short messages that predict the future and they provide lots of fun for children and adults alike.

1 Spread out teaspoonfuls of tuile mixture to 7.5cm/3in rounds on greased or lined baking sheets and bake until the edges are just turning brown.

2 Working quickly so that the cookies do not cool before they are folded, lift the cookies off the sheets with a palette knife or metal spatula. Lay a folded paper fortune message in the centre and fold the cookie in half. Bend in half again over the edge of a bowl.

3 Leave the cookies to cool and harden, then lift them off the bowl and store in an airtight container.

Rolled Cookies

A cookie dough that is rolled and cut may be a creamed, melted or rubbed-in mixture, but it must have the right consistency. If the dough is too dry it will crack and crumble; too wet and it may stick when rolling and spread during baking.

SIMPLE ALMOND COOKIES
The addition of almonds gives these cookies a delicious crunch.

Makes 24
115g/4oz/½ cup butter, softened
50g/2oz/¼ cup caster (superfine) sugar
1 egg, lightly beaten
15ml/1 tbsp ground almonds
200g/7oz/1¾ cups plain (all-purpose) flour
30ml/2 tbsp cornflour (cornstarch)

1 Preheat the oven to 180°C/350°F/ Gas 4. Lightly grease two baking sheets or line them with baking parchment. Beat the butter and sugar together until creamy. Gradually add the egg, beating well after each addition, then beat in the almonds. Sift over the flour and cornflour and mix to a soft dough.

2 Lightly knead the dough on a floured surface for a few seconds, until smooth. Do not overwork the dough or the butter will start to melt and the gluten will "develop", giving the cookies a tough texture.

3 Shape the dough into a ball then flatten slightly into a round – this makes it easier when you begin to roll it out. Wrap in clear film (plastic wrap) to prevent the dough from drying out and chill for about 30 minutes, or until firm but make sure it is not too stiff to roll. If you are making a large amount of cookie dough, divide it into pieces so that you will be able to handle it more easily when rolling.

4 On a floured surface, roll out the dough lightly and evenly in one direction only to a thickness of about 3mm/⅛in. Roll from the centre to the far edge but not actually over the edge. Always roll away from you and rotate the cookie dough occasionally to prevent it from sticking and also to make sure it is evenly rolled. Avoid pulling the dough as you roll or rotate it, otherwise it may become misshapen when baked.

5 Stamp out 6.5cm/2½in rounds using a fluted cookie cutter, or use another similar-sized shape. Gather up the scraps and re-roll to make more cookies.

6 Transfer the cookies to the prepared baking sheets using a palette knife or metal spatula. Rolled out cookies shouldn't spread as much as drop cookies during baking, but you should still leave a space of at least 2.5cm/1in between each on the baking sheet. Chill the cookies for at least 30 minutes before baking them, as this helps to retain their shape.

7 Bake for 10 minutes until the cookies are a pale golden brown, making sure you rotate the baking sheets halfway through the cooking time. Remove the cookies from the oven and leave on the baking sheets for 2–3 minutes. This allows the biscuits to firm up so that they are less fragile when you handle them. Transfer the cookies to a wire rack using a metal spatula.

Cook's Tip
Cooling cookies on a wire rack allows air to circulate around them, preventing them from gathering moisture and becoming soggy as they cool.

ALL SHAPES AND SIZES

One of the greatest assets of rolled cookies is that they may be cut into any shape or size. There is a huge range of cutters available, but other ways of cutting and shaping cookies include using a pastry wheel or a knife, or even making your own template out of paper or card.

USING A KNIFE OR A PASTRY WHEEL TO SHAPE COOKIES

If you want to make squares, rectangles, triangles or bars, a sharp knife and a ruler are the perfect tools for the job. Instead of a knife, you could use a fluted pastry wheel to give an attractive edging.

1 Roll out the cookie dough to a square or rectangular shape, turning it frequently by 90 degrees. During the early stages of rolling out, push in the edges of the dough with your cupped palms to keep the shape.

2 To make square or rectangular cookies such as shortbread fingers or bourbons, use a ruler to measure the dough so that it is rolled to the appropriate shape and size, then cut with a sharp knife or pastry cutter. (For example, for custard creams, cut the dough into 4cm/1½in strips, then cut each strip at intervals of 5cm/2in to make rectangles.)

3 To make triangular cookies, cut the dough into strips then into squares, then cut each square in half diagonally to make triangles.

4 To make neat diamond-shaped cookies, cut the dough into strips and then cut diagonally across the strips to make diamonds.

MAKING A TEMPLATE

For special occasions you may want to create a more complex cookie shape for which you do not have a cutter. In this case you will need to make a template. It's probably best to avoid very intricate designs, especially those with small protrusions as these may distort or burn during baking, and will break off easily once cooked.

1 Select the design, then either draw the design straight on to a piece of thin cardboard or trace it on to tracing or greaseproof (waxed) paper first, then glue it on to cardboard. Wait for the glue to dry thoroughly before carefully cutting out the template.

2 Place the template on the rolled out cookie dough and hold it firmly in place. Using the point of a sharp knife, cut around the template to create the cookie shape.

MAKING RING COOKIES

It's hard to transfer ring cookies to baking sheets without pulling them out of shape. One solution is to place rounds of cookie dough on the baking sheet, then cut out the centres with a smaller cutter. To make perfect rings, bake round cookies, then stamp out the centres while the cookies are still warm.

1 Roll out the dough then stamp into rounds and transfer to a baking sheet. Bake the cookies according to the recipe instructions.

2 Remove the cookies from the oven and leave on the baking sheet. Using a small cookie cutter, stamp out the centres of the cookies before they have time to cool.

3 Leave the cookies on the baking sheet for 3–4 minutes, then transfer to a wire rack to cool completely.

Cook's Tips
• *To make pretty jammy sandwiches, only remove the centres from half the rounds, then sandwich the rounds and rings together with a little jam.*
• *Young children love the mini cookies that are left over after punching out holes in larger cookies. Drizzle with a little icing made from sugar and water for an extra special treat.*

MAKING MULTI-COLOURED ROLLED COOKIES

By using two or more different coloured doughs you can make a range of attractive cookies. The coloured doughs can be rolled, stamped out, then pieced together before baking, or the rolled doughs can be layered together then cut into cookie shapes.

TWO-TONE COOKIES

To make cookies with different coloured middles, leave half the dough plain and knead in a little cooled melted chocolate into the other half, or use a few drops of food colouring.

1 Roll out each piece of dough to about 3mm/⅛in thick. Stamp out an equal number of cookies (rounds or hearts) and place them on separate baking sheets. Chill for 30 minutes.

2 Using a smaller cutter, stamp out the centres from all of the cookies, then swap the plain centres for the flavoured or coloured centres and vice versa.

3 If you like, you can use a third, even smaller, cutter as well and swap the tiny centres once more to make triple-tone cookies.

PINWHEELS

These cookies are made by rolling together layers of coloured dough.

1 Divide the cookie dough into two. Leave half plain and flavour the other half by kneading in 15ml/1 tbsp sifted (unsweetened) cocoa powder and 5ml/1 tsp milk. Wrap and chill for about 30 minutes.

2 Roll out each piece of dough to a rectangle measuring 20 x 25cm/ 8 x 10in. Lightly brush the plain dough with lightly beaten egg white and place the coloured dough on top. Roll up tightly from a long side, then cut into 5mm/¼in thick slices.

NEAPOLITAN SLICES

These cookies resemble mini slices of Neapolitan ice cream.

1 Divide the dough into three. Leave one third plain, flavour one third with cocoa (as for pinwheels) and colour the remaining third pink. Wrap and chill for 30 minutes.

2 Roll out each piece of dough into a rectangle measuring 10 x 7.5cm/ 4 x 3in. Place the rectangles on top of each other, brushing between the layers with lightly beaten egg white. Cut the dough into 5mm/¼in thick slices, then cut each slice in half.

SEVEN STEPS TO SUCCESS

• Always chill the dough to firm it for at least 20 minutes and up to 1 hour before rolling. If you chill it for longer, leave it at room temperature for about 10 minutes before rolling out.

• Cookies should be rolled to a thickness of 3–5mm/⅛–¼in. Thicker cookies will have soggy centres when the outside has browned; thinner cookies will be very crisp and fragile.

• Use the minimum amount of flour when rolling out the dough. Lightly dust the work surface and the rolling pin using a flour dredger or fine sieve, sprinkling with a little more flour when needed. After cutting the cookies, brush off any excess flour with a dry pastry brush.

• If the dough is sticky, even after chilling, roll it out between two sheets of baking parchment or clear film (plastic wrap). After rolling, leave the parchment or clear film in place, slide the dough on to a baking sheet and chill before stamping out the cookies with a cookie cutter.

• When stamping out the cookies, dip the cutter into flour, then press down firmly to cut right through the dough.

• Cut cookies closely together to minimize re-rolling scraps. The first rolling is always better.

• If you haven't got a cutter, use a sharp knife or pastry wheel to cut the dough into squares or rectangles, or stamp out rounds using a thin-rimmed glass.

Piped Cookies

For this type of cookie the mixture needs to be soft enough to pipe but firm enough to keep its shape during baking. Piped cookies are usually made by the creaming method, which gives them a crumbly, airy texture and makes blending in flavourings easy. Make sure that the butter is very soft before you start as this will make mixing and piping quick and easy.

VIENNESE PIPED COOKIES

With a little practice, these cookies can be piped into any shape you like.

Makes 12

175g/6oz/¾ cup unsalted (sweet)
   butter, softened
40g/1½oz/3 tbsp icing (confectioners')
   sugar, sifted
2.5ml/½ tsp vanilla essence (extract)
175g/6oz/1½ cups plain (all-purpose) flour
40g/1½oz/3 tbsp cornflour (cornstarch)

1 Preheat the oven to 180°C/350°F/ Gas 4. Grease or line two baking sheets. Cream the butter and icing sugar together until very pale and fluffy. Add the vanilla essence and beat for a few more seconds.

2 Sift the flour and cornflour together over the butter mixture and mix together until smooth.

3 Spoon the mixture into a piping (pastry) bag fitted with a large, star-shaped nozzle and pipe into the required shapes on the prepared baking sheets. Make sure the shapes are spaced well apart.

4 Bake the cookies for about 12 minutes, or until they are a pale golden colour. Leave for a few minutes on the baking sheets to firm up slightly before carefully transferring them to a wire rack with a palette knife or metal spatula to finish cooling.

Variations

Once you have mastered making and piping the basic recipe, try adding flavourings to vary the cookie mixture.
Chocolate *Substitute 30ml/2 tbsp (unsweetened) cocoa powder for the same quantity of flour.*
Coffee *Omit the vanilla essence and blend 5ml/1 tsp instant coffee powder with 5ml/1 tsp just boiled water. Leave to cool, then add to the mixture with the flour and cornflour.*
Strawberry *Use 40g/1½oz/3 tbsp strawberry flavour blancmange powder instead of the cornflour.*
Orange or lemon *Beat the finely grated rind of half an orange or lemon into the creamed mixture.*
Caramel *To give the cookies a mild caramel flavour, use unrefined icing sugar.*

PERFECT PIPING

To perfect your piping technique, follow these three simple steps.

1 Drop the nozzle into the bag, pushing it down to fit firmly. Twist the nozzle end round so that there is a twist in the bag just above it, then push the twisted section of the bag inside the nozzle to close it off.

2 Fold the top of the bag over your hand to make a "collar". Spoon in the mixture. When the bag is about half full, gently twist the top to remove the air. Holding the top of the bag, push the mixture down.

3 To pipe, hold the twisted end firmly and use the other hand to guide the nozzle. Using firm, steady pressure, pipe the shape. Push down slightly then lift up.

PIPING SHAPES

Viennese cookie mixture can be piped into all manner of shapes.

VIENNESE COOKIES

Round swirls are the classic shape for Viennese cookies.

Spoon the mixture into a piping (pastry) bag fitted with a 12mm/½in star nozzle. Pipe rosettes 5cm/2in across on to greased baking sheets, spacing them well apart.

VIENNESE WHIRLS

Sandwich two Viennese cookies together with buttercream filling and a little sieved apricot jam.

SWISS FINGERS

Pretty piped fingers are very popular, and very simple to make.

Spoon the mixture into a piping bag fitted with a 1cm/½in star nozzle. Pipe 6cm/2¼in lengths on greased baking sheets, spacing well apart.

OYSTER COOKIES

These pretty, sophisticated cookies resemble oyster shells.

Spoon the mixture into a piping bag fitted with a 1cm/½in star nozzle and pipe about five lines to make shells. Make the shape wide at one end and tapered at the other.

CHOCOLATE VANILLA SWIRLS

These two-colour cookies look lovely piped into paper cake cases.

1 Divide the Viennese cookie mixture into two equal parts and beat 15ml/1 tbsp sifted (unsweetened) cocoa powder into half of it. Spoon the vanilla mixture down one side of a piping bag fitted with a 1cm/½in star nozzle and then spoon the chocolate mixture down the other side.

2 Pipe the mixture into 12 paper cake cases in a bun tray (muffin pan) to make pretty striped swirls.

OTHER PIPED COOKIES

Many other cookie mixtures are piped to give them an even length, width and shape.

LANGUES DE CHATS

These classic French cookies are long, thin ovals with a slightly rough texture (like a cat's tongue).

Makes 18
75g/3oz/6 tbsp unsalted (sweet) butter, softened
115g/4oz/1 cup icing (confectioners') sugar, sifted, plus extra for dusting
2 large (US extra large) egg whites
30ml/2 tbsp caster (superfine) sugar
75g/3oz/⅔ cup plain (all-purpose) flour, sifted

1 Preheat the oven to 200°C/400°F/ Gas 6. Grease two baking sheets or line them with baking parchment. Cream the butter and icing sugar together until pale and fluffy.

2 In a separate bowl, whisk the egg whites to soft peaks, then add the caster sugar 15ml/1 tbsp at a time, whisking between each addition. Fold the whites into the butter mixture, then fold in the flour.

3 Spoon the mixture into a piping (pastry) bag fitted with a 1cm/½in plain nozzle and pipe 6cm/2½in lengths on to the prepared baking sheets. Allow 5cm/2in between each cookie for spreading.

4 Bake for 5–7 minutes, or until the edges are lightly browned. Leave to cool on the baking sheets for 5 minutes before transferring to a wire rack to cool completely.

FILIGREE CROWNS

These delicate, shaped cookies are made from finely piped lines of cookie mixture, which are first baked and then moulded into crowns. They make stunning little containers for desserts such as ice cream, sorbet, mousse or fresh fruit.

Makes 6

1 egg white
50g/2oz/¼ cup caster
   (superfine) sugar
25g/1oz/¼ cup plain
   (all-purpose) flour

1 Preheat the oven to 200°C/400°F/ Gas 6. Draw six rectangles, each measuring about 20 x 7.5cm/8 x 3in, on six separate pieces of baking parchment.

2 Whisk the egg white and sugar together in a small mixing bowl until foamy. Sift the flour over the egg mixture and stir in thoroughly.

3 Spoon the cookie mixture into a greaseproof (waxed) paper piping (pastry) bag and snip off the tip to create a small hole. On each rectangle of baking parchment, carefully pipe thin wiggly lines from side to side to fill the marked shape, then pipe a little extra mixture down one of the long edges.

4 Bake the cookies for about 3 minutes. Remove the tray from the oven and immediately roll the cookie around a straight-sided glass.

5 Peel away the paper and stand the crowns upright. Remove the glass. If the mixture hardens before you've moulded the crowns, return to the oven for a few seconds. Cool and store in an airtight container.

SPANISH CHURROS

These little Spanish cake-cookies are made from sweetened choux pastry, which is piped into hot oil and then deep-fried. Serve sprinkled generously with cinnamon sugar.

Makes 25

75g/3oz/6 tbsp butter, diced
250ml/8fl oz/1 cup water
115g/4oz/1 cup plain
   (all-purpose) flour
50g/2oz/4 tbsp caster
   (superfine) sugar
3 eggs, lightly beaten
2.5ml/½ tsp ground cinnamon

1 Heat the butter and water in a small heavy pan until the butter has melted – do not allow the water to boil. Sift the flour and 15ml/1 tbsp of the caster sugar on to a piece of greaseproof (waxed) paper.

2 Once the butter has melted, bring to a boil, then add the flour and sugar. Remove the pan from the heat and beat the mixture vigorously. Leave to cool for 5 minutes, then gradually beat in the eggs until the mixture is smooth and glossy.

3 Half-fill a large, heavy pan or deep-fryer with oil and heat to 190°C/375°F. Spoon the mixture into a piping (pastry) bag with a 1cm/½in star nozzle. Pipe five 10cm/4in lengths of the mixture into the hot oil being careful not to cause the fat to splash or spit. Fry the churros for 2 minutes, or until golden and crisp.

4 Remove the churros from the oil with a slotted spoon and drain on kitchen paper. Repeat until all the mixture has been used. Mix the remaining caster sugar with the ground cinnamon and sprinkle over the churros. Serve warm.

Pressed Cookies

Shaped cookies are amazingly simple to make using a commercial cookie press. The press comes with a range of patterened discs and may have several settings so that a variety of shapes and sizes of cookie can be made. Choose soft-textured cookie doughs that will easily push through the press.

VANILLA FLOWERS
These pretty cookies use vanilla essence for an irresistible flavour.

Makes 25
90g/3½oz/scant ½ cup butter, softened
90g/3½oz/½ cup caster (superfine) sugar
1 egg yolk
165g/5½oz/scant 1½ cups plain
  (all-purpose) flour
5ml/1 tsp milk
5ml/1 tsp vanilla essence (extract)

1 Cream the butter and sugar together until pale and fluffy. Beat in the egg yolk. Sift the flour over the butter mixture and then fold in with the milk and vanilla essence to make a soft dough. Knead for a few seconds until smooth.

2 Fill the cookie press cylinder almost to the top with the dough and then screw on the plunger. Press out the dough on to greased baking sheets, spacing the cookies well apart.

3 Place the baking sheets in the refrigerator for at least 30 minutes, so that the cookies keep their shape while baking. Decorate with sugar or nuts, if using. Meanwhile, preheat the oven to 180°C/350°F/Gas 4.

4 Bake for 15 minutes, or until very lightly browned. Leave to cool on the baking sheets for 5 minutes, then transfer to a wire rack.

CHOCOLATE DAISIES
This dark chocolate mixture works perfectly in a cookie press.

Makes 12
175g/6oz/¾ cup unsalted (sweet)
  butter, softened
40g/1½oz/3 tbsp icing (confectioners')
  sugar, sifted
175g/6oz/1½ cups plain (all-purpose) flour
25g/1oz/2 tbsp cocoa powder
  (unsweetened)
40g/1½oz/3 tbsp cornflour (cornstarch)

1 Preheat the oven to 180°C/ 350°F/Gas 4. Grease or line two baking sheets. Cream the butter and icing sugar together until very pale and fluffy.

2 Sift the flour and cornflour together over the butter mixture and mix together until smooth.

3 Put enough of the dough into the press to fill it almost to the top, then screw on the plunger.

4 Press out the dough on to the greased baking sheets. Make sure the shapes are spaced well apart.

5 Bake the cookies for about 12 minutes until just beginning to change colour. Leave the cookies for a few minutes on the baking sheets to firm up slightly before carefully transferring them to a wire rack to cool completely.

PRESSED COOKIE TIPS AND TECHNIQUES
• To achieve a really short texture, thoroughly cream the butter and sugar until very light and fold in the flour gently.
• The dough must be very smooth to go through the fine holes in the cookie discs, so don't add chunky flavouring ingredients, such as chopped nuts, dried fruit, glacé (candied) cherries or chocolate chips.
• The dough must be sufficiently soft to be easily squeezed through the press, but firm enough to hold its shape.
• If the mixture is too firm to press, add a few drops of milk
• If the dough is slightly soft and sticks to the cookie disc, put it in the refrigerator for about 30 minutes until it has firmed.
• Pressed cookies can be decorated with ingredients such as chocolate chips, sugar crystals or nuts before baking.

Moulded Cookies

Shaping cookie dough in a mould gives a professional finish. The dough can be either shaped in a mould, then turned out for baking or baked in the shaped tin (pan) itself. It is not essential to buy special moulds, you can improvise with plain tins for both shaping and baking.

SHAPING SHORTBREAD

Shortbread moulds usually have a carved design of a thistle and are available in different sizes. The mould should be brushed with a flavourless oil the first time it is used, then wiped with kitchen paper.

1 Make one quantity of shortbread mixture and roll out to a 15cm/6in round. Press it firmly into an 18cm/7in shortbread mould. Line a baking sheet with baking parchment.

2 Invert the mould on to the baking sheet, tapping the mould firmly to release the dough. Chill for about 30 minutes until firm.

3 Preheat the oven to 160°C/325°F/ Gas 3. Bake the shortbread for 35–40 minutes, or until pale golden. Sprinkle the top with a little caster (superfine) sugar, then leave to cool.

SHAPING MADELEINES

These French lemon cookies are baked in shell-shaped tins (pans).

Makes 15
1 egg
65g/2½oz/generous ¼ cup caster (superfine) sugar
65g/2½oz/9 tbsp self-raising (self-rising) flour
1.5ml/¼ tsp baking powder
finely grated rind of ½ lemon
65g/2½oz/5 tbsp butter, melted and cooled

1 Preheat the oven to 220°C/425°F/ Gas 7. Brush the tins with melted unsalted (sweet) butter. Chill for 10 minutes, then brush lightly with butter again, dust with flour and shake off any excess.

2 Whisk the egg and sugar until thick and pale. (The mixture should leave a trail when the whisk is lifted.) Sift over half the flour with the baking powder and fold in the lemon rind. Pour half the melted butter around the edge of the bowl and fold in gently.

3 Sift over the remaining flour, then pour in the rest of the melted butter around the edge of the bowl. Fold in gently until combined.

4 Spoon the mixture into the moulds, filling them just to the top. Bake for 10 minutes until golden. Leave for a few moments, then ease out the madeleines with a palette knife or metal spatula and transfer to a wire rack.

MAKING PETTICOAT TAILS

Shortbread is traditionally made into wedge-shaped petticoat tails.

1 Press one quantity of shortbread mixture into an 18cm/7in loose-based fluted flan tin (quiche pan).

2 Prick the surface with a fork and mark the shortbread into eight wedges using a knife. If you do not have a fluted tin, use a straight-sided sandwich tin (layer pan) and press a pattern around the edge.

MAKING SQUARES AND BARS

Cookie dough can be baked in a loose-based square or rectangular tin (pan), then cut into pieces.

1 Press one quantity of shortbread mixture into a 15cm/6in square tin or two quantities into an 18 x 28cm/7 x 11in rectangular tin.

2 To cut into squares, make two cuts lengthways, then two cuts across for the square tin and four for the rectangular tin. To cut into bars, cut in half lengthways first, then cut across widthways into bars.

SMALL MOULDED COOKIES

These can be made in tiny tartlet tins (mini quiche pans) or pretty metal chocolate moulds.

Press shortbread dough into the tins or moulds until level, then bake. Alternatively, turn out the moulded rounds on to greased or lined baking sheets. Chill before baking.

SHAPING COOKIES BY HAND

You can model cookie dough into all manner of shapes. Classic hand-moulded cookies include jumbles and pretzels. Choose a dough that will retain its shape when baked.

FORK COOKIES

These are the simplest moulded cookies, made by rolling dough into balls, then flattening with a fork to make a pretty pattern on the top.

Makes 16

115g/4oz/½ cup butter, softened
50g/2oz/¼ cup caster (superfine) sugar
150g/5oz/1¼ cups self-raising (self-rising) flour, sifted

1 Preheat the oven to 180°C/350°F/Gas 4. Lightly grease two baking sheets. Beat the butter in a bowl until creamy, then beat in the sugar. Stir in the flour and bring the dough together with your hands.

2 Shape into walnut-size balls and place on the baking sheets, spacing well apart. Dip a fork in cold water and use to flatten the cookies.

3 Bake for 10–12 minutes, until pale brown. Leave to cool on the baking sheets for a few minutes, then transfer to a wire rack to cool.

PRETZELS

These are complicated shapes, so require a more pliable dough.

Makes 40

115g/4oz/½ cup butter, softened
115g/4oz/1 cup icing (confectioners') sugar, sifted
1 egg, lightly beaten
15ml/1 tbsp golden (light corn) syrup
1.5ml/¼ tsp vanilla essence (extract)
250g/9oz/2¼ cups plain (all-purpose) flour, sifted

1 Preheat the oven to 190°C/375°F/Gas 5. Beat the butter and sugar together until light and creamy. Beat in the egg, syrup and vanilla essence. Add the flour and stir to make a dough. Knead on a floured surface, then wrap and chill for 30 minutes.

2 Divide the dough into 40 pieces and cover the pieces that you aren't working on with clear film (plastic wrap). Roll one piece into a thin strand about 25cm/10in long.

3 Create a loop with the strand, bring the ends together and press them into the top of the circle. Make the rest of the pretzels in the same way. Chill for 30 minutes.

4 Bake for 10 minutes until lightly browned, then cool on wire racks.

Bar Cookies

These are a cross between a cake and a cookie; some are thin and crunchy, others thick and chewy or light and spongy. Some bar cookies, such as brownies and flapjacks, are just a single layer, but many have two or more different layers that combine tastes and textures. Sometimes this base is partially or fully cooked first before the topping is added, then the oven temperature is lowered so that the topping doesn't overcook.

Always make bar cookies in the recommended tin (pan) size; even a small change in size will affect the cooking time and final result.

LAYERED FRUIT AND NUT BAR COOKIE

This indulgent treat combines several flavours and textures.

Makes 15

250g/9oz/2¼ cups plain (all-purpose) flour
175g/6oz/¾ cup chilled butter or
  hard margarine, diced
75g/3oz/scant ½ cup caster (superfine)
  sugar or soft light brown sugar

For the filling

115g/4oz/½ cup glacé (candied) cherries,
  coarsely chopped
50g/2oz/⅓ cup sultanas (golden raisins)
50g/2oz/½ cup almonds, chopped

For the topping

115g/4oz/½ cup butter or hard
  margarine, softened
115g/4oz/generous ½ cup caster
  (superfine) sugar
2 eggs
50g/2oz/½ cup plain (all-purpose) flour
50g/2oz/½ cup ground almonds
icing (confectioners') sugar, for dusting

1 Preheat the oven to 180°C/350°F/Gas 4. Line the base and grease an 18 × 28 × 2.5cm/7 × 11 × 1in cake tin (pan). To make the base, sift the flour into a bowl. Additional dry flavourings such as ground spices or (unsweetened) cocoa powder (substitute for an equal quantity of flour) can be added at this stage.

2 Rub in the butter or margarine pieces until the mixture resembles breadcrumbs. Stir in the sugar. If you are adding chunky flavourings, such as coconut or chocolate chips, stir them in with the sugar. Mix with your hands until the dough comes together.

3 Press the mixture into the base of the tin. Level with the back of a spoon or a potato masher. Prick the base with a fork to let out the steam and to make sure it remains level as it cooks, then bake for 10 minutes. Remove from the oven.

4 Reduce the temperature to 160°C/325°F/Gas 3. Mix together the filling ingredients, then sprinkle evenly over the base. To make the topping, cream the butter and sugar together until pale and fluffy, then beat in the eggs. Sift over the flour and fold in with the ground almonds. Spread the topping carefully over the fruit and nuts.

5 Bake for 30 minutes, or until a light golden brown colour and firm to the touch. Check the topping is cooked by inserting a wooden cocktail stick (toothpick) into it and leaving for a few seconds; it should come out clean. Leave to cool in the tin for 15 minutes. Lightly dust with icing sugar and cut into bars.

Variations
• *Use chopped dried fruit or spread over a thick layer of jam for the filling.*
• *Try flavouring the sponge cake topping with a little finely grated citrus rind.*

TOPPING IDEAS

There are dozens of different toppings for bar cookies. The base must be fairly firm but the topping can be softer, ranging from sponge cake to caramel, and from sticky meringue to chocolate. The following ideas are sufficient for an 18 × 28cm/7 × 11in tin (pan).

CRUMBLE OR STREUSEL

This works best on top of a slightly soft or sticky base or filling such as jam, fruit purée or soft caramel.

Beat 115g/4oz/½ cup butter until creamy, then mix in 50g/2oz/¼ cup soft light brown sugar. Stir in 115g/4oz/⅔ cup semolina and 115g/4oz/1 cup plain wholemeal (whole-wheat) flour until the mixture resembles breadcrumbs. Add 2.5ml/½ tsp ground ginger. Sprinkle over the base and press down. Bake at 160°C/325°F/Gas 3 for 40 minutes.

COCONUT

This light topping has a delicate flavour and lovely texture. Beat two eggs, then stir in 115g/4oz/generous ½ cup demerara (raw) sugar, 25g/1oz/3 tbsp ground rice, and 150g/5oz/1⅔ cup desiccated (dry unsweetened shredded) coconut. Spread over the base and bake at 180°C/350°F/Gas 4 for 25 minutes.

MERINGUE

This produces a wonderfully light, topping that melts in the mouth,

Whisk two egg whites with a pinch of salt in a clean bowl until they form soft peaks. Gradually whisk in 115g/4oz/generous ½ cup caster (superfine) sugar, a spoonful at a time, until the mixture is stiff and glossy. Fold in 2.5ml/½ tsp cornflour (cornstarch) and 5ml/1 tsp lemon juice. Spread over the base and swirl with a metal spatula to form soft peaks. Bake at 140°C/275°F/Gas 1 for 40 minutes until the meringue is set and tinged brown.

GRATED SHORTBREAD

To make this rich, buttery filling, cream together 115g/4oz/½ cup softened butter and 40g/1½oz/3 tbsp soft light brown sugar. Combine 5ml/1 tsp sunflower oil, 5ml/1 tsp vanilla essence (extract) and 1 egg yolk and beat into the butter mixture. Sift over 200g/7oz/1¾ cups plain (all-purpose) flour, 25g/1oz/¼ cup cornflour (cornstarch) and 2.5ml/½ tsp baking powder. Mix well and knead on a lightly floured surface for 30 seconds. Wrap in clear film (plastic wrap) and chill for about 30 minutes. Grate over the base or filling and press down. Bake at 150°C/300°F/Gas 2 for 45 minutes.

CITRUS CHEESECAKE

To make this zesty topping, put the finely grated rind of two lemons and two limes in a bowl with 225g/8oz/1 cup melted butter, 30ml/2 tbsp caster (superfine) sugar and three eggs. Whisk until thick and mousse-like. Sift over 40g/1½oz/⅓ cup plain (all-purpose) flour and 2.5ml/½ tsp baking powder and fold in with 30ml/2 tbsp lemon or lime juice. Pour over the base and bake at 180°C/350°F/Gas 4 for 25 minutes.

NUT CARAMEL

Put 175g/6oz/⅔ cup soft light brown sugar, 30ml/2 tbsp golden (light corn) syrup and 175g/6oz/¾ cup butter in a pan. Heat gently until the sugar has dissolved, then bring to the boil and simmer for 5 minutes, until a rich golden colour. Stir in 175g/6oz/1 cup chopped roasted unsalted peanuts. Immediately spread over base and leave to cool.

CHOCOLATE

This topping is incredibly simple and always produces great results.

Chop 350g/12oz plain (semisweet), milk or white chocolate. Sprinkle over the hot cookie base, then return to the oven for 1 minute until melted. Mark into bars when the chocolate is almost set.

BAKING THE PERFECT BROWNIE

Brownies, named after their dark rich colour, should be moist and chewy; with a sugary crust on the outside, but squidgy on the inside. There are many different recipes for brownies, varying in richness. Plainer ones rely on (unsweetened) cocoa powder alone, others on vast quantities of melted chocolate. Often, a small amount of coffee is added that is barely perceptible to the taste, but cuts through the sweetness a little. True brownies have a very high proportion of sugar and fat and most contain nuts, usually walnuts or pecan nuts.

Light versions and those made from white chocolate are often referred to as blondies. It is important to remove brownies from the oven as soon as the cooking time is up, even though they will still seem quite soft. They will firm up on standing and, if overcooked, the characteristic gooey texture will be ruined.

BROWNIE VARIATIONS

Double chocolate Add chocolate chips in place of the chopped walnuts.

Chunky choc and nut Use coarsely chopped chunks of white chocolate in place of half the walnuts.

Macadamia nut Replace the chopped walnuts with whole macadamia nuts.

Almond brownies Use almond essence and almonds instead of vanilla and walnuts.

CLASSIC CHOCOLATE BROWNIES

Richly coloured and flavoured, these are deliciously gooey and moist.

Makes 24

225g/8oz plain (semisweet) chocolate
225g/8oz/1 cup butter, diced
3 eggs
225g/8oz/generous 1 cup caster (superfine) sugar
30ml/2 tbsp strong black coffee
75g/3oz/⅔ cup self-raising (self-rising) flour
pinch of salt
150g/5oz/1¼ cups chopped walnuts
5ml/1 tsp vanilla essence (extract)

1 Preheat the oven to 180°C/375°F/Gas 5. Grease and line a 18 × 28cm/7 × 11in tin (pan). Break the chocolate into squares and place in a heatproof bowl with the butter.

2 Set the bowl over a pan of barely simmering water and leave for 5–10 minutes, stirring occasionally until the mixture is melted and smooth. Remove the bowl from the pan and then leave the chocolate mixture to cool for 5 minutes.

3 In a large bowl, beat the eggs, sugar and coffee until smooth, then gradually beat in the cooled melted chocolate mixture.

4 Sift the flour and salt over the mixture, then fold in together with the walnuts and vanilla essence.

5 Spoon the mixture into the prepared tin and bake for about 35 minutes, or until just firm to the touch in the centre. (Don't bake it for any longer than this as the mixture will still be soft under the crust, but will firm up as it cools. Overcooking gives a dry result.)

6 Leave the brownies to cool in the tin then turn out on to a board, trim off the crusty edges and cut into squares. using a serrated knife and a gentle sawing action.

GREASING, LINING AND REDUCING THE SIZE OF TINS

When making bar cookies, it is imporant to line the baking tin (pan) with greaseproof (waxed) paper or baking parchment. This makes it much easier to lift the baked brownies or bars from the tin. If you use greaseproof paper, you will need to brush a little flavourless oil over the paper before pouring in the mixture. If you use baking parchment, the paper does not need to greased.

Base-lining Some recipes only require the base of the tin to be lined. This technique can be used to line any shape of tin, whether rectangular, square or round. Place the tin on a sheet of greaseproof (waxed) paper or baking parchment and, using a pencil, carefully draw around the tin. Using a pair of scissors, cut just inside the drawn line so that it will fit neatly inside the tin.

Using a sheet of buttered paper or a piece of kitchen paper drizzled with a flavourless oil such as sunflower or vegetable oil, grease the inside of the tin and place the lining paper in the base, pressing it into the corners.

Square and rectangular tins
To line both the base and sides of a square or rectangular tin, place the tin on a piece of greaseproof paper or baking parchment that is considerably larger than the tin. Using a pencil, draw around the tin. Cut a straight line from the edge of the paper to each corner of the square or rectangle. Turn the piece of paper over so the side marked with pencil is facing downwards. Fold in each side along its pencil line.

Grease the tin, then fit the paper inside the tin, folding the corners to fit neatly.

Round tins To line a round tin, place the tin on a piece of greaseproof paper or baking parchment and use a pencil to draw around it. Cut out the circle just inside the line. Next cut a long strip of paper about 2cm/¾in wider than the depth of the tin. (It must be long enough to wrap around the outside of the tin with 3cm/1¼in to spare.) Fold up the lower edge by 1cm/½in, then make cuts about 2.5cm/1in apart from the edge to the fold.

Grease the tin, then position the paper strip(s) around the side of the tin, so that the snipped edge sits flat on the base. Place the paper circle in the base of the tin, covering the snipped paper. Lightly grease all the paper if necessary.

Reducing tin size If the tin you are using is larger than the size required, you can reduce its size by fitting a strip of foil across the tin to make it the correct size. Make a long strip of triple thickness foil and cut it to fit three sides of the required tin.

Fold the strip of foil along one of the long edges to make a lap and fit it inside the tin to make it the required size. The weight of the mixture will hold the lap down and keep the divider in place.

Short-cut Cookies

There are occasions when you may want to make cookies in a hurry and you either don't want to turn on the oven just to bake a single batch of cookies or take the time and trouble measuring and mixing. Using ready-made cookie dough that you've either made in advance or bought, baking in a microwave oven or following a no-bake cookie recipe may provide you with the perfect solution.

REFRIGERATOR COOKIES

These are so called because the dough can be made in advance and kept in the refrigerator for up to 2 weeks before being cooked. It means that cookies can be freshly baked on demand. They are ideal for those who enjoy the pleasures of home-baked cookies, but don't always have time to make them from scratch.

The cookie dough is shaped into a log, wrapped in clear film (plastic wrap) and chilled in the refrigerator. Because the dough has a high fat content it should be chilled for at least 1 hour and preferably for longer. This will firm it to make slicing easier and will also ensure that the cookies hold their shape when cooked. The texture of the cookies is partly determined by the thickness of the slices: thinner slices will make fairly crisp cookies, thicker ones will be slightly less crisp. Some cookies such as those with chunks of chocolate or nuts are best cut in thicker slices. When baking thicker cookies, lower the temperature slightly and cook for a few minutes longer to make sure that they're cooked through.

QUICK VANILLA COOKIES

Just a few drops of vanilla essence (extract) is needed for these.

Makes 32
150g/5oz/10 tbsp butter, softened
150g/5oz/¾ cup caster (superfine) sugar
1 egg, lightly beaten
2.5ml/½ tsp vanilla essence (extract)
225g/8oz/2 cups plain (all-purpose) flour, sifted

1 Put the ingredients in a bowl and mix to a smooth dough. Lightly knead on a floured surface then roll the dough into a log shape about 5cm/2in diameter and 20cm/8in long. Wrap the log in clear film (plastic wrap) and chill for at least 1 hour or until firm enough to slice. For mini cookies, divide the dough in half and make two thinner logs.

2 Preheat the oven to 190°C/375°F/Gas 5. Cut the dough into 5mm/¼in slices. You can dip the knife in water and wipe it dry for a clean cut.

3 When you have cut the required number of cookies, re-wrap the remaining dough and put it back in the refrigerator.

4 Place the cookies about 2.5cm/1in apart on ungreased baking sheets. Bake for 12 minutes, or until just golden around the edges. Leave on the baking sheets for 2–3 minutes, then transfer to a wire rack to cool completely. Use the remaining cookie dough within 1 week of making, or double-wrap and freeze for up to 3 months.

BOUGHT COOKIE DOUGH

If you do not have the time to make your own cookie dough, ready-made chilled or frozen dough can be bought instead. This usually comes in tubs and, although several different varieties are available, chocolate chip cookie dough is the most popular. The mixture is ready to be spooned on to greased baking sheets, then baked according to the manufacturer's instructions. Once opened, the dough can be kept in its tub in the refrigerator for several days, so that you can bake fresh batches when required.

NO-BAKE COOKIES

A range of cookies can be made by mixing melted ingredients with dry ingredients and leaving them to set. The setting agent may be chocolate, which sets firm, or syrups and marshmallows, which set to create a chewier cookie. The mixture may be spooned into paper cake cases or into a greased and base-lined shallow tin (pan), then cut into squares, bars or triangles when set.

SETTING COOKIES WITH CHOCOLATE

The simplest no-bake cookies are made with breakfast cereals such as cornflakes combined with melted plain (semisweet) chocolate, golden (light corn) or maple syrup and butter. Others may contain crushed or broken plain cookies, dried fruit and nuts rather than cereal. Always leave the melted chocolate to cool before adding the dry ingredients.

To make a basic mixture, melt 65g/2½oz/5 tbsp unsalted (sweet) butter and 175g/6oz plain chocolate together, then cool. Stir in 75g/3oz broken digestive biscuits (Graham crackers), 50g/2oz/½ cup flaked (sliced) almonds, 50g/2oz/⅓ cup chopped dried fruit and 50g/2oz roughly chopped white chocolate.

SETTING COOKIES WITHOUT CHOCOLATE

No-bake cookies can be set with a mixture of cooked sugar or golden (light corn) syrup combined with melted butter, marshmallows and soft toffees. The most effective mixture uses equal quantities of toffees, butter and marshmallows mixed with puffed rice cereal.

To make a basic mixture, melt 115g/4oz each of butter, marshmallows and toffees in a pan, then stir in 115g/4oz/2 cups puffed rice cereal.

MAKING ROUND COOKIES

Spoon the no-bake cookie mixture on to a sheet of greaseproof (waxed) paper or baking parchment and wrap the mixture, packing it into a fat log-shape roll about 20cm/8in long. Chill until firm, then cut into 1cm/½in slices.

MAKING COOKIE WEDGES

Some cookies are made in a round, then sliced into wedges like cakes.

1 Spoon the cookie mixture into a lightly greased and lined shallow 20cm/7in round or 15cm/6in square tin (pan). Chill for 1–2 hours, or until very firm, but not rock hard.

2 Remove the mixture from the tin, then cut into thin wedges using a sharp knife.

MAKING COOKIE TRIANGLES

Rather than making individual cookies, you can make a triangular block of cookie mixture, then slice it once it has set.

1 Line the base and three sides of a deep, greased 18cm/7in square tin (pan) with clear film (plastic wrap). Prop up one side of the tin on a box so that it is at an angle of about 45 degrees.

2 Spoon the mixture into the tin and level the surface with the back of the spoon. Leave to stand until firm, then chill until completely set. To serve, remove the block from the tin, peel off the clear film and cut into 1cm/½in triangular slices.

LAYERED NO-BAKE COOKIES

Most no-bake cookies are single-layered affairs but some are richer and have two or more layers. Bear in mind that you need to be able to slice through the cookies cleanly; so don't make one layer much more fragile than the others. Canadian nanaimo bars are a classic layered no-bake cookie. The base is made of a non-crumbly cookie and nut mixture, the filling is firm and smooth, and the chocolate topping has a little oil added to it so it doesn't crack when cut.

MICROWAVE COOKIES

Many traditional cookie recipes written with oven-baking in mind need to be adjusted for microwave cooking and there are some that simply cannot be converted successfully. Others, however, will turn out every bit as good but in a fraction of the time.

The key to cooking round cookies in a microwave is to arrange them in circles so that they cook evenly. Don't be tempted to add a cookie to the middle as it will cook more slowly than the rest.

SOFT ALMOND COOKIES

These almond cookies remain soft for some time after cooking.

Makes 12

50g/2oz/¼ cup butter, softened
50g/2oz/¼ cup soft light brown sugar
1 egg yolk
75g/3oz/⅔ cup plain (all-purpose) flour
25g/1oz/¼ cup ground almonds

1 Cream the butter and sugar together in a large mixing bowl until light and fluffy. Beat in the egg yolk. Sift over the flour and gently fold into the mixture together with the ground almonds. If you like, fold in other ingredients such as chopped glacé (candied) cherries, a mixture of dried fruit or chopped nuts.

2 Place six tablespoonfuls of the mixture in a circle on a microwave-proof dish or a piece of baking parchment cut to fit the base of the oven. Cook for 1¾–2½ minutes on high (100 per cent power) or until the surface of the cookies is dry.

3 Remove the cookies carefully from the microwave as the edges will still be soft, leave to stand for 1 minute before lifting them on to a wire rack. They will finish cooking and become firmer as they cool.

BAR MICROWAVE COOKIES

To achieve the best results with bar cookies and traybakes in a microwave, bake them in a round flan dish (quiche pan), or 4cm/1½in-deep pie plate, then cut the cookies into wedges. The centre may be difficult to cook properly in recipes such as shortbread, but this isn't a problem with high-fat, syrupy mixtures such as flapjacks.

STICKY LEMON FLAPJACKS

Made with rolled oats, flapjacks are deliciously thick and chewy.

Makes 8

75g/3oz/6 tbsp butter, diced
60ml/4 tbsp golden (light corn) syrup
115g/4oz/generous ½ cup demerara (raw) sugar
175g/6oz/1½ cups rolled oats
juice and finely grated rind of ½ lemon

1 Put the butter, syrup and sugar in a heatproof bowl. Microwave on medium (50 per cent) power for 3–4 minutes, stirring halfway through.

2 Stir in the oats, lemon rind and juice. Spoon the mixture into a 20cm/8in microwave flan dish and spread out.

3 Cook on full (100 per cent) power for 3–3½ minutes, or until bubbling all over. Remove from the oven and mark into wedges when warm. Leave to cool in the dish.

DIFFERENT-SHAPED COOKIES

Microwave cookies don't have to be round, but whatever the shape, they should still be arranged in a ring. Irregular-shaped cookies should be positioned with the widest part towards the outer edge of the dish. When microwaving finger or stick-shaped cookies, avoid arranging them like the spokes of a wheel; instead, place them around the edge of the dish in one or two rows.

SESAME CHEESE TWISTS

These savoury snacks are perfect to serve with soups or salads.

Makes 36

115g/4oz/1 cup plain (all-purpose) flour
1.5ml/¼ tsp salt
pinch of mustard powder
50g/2oz/¼ cup butter, diced and chilled
50g/2oz/½ cup finely grated strong-
   flavoured cheese, such as Cheddar
1 egg yolk
10ml/2 tsp cold water
30ml/2 tbsp sesame seeds

1 Sift the flour, salt and mustard powder into a bowl. Rub in the butter until the mixture resembles fine breadcrumbs, then stir in the cheese. Mix the egg yolk and water together, sprinkle over the dry ingredients and mix to a firm dough. Lightly knead on a floured surface.

2 Roll out the dough to 5mm/¼in thickness and cut into sticks about 7.5cm/3in long and 5mm/¼in wide.

3 Hold the ends of the sticks and twist them in opposite directions. Sprinkle the sesame seeds on a plate and roll the twists in them until coated. Line a microwave tray with baking parchment and arrange 12 twists in a circle on it.

4 Cook on full (100 per cent) power for 2–2½ minutes, until firm to the touch. Leave to stand for 2 minutes, then transfer to a wire rack to cool. Cook the remaining cheese twists in the same way.

Cook's Tip

There isn't a standard output or name or number for settings used by all microwave manufacturers, so cooking times are only a guide. The recipes given here are for 750-watt microwave ovens.

GETTING GOOD RESULTS

• Always use microwave-proof cookware. Glass and china are suitable, but avoid melamine, plastic and any dishes that contain metal.
• Microwaved cookies don't brown in the same way as conventionally baked ones, so coloured mixtures such as ginger and chocolate work best.
• Improve the look of microwave cookies by icing them after cooking or adding a dusting of sugar.
• Added ingredients such as chocolate, nuts and dried fruit should be cut into small, even-sized pieces.
• Don't cover the cookies during cooking to allow the steam to escape.
• Microwaved cookies continue cooking for a short time after the machine is switched off, so stop microwaving just before they are ready. Open the door during cooking to check progress. The best way to discover whether they are done is to sacrifice one and break it open; if the centre is beginning to change colour, the cookies are ready. Use the same cooking time for subsequent batches.
• Foods with a high fat or sugar content cook very quickly in a microwave and can burn easily. Always cook for the minimum time and watch carefully. Remember, if you reduce the number of cookies, the cooking time must also be reduced.

Baking Cookies

To make perfect cookies, you must take as much care with cooking them as you did with mixing and shaping the dough.

USING THE OVEN

Always allow time to preheat the oven; it will take about 15 minutes to reach the required temperature (although fan-assisted ovens may heat more quickly).

Unless the recipe instructs otherwise, bake cookies in the middle, or just above the middle, of the oven. If you are baking large quantities of cookies, do not put more than two baking sheets in the oven at once because this can cause the oven temperature to drop. This particularly applies to cookies that have been chilled beforehand.

USING BAKING SHEETS

If you are using a new baking sheet, check that it fits into the oven before you arrange the cookies on it; ideally, there should be a small gap at either side and at the back of the baking sheet to allow hot air to circulate. If you need to divide the cookies between two or more baking sheets, put the same number of cookies on each sheet, so the batches cook at the same rate. If you put two baking sheets of cookies in the oven at the same time, switch them around halfway through the cooking time. If you need to cook a second batch of cookies straight away, let the baking sheet cool before placing the next batch of raw cookies on it; a hot baking sheet might make the raw cookies spread, which will result in thin, irregular-sized cookies.

TIME AND TEMPERATURE

Baking times may vary slightly with different ovens, and can depend on how chilled the cookies were when cooking commenced. Get to know your oven. If you feel that it is either too cool or too hot, use an oven thermometer to check the temperature. If it needs adjusting, change your oven temperature dial accordingly to correct this.

Always check cookies a few minutes before the end of the suggested cooking time. Unlike cakes, they will not loose volume or sink if the oven door is opened, although you should avoid doing this too frequently or the temperature will drop and the cookies will be less crisp. Second and subsequent batches of cookies may take slightly less time to cook.

COOKING GUIDELINES

Not all cookies are the same. Different types of cookie need to be cooked in different ways and at different temperatures.

DROP COOKIES

These are baked in a moderate oven, around 180°C/350°F/Gas 4. This gives them a chance to spread out a little before they set. To make cookies that are crisp on the outside, but with a slightly soft and chewy centre, remove from the oven as soon as the edges are dark golden but the middle is still a little pale. For crisp cookies, wait until the whole cookie is lightly browned before removing from the oven. To achieve an even crisper result, spread out the mixture slightly to make a thinner layer before baking.

ROLLED, PIPED AND PRESSED COOKIES

These are usually chilled before baking to prevent them spreading too much during cooking. They are cooked in a moderate to hot oven, between 180°C/350°F/Gas 4 and 200°C/400°F/Gas 6.

1 Place the cookies on a baking sheet, then chill for 30 minutes.

2 Bake until pale golden; do not allow to colour too much.

3 Leave to cool slightly on the baking sheets, then carefully transfer to wire racks to cool completely.

REFRIGERATOR COOKIES

These cookies have a relatively high fat content and so are baked at a moderately high temperature, around 190°C/375°F/Gas 5.

1 Slice the chilled cookie mixture and arrange on ungreased baking sheets. Do not use non-stick sheets or line the sheets with baking parchment because this will make the cookies spread.

2 The cookies must be well chilled before baking, so either cook them as soon as they have been sliced or place the baking sheets in the refrigerator until ready to bake.

BAR COOKIES

This type of cookie is usually baked in a moderate to moderately low oven, between 160°C/325°F/Gas 3 and 180°C/350°F/Gas 4.

1 Bar cookies with a shortbread, pastry or crumb base are often partially baked before the topping is added. This allows the base to be cooked until crisp and firm without the topping becoming overcooked.

2 To test whether sponge or brownie mixtures are cooked, insert a cocktail stick (toothpick) into the mixture. It should come out clean.

COOLING COOKIES

Always follow the instructions in the recipe when cooling cookies. Most cookies are quite delicate so benefit from being left on the baking sheets for a minute or two to firm up, before removing to a wire rack to cool completely.

Use a thin palette knife or metal spatula to transfer cookies to wire racks. Placing them on a wire rack allows air to circulate around the them, and prevents moisture being trapped, which can make them lose their crisp texture. Don't cram too many cookies on the rack at any one time and avoid placing hot cookies on top of each other; they are likely to lose their crispness.

Cookies such as tuiles that are to be moulded into shape should be removed from the baking sheets after 30 seconds, while they are still warm and pliable. Others such as bar cookies may benefit from being allowed to cool in the baking tins (pans). Placing the whole tin on a wire rack can speed the cooling.

BAKING COOKIES AT HIGH ALTITUDE

At 3,000m/9,800ft above sea level, atmospheric pressure becomes lower, which makes liquid boil faster and causes greater evaporation. This affects cookie baking in several ways: flavours, especially sweet ones, are more concentrated; slightly more liquid is necessary; and smaller quantities of raising agents are needed. It also helps if you marginally reduce the amount of fat in recipes and increase the quantity of flour.

	ALTITUDE		
	3,000m/9,800ft	**5,000m/16,350ft**	**7,000/22,900ft**
Sugar For each 115g/4oz/ generous ½ cup, reduce by:	10ml/2 tsp	115ml/1 tbsp	30ml/2 tbsp
Baking powder For each 5ml/1 tsp, reduce by:	0.75ml/⅛ tsp	1.5ml/¼ tsp	1.5ml/¼ tsp
Liquid For each 75ml/5 tbsp, reduce by:	5ml/1 tsp	110ml/2 tsp	30ml/1tbsp
Oven temperature Increase by:	5°C/10°F/Gas ¼	15°C/25°F/Gas ½	20°C/35°F/Gas 1½

Cookie Decoration

Decorating cookies can add the final flourish to home-made cookies and can be one of the most enjoyable aspects of cookie-making. Cookies can be decorated before baking, while the cookies are still warm from the oven, or when they are completely cool.

DECORATING COOKIES BEFORE BAKING

Techniques for decorating unbaked cookies can range from the most simple sprinkling of sugar or nuts to brushing with a glossy glaze or painting intricate designs with edible food colouring.

SUGAR

A crunchy sugar topping is one of the easiest and most effective ways to decorate unbaked cookies. (It is also one of the most popular decorations for baked cookies.) Many different sugars can be used.

Caster (superfine) sugar can be sprinkled straight over raw cookies to give a subtle, crunchy texture. Coarse sugars such as demerara (raw) sugar and irregular-shaped coffee crystals give a crunchier result. Pretty coloured sugars and crushed white and brown sugar lumps also produce a lovely effect when sprinkled over raw cookies.

Moist cookie doughs can simply be sprinkled with sugar; drier cookies such as refrigerator or rolled cookies may benefit from being lightly brushed with a little water or milk before they are sprinkled with sugar. Alternatively, after rolling the dough, sprinkle it with sugar, then roll very lightly before cutting out the cookies.

Cookie dough that is shaped into a log before slicing can be rolled in sugar before the log is chilled and sliced. This will produce cookies with a crisp, sugary edge.

Cookies such as macaroons that produce a cracked surface during baking look particularly attractive dusted with sugar before baking. The sugar helps to accentuate the cracked effect. Flatten the balls of dough slightly, brush each with a little water and sift over a fine and even layer of icing (confectioners') sugar before baking.

NUTS

Chopped and flaked (sliced) nuts can be sprinkled over cookies in the same way as sugar. Nuts brown during baking, so avoid using on cookies that are baked at a high temperature or on cookies that are baked for a long time as the nuts may overcook.

A whole nut can be pressed into the top of each individual cookie. (This technique is best suited to soft cookie doughs.) The nuts may be decorative, or they can be used to indicate the type of cookie. For example, you might want to press a whole hazelnut into a hazelnut cookie, or an almond into an almond flavoured cookie.

Flaked (sliced) almonds look stunning sprinkled over cookies but should be baked for no longer than 10 minutes in a moderately hot oven or they will burn. This is the classic topping for tuiles.

GLAZES

Brushing a glaze over cookies can serve two purposes, either to provide a sticky surface that nuts or sugar can stick to, or simply to give an attractive finish.

To give cookies a rich, glossy finish, use a whole beaten egg or yolk. Brush the glaze lightly and evenly on the top, without it dripping over the edges – this is especially important where raising agents have been used because it will prevent the cookies rising evenly. You can dilute the glaze by adding 15ml/1 tbsp cold water or milk and adding a pinch of caster (superfine) sugar for sweet cookies; salt for savoury ones.

Lightly beaten egg white produces a clear, shiny finish. Brush over the cookies halfway through the baking time, so that it soaks into the cookies slightly and does not set to a crackled glaze. It looks effective sprinkled with a little sugar.

PAINTED COOKIES

Edible food colouring can be painted directly on to unbaked cookies to make pretty patterns. This technique is best suited to drier, firmer cookie doughs such as rolled and refrigerator cookies.

To decorate cookies, cut the dough into shapes, place them on baking sheets and chill for 30 minutes. Beat an egg yolk and mix in a few drops of food colouring. Using a fine paintbrush, paint patterns on to the cookies, and then bake. (Remember that the yellow egg yolk may affect the colour of the food colouring.)

CANDY CENTRES

This technique is very simple to do, yet is extremely effective.

Cut out the centre of each cookie and fill it with crushed boiled sweets (hard candy). The sweets will melt during baking, then harden when cooled to make a colourful centre.

SIMPLE WAYS TO DECORATE COOKIES BEFORE BAKING

• Chopped fudge, toffee and chocolate chunks and chips add a delicious, decorative finish to drop cookies.

• Candy-coated chocolate buttons retain their bright colours when baked in cookies and are especially popular with young children. Mix into the dough or gently press them into the surface of the cookies.

• Halved or sliced glacé (candied) cherries and candied angelica diamonds are effective and colourful decorations.

• Pressing a pattern with the tines of a fork or marking lines on cookies with a knife look great. This also helps to prevent the cookies from rising unevenly.

SIMPLE BAKED COOKIE DECORATIONS

As with unbaked cookies, you can transform simple baked cookies into something really special with just a few simple decorating techniques. A sprinkling of sugar takes just a few seconds, while dusting a design using a stencil or writing a simple message with a food colouring pen takes only a little longer. Food colouring pens work best on refrigerator or rolled cookies that have been only lightly baked, or on firm icing.

DECORATING COOKIES WITH SUGAR

Different types of sugar can be used to give a range of effects on various baked cookies.

Icing/confectioners' sugar

A light dusting of icing sugar gives plain cookies a wonderfully professional finish and is a useful way of disguising any imperfections.

Use a fine sieve or sugar dredger to give an even coating. If you want a very light layer, hold the sieve or dredger high and shake gently; for a thicker finish, keep the sieve or dredger closer to the cookies. If you are dusting pairs of cookies sandwiched together, fill them first, then sprinkle with sugar.

Caster/superfine sugar

Simply sprinkling freshly baked cookies with a little caster (superfine) sugar is perhaps one of the quickest and easiest decorations to use.

Sprinkle sugar over the cookies while they are still warm so that the sugar sticks to them. (Soft light and dark brown sugars can also be used but, because they are so moist, even sprinkling is very difficult. Push through a medium sieve rather than sprinkling by hand.)

FLAVOURED SUGARS

These are a good alternative to plain caster (superfine) sugar and give cookies a subtle hint more flavour. It is possible to buy flavoured sugars, but it is just as easy to make your own.

Vanilla Put a vanilla pod (bean) in a jar of caster sugar and leave for at least 2 weeks. Refill the jar with sugar as you use it.

Sweet spice Infuse (steep) the sugar for two weeks with whole spices such as cloves. To make instant spiced sugar, use about 2.5ml/½ tsp ground cinnamon or mixed (apple pie) spice for every 30ml/2 tbsp sugar.

Coarse-grained sugars

Granulated and demerara (raw) sugar look pretty sprinkled over cookies but, because the grains are so large, they will not stick to the cookie on their own. The easiest way to overcome this problem is to use a glaze such as beaten egg white to stick the sugar to the cookie, then return the cookies to the oven for 2–3 minutes.

Cookies such as sweet pretzels are usually coated with sugar, then grilled (broiled) until the it starts to caramelize. Brush the cooled cookies lightly with egg white and sprinkle generously with demerara sugar. (Sprinkle on plenty of sugar to protect the cookie from the heat.) Place under a hot grill (broiler) for about 1 minute until the sugar is just starting to bubble. Return to wire racks to cool.

Citrus Add a strip of orange or lemon rind to the sugar and leave for 3 days. Shake the sugar before use as it may have become slightly damp from the rind.

Rosemary Add a sprig of fresh rosemary to the sugar and leave for 3–4 days.

Lavender Add lavender (about five heads) to the sugar and leave for 3–4 days.

DECORATING COOKIES WITH SUGAR GLAZES

Cookies such as Lebkuchen are sometimes given a slightly shiny finish with a sugar glaze. These glazes may be clear or opaque and are usually brushed over the cookies while they are still hot or warm.

LEBKUCHEN GLAZE

This semi-opaque glaze gently softens the surface of the cookie, giving it a chewy texture.

Sift 175g/6oz/1½ cups icing (confectioners') sugar into a bowl. Add 2.5ml/½ tsp almond essence (extract), 5ml/1 tsp lemon juice and 30ml/2 tbsp hot water. Mix together until smooth, then brush over the hot Lebkuchen and leave to cool.

CLEAR GLAZE

This simple sugar glaze gives cookies a lovely, glossy finish.

1 Heat 25g/1oz/2 tbsp sugar in 60ml/4 tbsp water until the sugar dissolves. Boil rapidly for 5 minutes, or until reduced by half. (The glaze can be flavoured with a strip of lemon or orange rind if you like).

2 Remove from the heat and leave to cool. Gradually beat in 115g/4oz/1 cup sifted icing sugar, then brush over warm cookies and leave to set.

STENCILLING DESIGNS

This is an easy way to decorate cookies. You can buy stencils that are specially made for cake and cookie decorating, or make your own by drawing a small design on thin cardboard and cutting it out. Make sure there is a contrast between the colour of the cookie and the dusting ingredient; icing sugar works well on chocolate cookies, while (unsweetened) cocoa powder is better on pale cookies. You can also colour icing sugar by blending cake decorator's colouring dust (petal dust) with the sugar.

Place the stencil over the cookie. Dust with icing sugar or cocoa powder through a fine sieve, then carefully remove the cardboard.

Paper doilies can be used to make an attractive lacy pattern. Place a large doily over several cookies at once and dust liberally with icing sugar or cocoa powder.

To create a dramatic light and dark effect on cookies, lightly dust a whole cookie with icing sugar, then cover half of it with a piece of cardboard or a sheet of paper and carefully dust the other half with cocoa powder.

FOOD-COLOURING PENS

These pens look like felt-tipped pens but they are filled with edible food colouring. They come in a range of colours from primary to pastels and some are flavoured.

They can be used directly on to the cookies or on to icing. They are most effective used on rolled and cut cookies that have been baked only until light golden rather than well browned; icing must be dry and firm.

Use the decorating pens in the same way as an ordinary pen. Draw designs, write messages, or use to colour in shapes.

DECORATING COOKIES WITH ICING

Cookies can look lovely decorated with pretty coloured icing. It is important to get the consistency of icing exactly right; too thick and it will be difficult to spread; too thin and it will run off the edges and soak into the cookie.

There are many different types of icing that can be used to decorate cookies and they can range in colour from the palest pastels to vibrant primary colours. Glacé or fondant icings give a smooth, glossy finish and can be used to create simple finishing touches to the cookies, while royal icing can be swirled to give a textured pattern or piped into delicate and intricate designs. Whatever type of icing you use, iced cookies should usually be eaten within 3 or 4 days.

GLACÉ ICING

This is the simplest type of icing to make and use. It is perfect for the tops of cookies, or for drizzling and piping simple designs.

To cover 24 cookies
115g/4oz/1 cup icing
(confectioners') sugar
a few drops of vanilla essence
(extract) (optional)
15ml/1 tbsp hot water
a few drops of food colouring (optional)

Sift the icing sugar into a bowl, then add the vanilla essence, if using. Gradually stir in the hot water until the mixture is the consistency of thick cream. Add the food colouring, and continue stirring until smooth.

Top coating This is the simplest technique for coating the top of cookies with glacé icing.

Spoon a little icing on to the centre of the cookie, then carefully spread it out almost to the edges using the back of the spoon. (To make a perfect shape, pipe the outline of the shape first. Leave to dry for 1–2 minutes, then spoon in the icing and spread out to fill the shape.)

Feathered glacé icing Spoon a little icing over a cookie to cover it completely, then pipe several thin, straight parallel lines of icing in a contrasting colour across the top of the cookie.

Starting at the middle of the cookie, draw a wooden cocktail stick (toothpick) or fine skewer through the lines in the opposite direction, gently dragging the colour through the icing and creating a feathered effect on the cookie.

Cobweb icing Cover a cookie in icing, then pipe on fine, concentric circles of icing in a contrasting colour, starting from the centre and working outwards.

Draw a cocktail stick (toothpick) from the centre of the cookie to the outside edge, dividing the cookie into quarters, then repeat to divide it into eighths.

Drizzled icing Glacé icing can be drizzled or piped over cookies to give a pretty finish.

Place the cookies on a wire rack. Using a paper piping (pastry) bag or teaspoon, drizzle fine lines of icing over the cookies. You can then drizzle more icing at right angles to these first lines, if you like.

Variation
To make white glacé icing, add a few drops of lemon juice instead of vanilla essence; this enhances the whiteness.

ICING GLAZE

This is similar to glacé icing, but is flavoured with lemon juice and thinned with egg white, giving it a shinier, slightly harder set.

To cover 12 cookies

15ml/1 tbsp lightly beaten egg white
15ml/1 tbsp lemon juice
115g/4oz/1 cup icing (confectioners') sugar, sifted

Mix together the egg white and lemon juice in a bowl. Gradually beat in the icing sugar until the mixture is completely smooth, then place the cookies on a wire rack. Spoon the icing evenly over the cookies and leave to set.

ROYAL ICING

This icing sets hard to give a good finish so is perfect for piping designs and messages on cookies such as gingerbread. It can be coloured with a few drops of food colouring but is better left unflavoured.

To cover 30 cookies

1 egg white, at room temperature or 7.5ml/1½ tsp albumen powder
225g/8oz/2 cups icing (confectioners') sugar, sifted, plus extra if necessary

1 Beat the egg white for a few seconds with a fork. (If using albumen powder, mix according to the instructions.) Mix in the icing sugar a little at a time until the mixture stands in soft peaks and is thick enough to spread. If the icing is for piping, beat in a little more icing sugar until the icing will stand in stiff peaks. Spread or pipe the icing over the cookies. Leave to set.

MAKING AND USING A PAPER ICING BAG

A paper bag for piping is easy to make once you know how.

1 Cut a piece of greaseproof (waxed) paper or baking parchment into a 25cm/10in square, then cut it in half diagonally so that you have two triangles. Hold one triangle with the longest side away from you. Curl the left-hand point over into a cone to meet the point nearest you. Curl the right-hand point over the cone.

2 Bring the points of the folded triangles together to make a neat, narrow cone. Tuck the point of paper inside the cone, fold it over and secure with sticky tape.

3 If using a nozzle, cut off the pointed end of the bag. Position the nozzle so that it fits snugly.

4 Using a palette knife or metal spatula, fill the bag with icing. Take care not to overfill the bag; half to two-thirds full is ideal.

5 Fold the top corners of the bag in towards the centre, then fold over the top, firmly pushing the icing down towards the tip. Fold over the top corner again, making a pad to push with your thumb.

6 If you have not inserted a nozzle into the bag, snip a small, straight piece off the end of the bag for the icing to pass through. (It is better to snip off the small tip first. If the line of icing is too narrow, snip off a little bit more.)

7 Hold the piping bag between your middle and forefingers and push down with your thumb. Place the tip in position over the cookie, then gently push the icing through the bag using your thumb. To stop the flow of icing, release the pressure from your thumb. The icing will continue to flow for a few seconds after the pressure has stopped so you should release your thumb before you reach the end of the line.

DECORATING COOKIES WITH CHOCOLATE

The taste, texture and versatility of chocolate makes it one of the most popular ingredients for decorating cookies. It can be used to coat cookies, pipe or drizzle patterns, or even write short messages.

MELTING CHOCOLATE

For most decorating techniques, chocolate needs to be melted. Take care doing this as overheating will spoil both the texture and flavour. When melting chocolate, choose a variety with a high proportion of cocoa butter as this will melt much more easily and smoothly.

Using a double boiler Break the chocolate into pieces and put it in the top of a double boiler or in a heatproof bowl set over a pan of hot water; the water should not touch the top container. Bring the water to simmering point, then turn down the heat to keep the water at a very gently simmer.

Check the chocolate every few minutes, turning off the heat if necessary. Stir once or twice during melting until the chocolate is completely smooth. Do not cover the bowl once the chocolate has melted or condensation will form.

Using a microwave This is a quick and simple way of melting chocolate. Bear in mind that microwaved chocolate will retain its shape, so you will need to stir the chocolate to see if it has melted.

Break the chocolate into pieces and place in a microwave-safe bowl. Melt in bursts of 30–60 seconds, checking often and reducing the time as the chocolate begins to soften. Stop microwaving before all the chocolate has melted; the residual heat in the chocolate should complete the process.

As a guide, 115g/4oz chocolate will take about 1½ minutes on full (100 per cent) power and 225g/8oz will take 2–2½ minutes. White chocolate should be melted on medium (50 per cent) power.

Using direct heat This method is only suitable for recipes where the chocolate is melted with another liquid such as milk or cream, or with other ingredients such as butter and golden (light corn) syrup.

Put the liquid ingredients in the pan, then add the chopped or broken chocolate and melt slowly over the lowest heat. When the chocolate has started to melt, turn off the heat and stir constantly until the mixture is completely smooth.

Tempering chocolate This technique is used for couverture chocolate, making it easier to work with and giving it a glossy appearance when set.

Melt the chocolate in the usual way, then pour about two-thirds of it on to a marble slab or cold surface. Using a palette knife or metal spatula, move the chocolate back and forth until it is thick and beginning to reach setting point. Return the chocolate to the bowl and melt again, stirring constantly.

USING MELTED CHOCOLATE

When you are decorating cookies with melted chocolate, handle the chocolate as little as possible and use a palette knife or metal spatula to lift and move the decorated cookies around; the warmth of your fingers will leave prints on the chocolate and make the surface dull.

Always leave chocolate-coated cookies to set at room temperature and do not store in the refrigerator unless it is exceptionally warm; chilling will cause the chocolate to lose its glossy appearance. Also make sure that the cookies are at room temperature rather than still warm from the oven or cold (if they have been stored in the refrigerator or freezer).

Coating cookies with chocolate

Before coating cookies in melted chocolate, make sure that the chocolate is just starting to cool; chocolate that is hot or even very warm will soak into the cookies and spoil the texture.

1 Place the cookies on a wire rack with a sheet of baking parchment underneath. Spoon cooled melted chocolate over each cookie, then tap the rack to help it run down the sides and to level the top. Leave to set on the rack, then cover with a second coat, if you like. Scrape the chocolate off the baking parchment, return to the bowl and re-melt to coat more cookies.

2 To decorate coated cookies, drizzle or pipe with a contrasting colour of chocolate. For a smooth surface, do this before the first layer of chocolate has set; for a raised surface, wait until the first layer of chocolate has hardened.

Dipping cookies in chocolate

Round or shaped cookies are often half-coated in chocolate and finger cookies sometimes have one or both ends dipped in chocolate. This method is simpler than completely covering cookies in chocolate. If you're planning to sandwich cookies together, they are best dipped in chocolate before filling as the warmth of the chocolate may melt the filling if dipped afterwards.

1 Melt the chocolate in a narrow deep bowl. Holding the cookie by the part that you don't want to coat, dip it briefly in the melted chocolate, then allow any excess to drip back into the bowl.

2 Place the cookie on a sheet of baking parchment and leave to set. When the chocolate is firm carefully peel off the paper. If you want to sprinkle chopped nuts or other decorations on the top, do this before the chocolate sets.

Coating florentines with chocolate

The flat underside of florentines is traditionally coated with chocolate.

Holding the florentine between finger and thumb, spread the flat base with chocolate. With the prongs of a fork, create wavy lines in the chocolate. Place the florentine on a wire rack, and leave to set

Piping chocolate

Use a small paper piping (pastry) bag with the end snipped off to pipe thin lines of chocolate.

Place cookies on a sheet of baking parchment and pipe over thin lines, first in one direction, then the other.

Colouring white chocolate

You can colour melted white chocolate with cake decorator's colouring dust (petal dust). Do not use liquid or paste food colourings as these will spoil the texture of the chocolate.

Cookie Fillings

From smooth custard creams to sticky jammie sweethearts, two cookies sandwiched together are better than one. The key to a good cookie filling is to make the mixture soft enough to spread or pipe but not too moist because this can make the cookies soft and crumbly.

BUTTERCREAM

This simple cookie filling is very easy to make. Once filled, the cookies should be eaten within 3 days.

1 To make enough filling for about 12 pairs of average-size cookies, put 50g/2oz/¼ cup softened unsalted (sweet) butter in a bowl and beat with a wooden spoon until very soft, smooth and creamy.

2 Gradually stir in 90g/3½oz/scant 1 cup icing (confectioners') sugar and 5ml/1 tsp vanilla essence (extract). Beat the ingredients well with an electric mixer until they are very light and smooth.

Variations
Orange, lemon or lime buttercream
Add 15ml/1 tbsp finely grated citrus rind and replace the vanilla with juice, beating well to avoid curdling. The buttercream cannot be piped through a small nozzle because of the citrus rind.
Chocolate buttercream Blend 10ml/ 2 tsp (unsweetened) cocoa powder with 20ml/4 tsp boiling water until smooth Cool, then beat into the buttercream.
Coffee buttercream Replace the vanilla essence (extract) with 10ml/2 tsp instant coffee powder dissolved in 15ml/ 1 tbsp near-boiling water. Cool before adding to the mixture.

CRÈME AU BEURRE

This delicious buttercream has a rich taste and very smooth texture.

1 To make enough filling for about 12 pairs of average-size cookies, put 40g/1½oz/3 tbsp caster (superfine) sugar and 30ml/2 tbsp water in a small, heavy pan and heat gently until the sugar has completely dissolved. Bring to the boil and boil steadily for 2–3 minutes, until the syrup reaches 107°C/225°F on a sugar thermometer or when a little syrup pulled apart between two dry teaspoons makes a fine thread.

2 Beat 1 egg yolk in a heatproof bowl for a few seconds. Gradually pour over the syrup in a steady, narrow stream, whisking constantly. Continue whisking until the mixture is thick and cold. Beat 75g/3oz/ 6 tbsp unsalted (sweet) butter until creamy. Gradually add the egg yolk mixture to the butter, whisking well after each addition.

CHOCOLATE GANACHE

This filling is a fairly soft so chill for a few minutes before using to fill cookies. It is rich, so spread thinly.

1 To make enough filling for about 20 pairs of average-size cookies. Pour 120ml/4fl oz/½ cup double (heavy) cream into a small pan and bring to the boil. Remove the pan from the heat and add 115g/4oz plain (semisweet) chocolate. Stir until melted and smooth.

2 Return the mixture to the heat and bring back to the boil. Transfer to a bowl and leave to cool. Chill for 10 minutes before using.

FILLING COOKIES WITH JAM

To make a smooth, slightly set jam filling, the jam needs to be boiled briefly to thicken it.

1 To makes enough for 16 pairs of cookies, put 120ml/8 tbsp jam in a small, heavy pan. Add 5ml/1 tsp lemon juice. Heat gently until runny, then boil for 3–4 minutes.

2 Remove the pan from the heat and leave to cool slightly, then push the jam through a fine sieve to remove any lumps. Leave the jam until barely warm, then use to sandwich the cookies together.

FILLING BRANDY SNAPS

Whipped cream, sometimes sweetened with a little sugar and flavoured with brandy or a few drops of vanilla essence (extract), makes a simple filling for these crisp rolled cookies. Using a well-chilled bowl for whipping the cream will give a lighter result.

1 To make enough cream to fill about 20 brandy snaps, pour 250ml/ 8fl oz/1 cup whipping cream into a large chilled bowl. Sift 10ml/2 tsp icing (confectioners') sugar over the cream and add about 30ml/2 tbsp brandy. Whip the mixture using an electric mixer or balloon whisk until the cream just forms soft peaks.

2 Spoon the cream into a piping (pastry) bag fitted with a large star nozzle. Push the end of the nozzle into the end of the brandy snap and squeeze gently until the brandy snap is filled to the middle. Repeat with the other end of the brandy snap.

CHOCOLATE-FILLED COOKIES

Chunks of chocolate can be baked inside the cookie to make a delicious surprise filling.

Makes about 16
150g/5oz/10 tbsp butter, softened
150g/5oz/¾ cup caster
  (superfine) sugar
1 egg yolk
15ml/1 tbsp ground almonds
225g/8oz/2 cups self-raising
  (self-rising) flour
25g/1oz/¼ cup (unsweetened)
  cocoa powder
150g/5oz plain (semisweet) chocolate
icing (confectioners') sugar, for dusting

1 Preheat the oven to 190°C/375°F/ Gas 5 and grease or line two baking sheets. Cream the butter and sugar until pale and fluffy. Beat in the egg yolk and ground almonds. Sift over the flour and cocoa powder and fold into the mixture to make a firm dough. Knead for a few seconds, then wrap in clear film (plastic wrap) and chill for 30 minutes.

2 Roll out just over a third of the dough to a thickness of 3mm/⅛in and stamp out 16 rounds using a 4cm/1½in cookie cutter. Break the chocolate into squares and put one in the centre of each cookie round.

3 Roll out the remaining dough and cut into 16 larger rounds using a 5cm/2in cutter. Place these over the chocolate-covered cookie rounds and press the edges together. Bake for 10 minutes until firm. Dust the cookies with icing sugar and transfer to a wire rack. Serve warm while the filling is still soft and melted.

CLASSIC COOKIE FILLINGS

These recipes will make enough to fill 12–15 pairs of cookies.
Custard cream Melt 25g/ 1oz/2 tbsp butter in a small pan, then beat in 225g/8oz/2 cups sifted icing (confectioners') sugar, 30ml/2 tbsp milk and a few drops of vanilla essence (extract) until smooth.
Chocolate bourbon Beat together 50g/2oz/¼ cup of softened butter, 75g/3oz/¾ cup sifted icing (confectioners') sugar, 15ml/1 tbsp sifted (unsweetened) cocoa powder and 5ml/1 tsp golden (light corn) syrup until smooth.
Chocolate and orange Bring 120ml/4fl oz/½ cup whipping cream to the boil. Remove from the heat and stir in 200g/7oz chopped white chocolate until smooth. Stir in 5ml/1 tsp orange essence (extract) or liqueur.
Fudgy mocha Dissolve 10ml/ 2 tsp instant coffee powder in 5ml/1 tsp water in a heatproof bowl set over a pan of boiling water. Add four chopped chocolate-coated fudge fingers. Stir until melted, remove from the heat and whisk in 30ml/ 2 tbsp double (heavy) cream. Chill until firm enough to spread.
Honey and ginger Beat together 75g/3oz/6 tbsp softened butter, 75g/3oz/¾ cup set honey and 75g/3oz/¾ cup icing (confectioners') sugar until light and creamy. Beat in 40g/1½oz finely chopped, preserved stem ginger.

Storing Cookies

With few exceptions, cookies are best eaten on the day that they are made. Some such as American-style soft cookies are delicious when still slightly warm from the oven, but most cookies need to be cooled first to allow them to crisp. If you're not planning to eat them straight away, store them as soon as they have cooled. This will prevent crisp cookies from becoming soft and soft ones from drying out and hardening. Store crisp and soft cookies separately; if kept together, not only will their texture suffer, but the flavours may mingle as well.

SOFT COOKIES

It is essential to keep these cookies in an airtight container and, if possible, they should also be stored in the refrigerator to retain the freshly baked flavour.

Carefully pack cookies into an airtight container and seal. If the lid of the container isn't tight-fitting, put the cookies inside a plastic bag first, or cover the whole container with clear film (plastic wrap) before closing the lid. To restore the texture of soft cookies that have hardened – this may happen very quickly in dry climates – add a slice of brown bread to the container. Replace the bread daily.

CRISP COOKIES

The container for this type of cookie does not need to be absolutely airtight; unless the atmosphere is very humid, a slight flow of air will help them stay crisp.

Glass jars and ceramic containers with cork stoppers are ideal for storing crisp cookies. Place a little crumpled tissue paper in the base of the jar to help absorb any moisture. If cookies become soft, place them on a baking sheet and put in a preheated oven at 150°C/300°F/Gas 2 for about 3 minutes to re-crisp. Remove and cool on a wire rack before storing.

COOKIES IN THE FREEZER

Undecorated baked cookies can be frozen successfully. Freeze the cookies on trays, then pack into an airtight container interleaving with greaseproof (waxed) paper or baking parchment. (Avoid freezing cream-filled cookies such as brandy snaps as these will quickly become soggy.) To thaw, leave at room temperature for about 20 minutes.

Iced cookies can also be frozen in the same way, but they should be removed from the airtight container and thawed on a wire rack – the icing may be spoiled if they are left to thaw while still packed in layers.

CHILLING AND FREEZING COOKIE DOUGH

As long as cookie dough doesn't contain leavening ingredients, it can be stored in the refrigerator overnight or, in some cases, for up to a week. Cookie dough can also be frozen for up to 3 months but the flavours tend to lose their intensity after a month so, for optimum results, the dough is best frozen for just a few weeks.

To store cookie dough in the refrigerator, wrap it in clear film (plastic wrap) or place it in a bowl and cover it tightly with clear film. To freeze, wrap the dough in a double wrapping of clear film, then store in an airtight container.

To freeze unbaked cookies, open-freeze them on trays, then pack into airtight containers, interleaving them layers with greaseproof (waxed) paper or baking parchment. Thaw unbaked cookies on baking sheets.

WHAT WENT WRONG AND WHY

Occasionally cookies don't turn out quite as you had hoped. If you have a problem when baking, try to work out why so that you can either remedy it at the time, or at least avoid it next time you bake cookies.

Problem	Cause	Remedy
The dough is very soft and won't hold its shape.	Too much liquid or fat or too little flour, or the dough has become too warm.	Always measure ingredients carefully. Chill the dough for 30 minutes before baking. If it is still too soft, work in a little extra flour.
The dough is dry and crumbly and won't hold together.	Not enough liquid or fat or too much flour, or the dough may not have been kneaded sufficiently.	Try gently kneading the dough; the warmth of your hands may bring it together. If the dough includes egg, check the right size was used. Knead in a little beaten egg, milk or soft butter.
The cookies are not evenly cooked.	The cookies are either of uneven sizes on the baking sheet; or some cookies were placed too near the edge of the sheet.	Make sure that all the cookies on a baking sheet are an even size. Leave at least a 2.5cm/1in gap around the edge of the baking sheet and turn the sheets around halfway through baking.
The cookies stick to the baking sheet.	The baking sheet was not greased or greased unevenly. Alternatively, it may have been greased with salted butter.	Use melted, unsalted (sweet) butter or oil for greasing or line the sheet with baking parchment.
The cookies crumble when removed from baking sheet.	Cookies that have a very high butter content are often more fragile than less rich ones.	Leave fragile cookies to cool on the baking sheet for at least 3 minutes before transferring to a wire rack.
The cookies are dry and too crisp on top.	The oven was too hot or the cookies were baked for too long.	If you have concerns about the temperature of your oven, use an oven thermometer. Check cookies a few minutes before end of cooking time.
The cookies spread out too much on the baking sheet.	The cookies were not chilled before baking, or, the baking sheet was over-greased when the cookies were added.	Most cookies benefit from chilling before baking. Grease baking sheets only lightly. Some cookies such as refrigerator cookies should be baked on ungreased baking sheets. Always use cold baking sheets.
The cookies are burnt on the base but not on the top.	There are a number of possible causes: baking too low down in the oven, or at too low a temperature; the baking sheets may be poor quality, or you may have used salted butter for greasing.	Check the oven temperature and bake cookies on the middle shelf. Avoid thin or very dark baking sheets. Butter burns at a lower temperature, so use oil for cookies baked at high temperatures or for a long time.

Presentation and Packaging

Whether you're making cookies to serve to guests, give as a gift or sell at a fundraising event, it is worth spending a little time on pretty presentation and attractive and elegant packaging.

All cookies should be properly stored as soon as they have cooled or, if iced or decorated, as soon as they have set and hardened. Leave gift wrapping and packaging until the last minute so that the cookies are as fresh as possible. It is often useful to include information about the cookies as well, including a list of ingredients and advice on storing.

GIFT BOXES

You can buy a huge range of pretty storage containers that make perfect packaging for cookies. Stationers and department stores sell a range of beautiful gift boxes and containers in all shapes and sizes, patterns and colours. These are the simplest way to package cookies and look stunning tied with curled ribbon or raffia.

Line the box with either crumpled tissue paper or several layers of greaseproof (waxed) paper. If the cookies are iced or fragile, then shallow boxes that will hold the cookies in one or just a few layers are better than very deep ones.

Certain types of cookie can be individually wrapped in tissue paper or cellophane before packing into the box. Amaretti, for example, are usually wrapped in pairs in twists of fine tissue paper.

JARS, TINS AND OTHER CONTAINERS

Reusable containers such as glass or ceramic storage jars or tins, are more practical than simple cardboard boxes, as they have the advantage of being airtight. They also have the advantage of becoming part of the gift as well.

As well as packaging cookies in more conventional jars and tins, you could also consider packing cookies into a container such as a cup. Wrap the cookies in cellophane and tie with a ribbon, then place in the container. (This form of packaging is not airtight, so the cookies should be wrapped at the last minute.)

MAKING BOXES

It can be great fun making your own boxes or cartons to pack cookies in. It is also much cheaper than buying ready-made gift boxes, which can be surprisingly expensive. All you need is some fine cardboard, a metal ruler and a sharp knife.

MAKING A CUBE BOX

Following the template on the opposite page, draw the outline of the cube box on the back of a piece of coloured, patterned or plain cardboard. Cut out the shape and carefully score along the dotted lines with a sharp craft knife.

1 Fold along the dotted lines, sticking tab A to edge A (keeping the tab inside the box), then tab B to edge B. Repeat with tab C to edge C and tab D to edge D.

2 To create the lid, simply fold in tabs E and tuck the flap inside the box to hold the lid in place.

MAKING A CARTON

Following the template shown below, draw the outline of the carton on the back of a piece of fine cardboard and carefully cut out.

1 Score along the dotted lines using a sharp craft knife and cut out the four slots. You can use a hole punch to make the four holes as marked on the diagram.

2 Fold the carton along the scored lines, tucking tongue A into flaps B and tongue C into flaps D, so that the end of the tongue is on the inside of the carton. Fill the carton with cookies, then you can thread fine ribbon through the punched holes and tie together.

DECORATING BOXES

If you don't have time to make a box, you can cover a used box with coloured paper. Stick on gift wrap or coloured paper, then trim the paper back to the edges of the box.

CUBE BOX TEMPLATE

CARTON TEMPLATE

BAGS

You can buy pretty ready-made bags made out of paper, cardboard and cellophane, which look very attractive filled with cookies. Fabric bags can also look very pretty. Both are ideal for cookies that are to be given and eaten on the same day.

SIMPLE BAGS

These are best made from clear or coloured cellophane and make a perfect quick and easy wrapping for square or round cookies.

1 Cut a 25cm/10in square of cellophane. Put a pile of about six cookies in the centre.

2 Gather up the edges around the cookies, then tie a ribbon tightly where you've gathered the cellophane together. If you use curling ribbon, pull the ribbon between your thumb and the blade of a pair of scissors to create very pretty corkscrew curls.

POINTED BAGS

These are perfect for wrapping small cookies and long, thin fingers.

1 Cut a 40cm/16in square of cellophane. Fold it in quarters, hold the corner where the folds join and cut a quarter circle.

2 Open out and cut in half. Pull the two points of one half to meet. Slide one of the points behind the other to make a cone. Secure with sticky tape. Half-fill with cookies, then gather and tie with ribbon.

TUBE BAGS

These little packages, tied at both ends, are perfect for wrapping long, thin finger-shaped cookies such as brandy snaps. Simply cut out a sheet of cellophane that is about twice the length of the cookies, then roll a few cookies together to make a little tube-shaped package. Tie each end of the tube with ribbon to keep the cookies in place.

GIFT TAGS

Adding a label or gift tag to gift-wrapped cookies is the final touch. They can either carry a message or information about the ingredients and advice on storing. You can buy ready-made gift tags, make your own from thin cardboard or even bake your own individual cookie gift tags and ice on a message.

EDIBLE GIFT TAGS

These are pretty and fun, and make a really unusual, themed label.

1 Sift 75g/3oz/⅔ cup plain (all-purpose) flour, a pinch of bicarbonate of soda (baking soda) and a pinch of salt into a mixing bowl. Rub in 30g/1¼oz chilled, diced butter until the mixture resembles fine breadcrumbs. Stir in 40g/1½oz/ scant ¼ cup caster (superfine) sugar.

2 Blend together 15ml/1 tbsp golden (light corn) syrup and ½ egg yolk in a separate bowl. Add these to the dry ingredients and mix to a firm dough. Knead the dough lightly, then wrap in clear film (plastic wrap) and chill for 30 minutes.

3 Roll the dough out on a lightly floured surface to a thickness of 5mm/¼in, then stamp out gift tag-size shapes using a cookie cutter.

4 Using a skewer, pierce a hole for the ribbon to thread through about 1cm/½in from the top. Place the cookies on lightly greased baking sheets and bake in a preheated oven at 180°C/350°F/Gas 4 for 12–15 minutes, or until lightly browned. Leave on the baking sheets for 3 minutes, then, using a palette knife or metal spatula, transfer to a wire rack to cool.

3 Put a little royal icing – either white or coloured – in a paper piping (pastry) bag fitted with a writing nozzle. Pipe on your message, then leave the icing to dry. Thread ribbon through the holes made with the skewer and tie on to the cookies' container.

Cook's Tip

If the gift tag hole closes up during baking, gently pierce it again while the cookies are still hot. They will be too brittle once they have cooled.

SENDING COOKIES BY POST

If you choose cookies that are robust, there is no reason why you can't post your gift of cookies as long as you package them carefully and send by next-day delivery. Delicate iced cookies are not ideal for sending via post because they are too likely to be damaged.

1 Line the base and sides of a strong box or tin with bubble wrap or plenty of crumpled tissue paper to stop the cookies moving around.

2 Pack the cookies tightly into a box or tin, interleaving the layers with baking parchment.

3 Cut a piece of corrugated paper or bubblewrap and place between the cookies and the lid, then place the box in a plastic bag. (This will protect the cookies against damp or rain should the package be left on a doorstep or leaking mail box.)

4 Put the wrapped box in a slightly larger box, surrounded by more bubblewrap, foam pieces or crumpled paper to stop the two boxes knocking against each other.

5 Clearly address the package and label it fragile, then take the box to the post office immediately and send it next-day delivery.

Cook's Tip

It is not really practical to send home-made cookies abroad, as the mail is often unreliable and the arrival of stale cookies would be very disappointing for the recipient. In addition, some countries will have very strict rules about the importation and transportation of foodstuffs, even home-baked gifts, to protect their indigenous agriculture and to abide by local health and safety rules.

LISTING INGREDIENTS

When offering cookies as a gift, particularly when you do not give them in person, it is best to include information about the ingredients. Many people suffer from allergies and intolerance to certain foods, and many of the main food culprits are included in cookies. The most common being gluten in flour, dairy products in the form of butter, and eggs and nuts.

Even if you know the person to whom you are giving the cookies has no allergy, it is best to let them know what they contain in case they share them with someone who does have an allergy or intolerance.

Teatime Treats

Whether you are taking a well-earned five-minute break, entertaining friends for afternoon tea – a sadly forgotten custom these days – or attempting to stem the hunger pangs of ravenous children returning from school, this is the chapter to turn to.

Tasty cookie treats range from Peanut Butter and Jelly Cookies – perfect for the kids – to Cappuccino Swirls – ideal for those with more sophisticated tastes.

Butter Cookies

These crunchy, buttery cookies make a delicious afternoon treat served with a cup of tea or a glass of milk. The dough can be made in advance and chilled until you are ready to bake the cookies.

Makes 25–30
175g/6oz/¾ cup unsalted (sweet) butter, at room temperature, diced
90g/3½oz/½ cup golden caster (superfine) sugar
250g/9oz/2¼ cups plain (all-purpose) flour
demerara (raw) sugar, for coating

1 Put the butter and sugar in a bowl and beat until light and fluffy. Add the flour and, using your hands, gradually work it in until the mixture forms a smooth dough. Roll into a sausage shape about 30cm/12in long, then pat the sides flat to form either a square or triangular log.

2 Sprinkle a thick layer of demerara sugar on a piece of greaseproof (waxed) paper. Press each side of the dough into the sugar to coat. Wrap and chill for about 30 minutes until firm. Meanwhile, preheat the oven to 160°C/325°F/Gas 3.

3 When ready to bake, remove the dough from the refrigerator and unwrap. Cut into thick slices and place slightly apart on non-stick baking sheets. Bake for 20 minutes until just beginning to turn brown. Transfer to a wire rack to cool.

Variations
• *To flavour the cookies, add ground cinnamon, grated lemon or orange rind, or vanilla or almond essence (extract) to the butter mixture, or add whole glacé (candied) cherries, chocolate chips, chopped nuts or dried fruit such as chopped apricots to the dough.*
• *As an alternative, coat the outside in granulated sugar or chopped toasted nuts.*

Peanut Butter and Jelly Cookies

These cookies are a twist on the original American peanut butter cookie and are a real hit with kids and adults alike. Give them a try – you'll love the crunchy nuts and sweet raspberry centres.

Makes 20–22

227g/8oz jar crunchy peanut butter
 (with no added sugar)
75g/3oz/6 tbsp unsalted (sweet) butter,
 at room temperature, diced
90g/3½oz/½ cup golden caster
 (superfine) sugar
50g/2oz/¼ cup light muscovado
 (brown) sugar
1 large (US extra large) egg, beaten
150g/5oz/1¼ cups self-raising
 (self-rising) flour
250g/9oz/scant 1 cup seedless
 raspberry jam

1 Preheat the oven to 180°C/350°F/ Gas 4. Line three or four baking sheets with baking parchment. Put the peanut butter and unsalted butter in a large bowl and beat together until well combined and creamy.

2 Add the caster and muscovado sugars and mix. Add the beaten egg and blend well. Sift in the flour and mix to a stiff dough.

3 Roll the dough into walnut-size balls between the palms of your hands. Place the balls on the prepared baking sheets and gently flatten each one with a fork to make a rough-textured cookie with a ridged surface. (Don't worry if the dough cracks slightly.)

4 Bake for 10–12 minutes, or until cooked but not browned. Using a palette knife (metal spatula), transfer to a wire rack to cool.

5 Spoon jam on to one cookie and top with a second. Continue to sandwich the cookies in this way.

Citrus Drops

These soft, cake-like treats are deliciously tangy, with a zesty, crumbly base filled with sweet, sticky lemon or orange curd. The crunchy topping of almonds makes the perfect finish.

Makes about 20

175g/6oz/¾ cup unsalted (sweet) butter,
  at room temperature, diced
150g/5oz/¾ cup caster
  (superfine) sugar
finely grated rind of 1 large lemon
finely grated rind of 1 orange
2 egg yolks
50g/2oz/½ cup ground almonds
225g/8oz/2 cups self-raising
  (self-rising) flour
lemon and/or orange curd
milk, for brushing
flaked (sliced) almonds,
  for sprinkling

1 Preheat the oven to 160°C/325°F/ Gas 3. Line two baking sheets with baking parchment. Beat the butter and sugar together until light and fluffy, then stir in the citrus rinds.

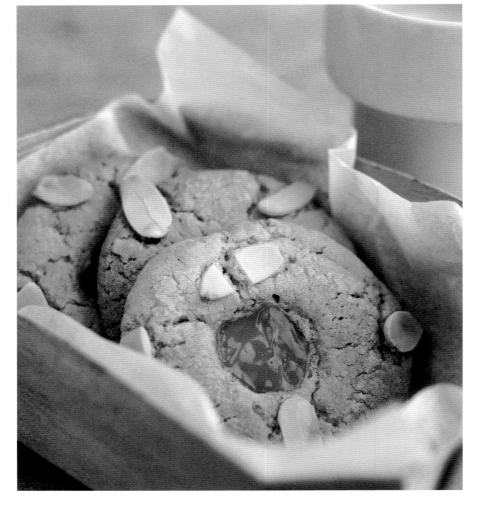

2 Stir the egg yolks into the mixture, then add the ground almonds and flour and mix well.

3 Divide the mixture into 20 pieces and shape into balls. Place on the baking sheets. Using the handle of a wooden spoon, make a hole in the centre of each cookie. Put 2.5ml/ ½ tsp lemon or orange curd into each hole and pinch the opening to semi-enclose the curd.

4 Brush the tops of each cookie with milk and sprinkle with flaked almonds. Bake for about 20 minutes until pale golden brown. Leave to cool slightly on the baking sheets to firm up, then transfer to a wire rack to cool completely.

Sugar-topped Vanilla Cookies

Buttery, crumbly vanilla cookies with an irresistible crunchy sugar topping, these are great with a cup of tea but also delicious served with luxury vanilla ice cream for a quick dessert.

Makes about 24

115g/4oz/½ cup unsalted (sweet) butter,
    at room temperature, diced
50g/2oz/¼ cup vanilla caster
    (superfine) sugar
1 egg, beaten
1.5ml/¼ tsp vanilla essence (extract)
200g/7oz/1¾ cups self-raising
    (self-rising) flour
45ml/3 tbsp cornflour (cornstarch)

For the topping

1 egg white
15ml/1 tbsp vanilla caster
    (superfine) sugar
75g/3oz sugar cubes, crushed

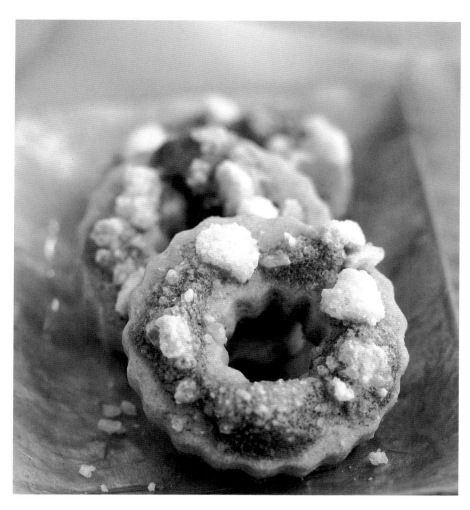

1 Preheat the oven to 180°C/350°F/ Gas 4. Put the butter and sugar in a bowl and beat until the mixture is light and fluffy. Beat in the egg and vanilla essence. Sift together the flour and cornflour over the mixture and mix to a soft but not sticky dough.

2 Roll the mixture out on a lightly floured surface. Using a flower biscuit (cookie) cutter or ring cutter, stamp out cookies and place on a non-stick baking sheet. Re-roll any trimmings and stamp out more cookies until you have used up all the dough.

3 For the topping, put the egg white in a small bowl and whisk until foamy. Whisk in the vanilla sugar. Using a pastry brush, spread generously on each cookie. Sprinkle with the crushed sugar cubes.

4 Bake for about 15 minutes, or until the topping is just beginning to turn golden brown. Remove from the oven and transfer to a wire rack to cool.

Cook's Tip

To make your own vanilla sugar, take a vanilla pod (bean) and split it open down one side. Place in a jar of sugar and use as necessary. If you don't have any vanilla sugar, increase the quantity of vanilla essence (extract) to 2.5ml/½ tsp.

Toffee Apple and Oat Crunchies

An unashamedly addictive mixture of chewy oats, soft apple and wonderfully crunchy toffee, this cookie won't win large prizes in the looks department but is top of the class for flavour.

Makes about 16

150g/5oz/10 tbsp unsalted
  (sweet) butter
175g/6oz/scant 1 cup light muscovado
  (brown) sugar
90g/3½oz/½ cup granulated sugar
1 large (US extra large) egg, beaten
75g/3oz/⅔ cup plain (all-purpose) flour
2.5ml/½ tsp bicarbonate of soda
  (baking soda)
pinch of salt
250g/9oz/2½ cups rolled oats
50g/2oz/scant ½ cup sultanas
  (golden raisins)
50g/2oz dried apple rings,
  coarsely chopped
50g/2oz chewy toffees, coarsely chopped

1 Preheat the oven to 180°C/350°F/ Gas 4. Line two or three baking sheets with baking parchment. In a large bowl, beat together the butter and both sugars until creamy. Add the beaten egg and stir well until thoroughly combined.

2 Sift together the flour, bicarbonate of soda and salt. Add to the butter, sugar and egg mixture and mix in well. Finally add the oats, sultanas, chopped apple rings and toffee pieces and stir gently until just combined.

3 Using a small ice cream scoop or large tablespoon, place heaps of the mixture well apart on the prepared baking sheets. Bake for about 10–12 minutes, or until lightly set in the centre and just beginning to brown at the edges.

4 Remove from the oven and leave to cool on the baking sheets for a few minutes. Using a palette knife (metal spatula), transfer the cookies to a wire rack to cool completely.

Apple and Elderflower Stars

These delicious, crumbly apple cookies are topped with a sweet yet very sharp icing. Packaged in a pretty box, they would make a delightfully festive gift for someone special.

Makes about 18

115g/4oz/½ cup unsalted (sweet) butter, at room temperature, diced
75g/3oz/scant ½ cup caster (superfine) sugar
2.5ml/½ tsp mixed (apple pie) spice
1 large (US extra large) egg yolk
25g/1oz dried apple rings, finely chopped
200g/7oz/1¾ cups self-raising (self-rising) flour
5–10ml/1–2 tsp milk, if necessary

For the topping

200g/7oz/1¾ cups icing (confectioners') sugar, sifted
60–90ml/4–6 tbsp elderflower cordial
granulated sugar, for sprinkling

1 Preheat the oven to 190°C/375°F/Gas 5. Cream together the butter and sugar until light and fluffy. Beat in the mixed spice and egg yolk. Add the chopped apple and flour and stir together well. The mixture should form a stiff dough but if it is too dry, add some milk.

2 Roll the dough out on a floured surface to 5mm/¼in thick. Draw a five-pointed star on cardboard. Cut out and use as a template for the cookies. Alternatively, use a star biscuit (cookie) cutter.

3 Place the cookies on non-stick baking sheets and bake for about 10–15 minutes, or until just beginning to brown around the edges. Using a palette knife (metal spatula), carefully transfer the cookies to a wire rack to cool.

4 To make the topping, sift the icing sugar into a bowl and add just enough elderflower cordial to mix to a fairly thick but still pourable consistency.

5 When the cookies are completely cool, trickle the icing randomly over the stars. Immediately sprinkle with granulated sugar and leave to set.

Greek Honey Crunch Creams

With its scent of liquorice and aniseed, Greek honey lends a wonderful flavour to these cookies. If you like your honey less strong, try using orange blossom or lavender instead.

Makes 20

250g/9oz/2¼ cups self-raising
  (self-rising) flour
10ml/2 tsp bicarbonate of soda
  (baking soda)
50g/2oz/¼ cup caster (superfine) sugar
115g/4oz/½ cup unsalted (sweet)
  butter, diced
finely grated rind of 1 large orange
115g/4oz/½ cup Greek honey
25g/1oz/¼ cup pine nuts or
  chopped walnuts

For the filling

50g/2oz/¼ cup unsalted (sweet) butter,
  at room temperature, diced
115g/4oz/1 cup icing (confectioners')
  sugar, sifted
15ml/1 tbsp Greek honey

1 Preheat the oven to 200°C/400°F/ Gas 6. Line three or four baking sheets with baking parchment. Sift the flour, bicarbonate of soda and caster sugar into a bowl. Add the butter and rub in until the mixture resembles breadcrumbs. Stir in the orange rind.

2 Put the honey in a small pan and heat until just runny but not hot. Pour over the dry mixture and mix to a firm dough.

3 Divide the dough in half and shape one half into 20 small balls about the size of a hazelnut in its shell. Place the balls on the baking sheets, spaced well apart, and gently flatten. Bake for 6–8 minutes, until golden brown. Leave to cool and firm up on the baking sheets. Use a palette knife (metal spatula) to transfer the cookies to a wire rack to allow them to cool completely.

4 Shape the remaining dough into 20 balls and dip one side of each one into the pine nuts or walnuts. Place the cookies, nut sides up, on the baking sheets, gently flatten and bake for 6–8 minutes, until golden brown. Leave to cool and firm up slightly on the baking sheets before carefully transferring the cookies to a wire rack, still nut sides up, to cool completely.

5 To make the filling, put the butter, sugar and honey in a bowl and beat together until light and fluffy. Use the mixture to sandwich the cookies together in pairs using a plain cookie for the base and a nut-coated one for the top.

Cook's Tip
Greek honey is also called Hymettus honey, named after the mountain. It is very dark and aromatic, with a unique taste, and is one of the most expensive honeys in the world.

Ginger Cookies

These are a supreme treat for ginger lovers – richly spiced cookies packed with chunks of succulent preserved stem ginger. Serve small cookies as an after-dinner treat.

Makes 30 small or 20 large cookies

350g/12oz/3 cups self-raising
  (self-rising) flour
pinch of salt
200g/7oz/1 cup golden caster
  (superfine) sugar
15ml/1 tbsp ground ginger
5ml/1 tsp bicarbonate of soda
  (baking soda)
115g/4oz/½ cup unsalted (sweet) butter
90g/3½oz/generous ¼ cup golden
  (light corn) syrup
1 large (US extra large) egg, beaten
150g/5oz preserved stem ginger in syrup,
  drained and coarsely chopped

1 Preheat the oven to 160°C/325°F/ Gas 3. Line three baking sheets with baking parchment or lightly greased greaseproof (waxed) paper.

2 Sift the flour into a large mixing bowl, add the salt, caster sugar, ground ginger and bicarbonate of soda and stir to combine.

3 Dice the butter and put it in a small, heavy pan with the syrup. Heat gently, stirring, until the butter has melted. Remove from the heat and set aside to cool until just warm.

4 Pour the butter mixture over the dry ingredients, then add the egg and two-thirds of the ginger. Mix thoroughly, then use your hands to bring the dough together.

5 Shape the dough into 20 large or 30 small balls, depending on the size you require. Place them, spaced well apart, on the baking sheets.

6 Gently flatten the balls, then press a few pieces of the remaining preserved stem ginger into the top of each of the cookies.

7 Bake for about 12–15 minutes, depending on the size of your cookies, until light golden in colour. Remove from the oven and leave to cool for 1 minute on the baking sheets to firm up. Using a palette knife (metal spatula), transfer to a wire rack to cool completely.

Fig and Date Ravioli

These melt-in-the-mouth cushions of sweet pastry are filled with a delicious mixture of figs, dates and walnuts and dusted with icing sugar. They are ideal for serving with coffee.

Makes about 20

375g/13oz packet sweet
  shortcrust pastry
milk, for brushing
icing (confectioners') sugar, sifted,
  for dusting

For the filling

115g/4oz/⅔ cup ready-to-eat dried figs
50g/2oz/⅓ cup stoned (pitted) dates
15g/½oz/1 tbsp chopped walnuts
10ml/2 tsp lemon juice
15ml/1 tbsp clear honey

1 Preheat the oven to 180°C/350°F/ Gas 4. To make the filling, put all the ingredients into a food processor and blend to a paste.

2 Roll out just under half of the shortcrust pastry on a lightly floured surface to a square. Place spoonfuls of the fig paste on the pastry in neat rows at equally spaced intervals, as when making ravioli.

3 Roll out the remaining pastry to a slightly larger square. Dampen all around each spoonful of filling, using a pastry brush dipped in cold water. Place the second sheet of pastry on top and press together around each mound of filling.

4 Using a zigzag pastry wheel or a pizza cutter, cut squares between the mounds of filling. Place the cookies on non-stick baking sheets and lightly brush the top of each with a little milk. Bake for 15–20 minutes until golden.

5 Using a palette knife (metal spatula), transfer the cookies to a wire rack to cool. When cool, dust with icing sugar.

Coconut and Lime Macaroons

These pretty pistachio nut topped cookies are crunchy on the outside and soft and gooey in the centre. The zesty lime topping contrasts wonderfully with the sweet coconut.

Makes 12–14

4 large (US extra large) egg whites

250g/9oz/3 cups sweetened desiccated (dry shredded) coconut

150g/5oz/¾ cup granulated sugar

10ml/2 tsp vanilla essence (extract)

25g/1oz/¼ cup plain (all-purpose) flour

115g/4oz/1 cup icing (confectioners') sugar, sifted

grated rind of 1 lime

15–20ml/3–4 tsp lime juice

about 15g/½oz/1 tbsp pistachio nuts, chopped

1 Preheat the oven to 180°C/350°F/ Gas 4. Line two baking sheets with baking parchment. Put the egg whites, desiccated coconut, sugar, vanilla essence and flour in a large, heavy pan. Mix well.

2 Place over a low heat and cook for 6–8 minutes, stirring constantly to ensure it does not stick. When the mixture becomes the consistency of thick porridge (oatmeal), remove from the heat.

3 Place spoonfuls of the mixture in rocky piles on the lined baking sheets. Bake for 12–13 minutes, until golden brown. Remove from the oven and leave to cool completely on the baking sheets.

4 To make the topping, put the icing sugar and lime rind into a bowl and add enough lime juice to give a thick pouring consistency. Place a spoonful of icing on each macaroon and allow it to drip down the sides. Sprinkle over the pistachio nuts and serve.

Variation
If you prefer, make Coconut and Lemon Macaroons by substituting grated lemon rind and juice.

Cappuccino Swirls

A melt-in-the-mouth, mocha-flavoured cookie drizzled with white and dark chocolate is just the thing to have with that mid-morning café latte, as well as with afternoon tea with friends.

Makes 18

10ml/2 tsp instant coffee powder
10ml/2 tsp boiling water
150g/5oz/1¼ cups plain
   (all-purpose) flour
115g/4oz/½ cup cornflour (cornstarch)
15ml/1 tbsp (unsweetened) cocoa
   powder
225g/8oz/1 cup unsalted (sweet) butter,
   at room temperature, diced
50g/2oz/¼ cup golden caster
   (superfine) sugar

For the decoration

50g/2oz white chocolate
25g/1oz dark (bittersweet) chocolate

1 Preheat the oven to 190°C/375°F/ Gas 5. Line two baking sheets with baking parchment. Put the coffee powder in a cup, add the boiling water and stir until dissolved. Set aside to cool. Sift together the flour, cornflour and cocoa powder.

2 Put the butter and sugar in a bowl and beat until creamy. Add the coffee and the sifted flour and mix well. Spoon into a piping (pastry) bag fitted with a plain nozzle.

3 Pipe 18 spirals, slightly apart, on to the prepared baking sheets.

4 Bake for 10–15 minutes, or until firm but not browned. Remove from the oven and leave on the baking sheets for 1 minute, then transfer to a wire rack to cool.

5 Melt the white and dark chocolate separately in heatproof bowls set over a pan of hot water.

6 Place the cooled cookies close together on kitchen paper. Using a teaspoon, take some white chocolate and flick over the cookies, moving your hand speedily from left to right to create small lines of chocolate drizzle over them.

7 When all the white chocolate has been used, repeat the process with the dark chocolate, flicking it over the cookies so the dark chocolate is at an angle to the white chocolate. Leave until the chocolate has set and then remove the cookies from the paper.

Chocolate Treacle Snaps

These elegantly thin, treacle-flavoured snap cookies have a delicate hint of spice and a decorative lick of chocolate on top. They are particularly good with a steaming cup of hot coffee.

Makes about 35

90g/3½oz/7 tbsp unsalted
   (sweet) butter, diced
175ml/6fl oz/¾ cup golden
   (light corn) syrup
50ml/2fl oz/¼ cup black
   treacle (molasses)
250g/9oz/2¼ cups plain
   (all-purpose) flour
150g/5oz/¾ cup golden caster
   (superfine) sugar
5ml/1 tsp bicarbonate of soda
   (baking soda)
1.5ml/¼ tsp mixed
   (apple pie) spice
100g/3½oz milk chocolate
100g/3½oz white chocolate

1 Preheat the oven to 180°C/350°F/Gas 4. Line two or three baking sheets with baking parchment. Put the butter, syrup and treacle in a small pan. Heat gently, stirring constantly, until the butter has melted. Remove from the heat and set aside until required.

2 Sift the flour into a large mixing bowl. Add the sugar, bicarbonate of soda and mixed spice, and mix well using a wooden spoon. Slowly pour in the butter and treacle mixture and stir to combine well.

3 Place large teaspoonfuls of the mixture well apart on the prepared baking sheets. Bake the cookies for 10–12 minutes until just beginning to brown around the edges. Leave them to cool for a few minutes on the baking sheets. When firm enough to handle, transfer the cookies to a wire rack to cool completely.

4 Melt the milk chocolate and white chocolate separately in the microwave or in heatproof bowls set over pans of hot water. Swirl a little of each into the centre of each cookie and leave to set.

Shape and Bake Cookies

The mixture for these simple Maryland-style cookies can be made and stored in the refrigerator. It's so easy to cook some each day – and there's nothing like a warm, freshly baked cookie.

Makes about 12 giant or
 20 standard size cookies

115g/4oz/½ cup unsalted (sweet) butter, at room temperature, diced

115g/4oz/generous ½ cup granulated sugar

115g/4oz/generous ½ cup light muscovado (brown) sugar

1 large (US extra large) egg

5ml/1 tsp vanilla essence (extract)

200g/7oz/1¾ cups self-raising (self-rising) flour

150g/5oz/scant 1 cup chocolate chips

50g/2oz/½ cup chopped toasted hazelnuts or walnuts

50g/2oz/scant ½ cup raisins

1 Preheat the oven to 180°C/350°F/ Gas 4. Line two baking sheets with baking parchment. Put the butter, granulated sugar and muscovado sugar in a large mixing bowl and beat together well until light and fluffy. Add the egg and vanilla essence and beat again until the mixture is well combined.

2 Add the flour, chocolate chips, chopped toasted hazelnuts or walnuts and raisins, and mix together until the ingredients have just blended. The dough will now have a slightly crumbly consistency.

3 Depending on whether you want giant or standard size cookies, place tablespoonfuls or teaspoonfuls of the mixture, spaced well apart, on the prepared baking sheets. Bake for 15 minutes until golden brown.

4 Leave the cookies on the baking sheets for 5 minutes, then use a palette knife (metal spatula) to transfer to a wire rack to cool.

Cook's Tip
If you don't want to bake the mixture all at once, simply spoon it into a plastic container, cover the surface with clear film (plastic wrap) to prevent it from drying out and replace the lid. Keep in the refrigerator for up to 1 week. When required, remove the dough from the refrigerator 15 minutes before you want to bake the cookies to soften slightly, and shape and bake as before.

Cookies for Kids

There's nothing quite like coming home from school to a plate of freshly baked cookies and a glass of milk. This chapter is packed with fabulous, fun ideas that kids will love, from simple cookies with pretty sugar icing to utterly adorable puppy faces and indulgent ice cream sandwiches.

Jammie Bodgers

These buttery cookies are an absolute classic. Sandwiched with buttercream and a generous dollop of strawberry jam, they make a perfect snack served with a glass of milk at teatime, or are equally good wrapped tightly, and popped in a lunchbox as a post-sandwich treat.

Makes 20

225g/8oz/2 cups plain (all-purpose) flour
175g/6oz/¾ cup unsalted (sweet) butter, chilled and diced
130g/4¼oz/⅔ cup caster (superfine) sugar
1 egg yolk

For the filling

50g/2oz/¼ cup unsalted (sweet) butter, at room temperature, diced
90g/3½oz/scant 1 cup icing (confectioners') sugar
60–75ml/4–5 tbsp strawberry jam

Cook's Tip

If you don't have a small cutter for the cookie centres, use a sharp knife to cut out triangles or squares instead.

1 Put the flour and butter in a food processor and process until the mixture resembles breadcrumbs. Add the sugar and egg yolk and process until the mixture starts to form a dough.

2 Turn out on to a floured surface and knead until smooth. Shape into a ball, wrap in clear film (plastic wrap) and chill for at least 30 minutes. Preheat the oven to 180°C/350°F/ Gas 4. Grease two baking sheets.

3 Roll out the dough thinly on a lightly floured surface and cut out rounds using a 6cm/2½in cookie cutter. Re-roll the trimmings and cut out more rounds until you have 40.

4 Place half the cookie rounds on a prepared baking sheet. Using a small heart-shaped cutter, about 2cm/¾in in diameter, cut out the centres of the remaining rounds. Place these rounds on the second baking sheet.

5 Bake the cookies for about 12 minutes until pale golden, then transfer to a wire rack and leave to cool completely.

6 To make the buttercream, beat together the butter and sugar until smooth and creamy.

7 Using a palette knife (metal spatula), spread a little buttercream on to each whole cookie. Spoon a little jam on to the buttercream, then gently press the cut-out cookies on top, so that the jam fills the heart-shaped hole.

Peanut Crunch Cookies

These delicious sweet and nutty cookies are so easy to make. They puff up into lovely domed rounds during baking, giving them a really professional look. If you prefer cookies with a slightly less "nutty" texture, use smooth peanut butter rather than the crunchy variety.

Makes 25

115g/4oz/½ cup unsalted (sweet)
   butter, at room temperature, diced
115g/4oz/generous ½ cup light
   muscovado (brown) sugar
1 egg
150g/5oz/1¼ cups self-raising
   (self-rising) flour
2.5ml/½ tsp baking powder
150g/5oz/generous ½ cup crunchy
   peanut butter
icing (confectioners') sugar, for dusting

1 Preheat the oven to 190°C/375°F/ Gas 5. Grease two baking sheets.

2 Put the butter and sugar in a mixing bowl and beat until pale and creamy. Beat in the egg, then add the flour, baking powder and peanut butter. Beat until the ingredients are thoroughly mixed.

3 Place heaped teaspoonfuls of the mixture on to the greased baking sheets; space well apart to allow the cookies to spread while baking. (If necessary, spoon the dough on to the baking sheets in batches.)

4 Bake the cookies for about 20 minutes until risen; they will still be quite soft to the touch.

5 Leave the cookies on the baking sheets for about 5 minutes, then transfer to a wire rack to cool. To serve, lightly dust with icing sugar.

Pink Sugared Hearts

Pretty and pink, these delightful cookies are always a hit with Barbie-loving girls. Rolling the edges of the cookies in coloured sugar to accentuate their shape really adds to the fun of decorating.

Makes 32
225g/8oz/2 cups plain
   (all-purpose) flour
175g/6oz/¾ cup unsalted (sweet)
   butter, chilled and diced
130g/4¼oz/⅔ cup caster
   (superfine) sugar
1 egg yolk

For the decoration
50g/2oz/¼ cup granulated sugar
pink food colouring
225g/8oz/2 cups icing
   (confectioners') sugar
30–45ml/2–3 tbsp lemon juice

1 Preheat the oven to 180°C/350°F/ Gas 4. Grease two baking sheets.

2 Put the flour and diced butter into a food processor, then process until the mixture resembles fine breadcrumbs. Add the sugar and egg yolk to the food processor and process until the mixture begins to form a ball.

3 Turn the dough out on to a lightly floured surface and knead until smooth. Shape the dough into a ball, wrap in clear film (plastic wrap) and chill for at least 30 minutes.

4 Working in batches, roll out the dough thinly on a lightly floured surface and cut out heart shapes using a 5cm/2in cutter. Transfer to the baking sheets, spacing them slightly apart. Bake for 10 minutes, or until pale golden. Transfer to a wire rack to cool.

5 To decorate, put the granulated sugar in a bowl and add a small dot of pink food colouring. Using the back of a teaspoon, work the food colouring into the sugar until it is completely pink.

6 Put the icing sugar in a separate bowl and add 30ml/2 tbsp of the lemon juice, stirring until smooth but spreadable. If the paste is too thick add a little more lemon juice and stir until well combined.

Cook's Tip
To make festive cookies, try cutting out tree shapes and use green food colouring instead of pink. Alternatively, cut out star shapes and use silver or gold food colouring to tint the sugar. Children will love these festive shapes and will enjoy leaving a plate of cookies and a glass of milk out for Santa.

7 Using a palette knife (metal spatula) spread a little icing on to each cookie, to within 5mm/¼in of the edge.

8 Turn each iced cookie on its side and gently roll in the coloured sugar so that the edges of the icing become coated in pink sugar. Leave the cookies to set for about 1 hour.

Butter Gems

These tiny shortbread-based cookies are topped with rosettes of soft buttercream and a pretty sprinkling of brightly coloured sugar. They make a great treat for even the smallest of mouths.

Makes about 40

115g/4oz/½ cup unsalted (sweet)
  butter, at room temperature, diced
50g/2oz/¼ cup caster (superfine) sugar
175g/6oz/1½ cups plain
  (all-purpose) flour

For the decoration

50g/2oz/4 tbsp unsalted (sweet) butter,
  at room temperature, diced
5ml/1 tsp vanilla essence (extract)
90g/3½ oz/scant 1 cup icing
  (confectioners') sugar
25g/1oz/2 tbsp granulated sugar
green, lilac or pink food colourings

1 Put the diced butter and the sugar in a large bowl and beat together until smooth and creamy. Add the flour to the creamed butter and mix well to form a thick paste.

2 Turn the dough on to a lightly floured surface and knead until smooth. Wrap the dough in clear film (plastic wrap) and chill for at least 30 minutes.

3 Preheat the oven to 180°C/350°F/Gas 4. Grease two baking sheets.

4 Roll out the dough on a lightly floured surface and cut out rounds using a 3.5cm/1¼in cookie cutter. Space slightly apart on the baking sheets and bake for 10 minutes, or until pale golden. Transfer to a wire rack to cool completely.

5 To decorate the cookies, beat the butter with the vanilla essence and icing sugar until smooth and creamy. Spoon the buttercream into a piping (pastry) bag fitted with a star-shaped nozzle, then pipe a rosette on to each cookie.

6 Put the granulated sugar into a small bowl and add several drops of the food colouring. Using the back of a teaspoon work the colouring into the sugar until it is deeply coloured. Sprinkle a little of the sugar over the cookies.

Alphabetinis

These funny little letters are great for kids – and might even be a good way to encourage them to practise their spelling. They are great fun to make and even better to eat.

Makes about 30

2 egg whites
15ml/1 tbsp cornflour (cornstarch)
50g/2oz/½ cup plain (all-purpose) flour
150g/5oz/¾ cup caster (superfine) sugar
10ml/2 tsp vanilla essence (extract)
90g/3½oz milk chocolate

1 Preheat the oven to 180°C/350°F/ Gas 4. Line two large baking sheets with baking parchment.

2 In a clean glass bowl, whisk the egg whites until peaking. Sift the cornflour and plain flour over the egg whites and add the sugar and vanilla essence. Fold in using a large metal spoon.

3 Spoon half the mixture into a plastic bag and gently squeeze it into a corner of the bag. Snip off the tip of the corner so that the cookie mixture can be squeezed out in a thin line, 1cm/½in wide.

4 Very carefully, pipe letters on to one of the lined baking sheets, making each letter about 6cm/ 2½in tall. Spoon the remaining cookie mixture into the bag and pipe more letters on to the second lined baking sheet.

5 Bake the cookies for 12 minutes, or until crisp and golden. Carefully transfer to a wire rack to cool.

6 Break the chocolate into pieces and put in a heatproof bowl set over a pan of simmering water. Heat, stirring frequently, until melted.

7 Spoon the melted chocolate into a small paper piping (pastry) bag (or use a smaller plastic bag) and snip off the merest tip.

8 Pipe the chocolate in lines over the cookies to highlight the shape of each letter. Leave to set for at least 1 hour.

Flower Power Cookies

Look out for little piped sugar flower decorations in the supermarket. Some are in pretty pale colours, while others are much brighter and more vibrant. The latter are best for these colourful cookies as they contrast better with the pretty pastel-coloured icing.

Makes 28
225g/8oz/2 cups plain (all-purpose) flour
175g/6oz/¾ cup unsalted (sweet)
*   butter, chilled and diced*
finely grated rind of 1 orange
130g/4¼oz/⅔ cup light muscovado
*   (brown) sugar*
1 egg yolk

For the decoration
30ml/2 tbsp orange juice
200g/7oz/1¾ cups icing
*   (confectioners') sugar*
green, yellow and orange food colourings
multi-coloured sugared flowers, to decorate

1 Put the flour, butter and orange rind into a food processor. Process until the mixture resembles fine breadcrumbs. Add the sugar and egg yolk to the food processor and process until the mixture starts to bind together.

2 Turn the mixture out on to a lightly floured surface and knead until it forms a dough. Shape the dough into a ball, wrap tightly in clear film (plastic wrap) and chill in the refrigerator for at least 30 minutes.

3 Preheat the oven to 180°C/350°F/ Gas 4. Grease two baking sheets. Roll out the dough thinly on a floured surface and cut out rounds using a fluted cookie cutter about 6cm/2½in in diameter.

4 Transfer the cookies to the baking sheets, spacing them slightly apart. Bake for 12–15 minutes until pale golden, then transfer to a wire rack to cool completely.

5 To decorate the cookies, put the orange juice in a bowl and gradually stir in the icing sugar until the mixture has the consistency of thick pouring cream. Divide the mixture among three bowls and stir a few drops of a different food colouring into each bowl.

6 Spoon a little green icing on to one third of the cookies, spreading it to within 1cm/½in of the cookie edges. Top each one with a sugared flower (ideally of a contrasting colour). Decorate the remaining cookies in the same way, using the yellow icing on half the cookies and the orange icing on the remaining half. Leave to set for about 1 hour.

Dolly Cookies

These pretty cookies look like they belong at a doll's tea party and are great fun for kids to make and decorate. The cookies are made by simply chilling a roll of dough, then slicing off pieces on to a baking sheet so you don't even need cookie cutters. Baking doesn't get much easier than this.

Makes 14
115g/4oz/½ cup unsalted (sweet)
   butter, at room temperature, diced
50g/2oz/¼ cup caster
   (superfine) sugar
pink food colouring
5ml/1 tsp vanilla essence (extract)
175g/6oz/1½ cups plain
   (all-purpose) flour
90g/3½oz white chocolate
75g/3oz multi-coloured
   sweets (candies)

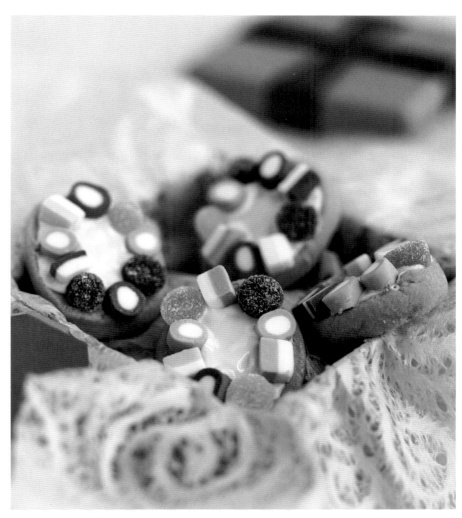

1 Put the butter and sugar in a bowl with a dash of pink food colouring and the vanilla essence. Beat together until smooth and creamy.

2 Add the flour to the butter and sugar mixture and stir well until thoroughly combined. Turn the dough out on to a lightly floured surface and knead until smooth.

3 Using your hands, roll the dough into a thick sausage shape, about 12cm/4½in long and 5cm/2in in diameter. Wrap the dough in clear film (plastic wrap) and chill for at least 30 minutes.

4 Preheat the oven to 180°C/350°F/ Gas 4. Grease two large baking sheets.

5 Cut the dough into 5mm/¼in slices and space them slightly apart on the baking sheets. Bake for 15–18 minutes, or until the cookies begin to colour. Transfer to a wire rack to cool completely.

6 Break the chocolate into pieces and put in a heatproof bowl set over a pan of simmering water. Heat, stirring frequently, until the chocolate has melted. Using a sharp knife, cut the sweets in half.

7 Using a small palette knife (metal spatula) swirl a little chocolate on to each cookie and decorate with a ring of sweets. Leave to set.

Gingerbread Family

You can have great fun with these cookies by creating characters with different features. By using an assortment of different gingerbread cutters you can make a gingerbread family of all shapes and sizes. If you want to make decorating the cookies simpler, use just one colour of chocolate rather than three. Coloured writer icing and candy are also good for decorating.

Makes about 12

350g/12oz/3 cups plain
   (all-purpose) flour
5ml/1 tsp bicarbonate of soda
   (baking soda)
5ml/1 tsp ground ginger
115g/4oz/½ cup unsalted (sweet)
   butter, chilled and diced
175/6oz/scant 1 cup light muscovado
   (brown) sugar
1 egg
30ml/2 tbsp black treacle (molasses)
   or golden (light corn) syrup
50g/2oz each plain, milk and white
   chocolate, to decorate

1 Preheat the oven to 180°C/ 350°F/Gas 4. Grease two large baking sheets.

2 Put the flour, bicarbonate of soda, ginger and diced butter into the food processor. Process until the mixture begins to resemble fine breadcrumbs.

3 If necessary, scrape down the sides of the food processor bowl with a wooden spoon or spatula to remove any crumbs that have become stuck to the sides.

4 Add the sugar, egg and black treacle or golden syrup to the food processor and process the mixture until it begins to form into a ball.

5 Turn the dough out on to a lightly floured surface, and knead until smooth and pliable.

6 Roll out the dough on a lightly floured surface (you might find it easier to roll half of the dough out at a time). Cut out figures using people-shaped cutters, then transfer to the baking sheets. Re-roll any trimmings and cut out more figures.

7 Bake for 15 minutes until slightly risen and starting to colour around the edges. Leave for 5 minutes, then transfer to a wire rack to cool.

8 To decorate the cookies, break each type of chocolate into a separate bowl. One at a time, set a bowl over a pan of simmering water and heat, stirring frequently, until melted. Spoon the melted chocolate into paper piping (pastry) bags, snip off the merest tip, then pipe faces and clothes on to the cookies. Leave to set.

Cook's Tip
You can use any colour of sugar for these cookies: the darker the sugar, the darker the final cookies will be. Similarly, black treacle will produce a darker cookie than golden syrup will.

Puppy Faces

Children of any age can have fun making these little pups – you could even use the family pet as a model. These cookies are decorated with the widely available, white "ready-to-roll" icing, but you can knead in a little black, brown or yellow food colouring to make different coloured dogs.

Makes 10

100g/3½oz/scant 1 cup plain
 (all-purpose) flour
50g/2oz/½ cup rolled oats
2.5ml/½ tsp mixed (apple pie) spice
50g/2oz/¼ cup unsalted (sweet) butter,
 chilled and diced
100g/3½oz/½ cup caster
 (superfine) sugar
1 egg yolk

For the decoration

60ml/4 tbsp apricot jam
250g/9oz white ready-to-roll icing
10 round coloured sweets (candies)
black and red writer icing tubes
icing (confectioners') sugar, for dusting

1 Put the flour, rolled oats, mixed spice and butter into the food processor. Process until the mixture resembles fine breadcrumbs.

2 Add the sugar, egg yolk and 5ml/ 1 tsp water to the food processor and blend until the mixture begins to form a ball.

3 Turn the dough out on to a lightly floured surface and knead until smooth. Wrap in clear film (plastic wrap) and chill for 30 minutes.

4 Preheat the oven to 200°C/400°F/ Gas 6. Grease a large baking sheet.

5 Roll out the dough on a floured surface and cut out rounds using a 6cm/2½in cutter. Transfer to the baking sheet, spacing slightly apart. Bake for 12 minutes until pale golden. Transfer to a wire rack to cool.

6 Press the jam through a sieve. Brush a little jam over each cookie to within 5mm/¼in of the edge.

7 Roll out half the icing as thinly as possible on a surface dusted with icing sugar. Cut out 10 rounds using the 6cm/2½in cutter and lay one over each cookie. To make the eyes, halve the coloured sweets, brush the icing lightly with water and press the sweets into the cookies.

8 Use the black writer tube to pipe the noses and mouths, finishing with little red tongues.

9 To make the ears, divide the remaining icing into 20 pieces. Roll each piece into a ball and flatten between the thumb and forefinger to make a flat pear shape. Lightly brush the icing with water and secure the ears. Arrange the cookies in a single layer on a tray.

Tree Cookies

These cookies look really effective with their chocolate cookie "trunks" and brightly coloured "fruits". Kids will love helping to decorate them. Arrange the cookies in a line on the tea table (preferably on a multi-coloured cloth if you have one).

Makes 10

50g/2oz/¼ cup unsalted (sweet) butter,
   at room temperature, diced
115g/4oz/½ cup light muscovado
   (brown) sugar
1 egg
150g/5oz/1¼ cups self-raising
   (self-rising) flour
2.5ml/½ tsp bicarbonate of soda
   (baking soda)
finely grated rind of 1 lemon

For the decoration

50g/2oz/½ cup icing
   (confectioners') sugar
10ml/2 tsp lemon juice
10 milk chocolate fingers
brightly coloured sweets (candies),
   such as m&ms

1 Preheat the oven to 180°C/350°F/ Gas 4. Grease two baking sheets.

2 In a large bowl, beat together the butter and sugar until smooth and creamy. Beat in the egg. Add the flour, bicarbonate of soda and lemon rind and mix until smooth.

3 Place 5 large spoonfuls of the mixture on to each baking sheet, spacing them well apart. Bake for 15 minutes until the cookies have risen. Leave on the baking sheet for 5 minutes to firm up, then transfer to a wire rack to cool.

Variation

To create pretty blossoming trees, attach pastel-coloured sugar flowers to the cookies instead of coloured sweets.

4 To decorate the cookies, mix together the icing sugar and lemon juice to make a thick paste. Use a little paste to secure one end of a chocolate finger to each cookie.

5 Attach the coloured sweets in the same way, securing each one with a little paste. Leave the cookies to set for at least 1 hour. (Handle the decorated cookies with care.)

Orange Biscotti

These crisp, crunchy cookies are based on a traditional Italian recipe in which the cookies are packed with nuts and twice baked. This version is flavoured with orange instead of the nuts and shaped into long, thin sticks. They are a little softer than the classic biscotti, which are very hard.

3 Bake the dough for 25 minutes, then remove from the oven and leave to stand for about 5 minutes until slightly cooled.

4 Using a sharp knife, carefully cut the mixture widthways into thin sticks, about 1cm/½in wide.

5 Space the cookies out slightly on the baking sheet so there's a gap in between each one allowing air to circulate, then return to the oven and bake for a further 20 minutes until crisp. Transfer the biscotti to a wire rack and leave to cool. Serve dusted with a little icing sugar.

Makes about 20

50g/2oz/¼ cup unsalted (sweet) butter, at room temperature, diced
90g/3½oz/½ cup light muscovado (brown) sugar
1 egg
finely grated rind of 1 small orange, plus 10ml/2 tsp juice
175g/6oz/1½ cups self-raising (self-rising) flour
7.5ml/1½ tsp baking powder
good pinch of ground cinnamon
50g/2oz/½ cup polenta
icing (confectioners') sugar, for dusting

1 Preheat the oven to 160°C/325°F/ Gas 3. Grease a large baking sheet. In a large bowl, beat together the butter and sugar until smooth and creamy. Beat in the egg, then the orange rind and juice, flour, baking powder, cinnamon and polenta.

2 Tip the mixture on to a lightly floured surface and knead. Place the dough on the baking sheet and flatten out with the palm of your hand to make a rectangle about 25 × 18cm/10 × 7in.

Ice Cream Sandwiches

Home-made wafer cookies have a flavour unlike anything you can buy at the supermarket. These crisp, nutty cookies make perfect ice cream sandwiches for a summer-time treat. They're also fun to make and are a good accompaniment to almost any fruity or creamy dessert.

Makes 6 sandwiches

50g/2oz/¼ cup unsalted (sweet) butter

2 egg whites

75g/3oz/scant ½ cup caster
  (superfine) sugar

50g/2oz/½ cup plain (all-purpose) flour

40g/1½oz/scant ½ cup ground almonds

30ml/2 tbsp flaked (sliced)
  almonds (optional)

raspberry ripple or vanilla ice cream,
  to serve

icing (confectioners') sugar, for dusting

1 Preheat the oven to 200°C/400°F/ Gas 6. Line two large baking sheets with baking parchment. Put the butter in a small pan and melt over a very low heat.

2 Put the egg whites and sugar in a bowl and whisk lightly with a fork until the egg whites are broken up. Add the flour, melted butter and ground almonds and mix until evenly combined.

3 Drop 6 level tablespoonfuls of mixture on to each baking sheet, spacing them well apart. Spread the mixture to circles about 7cm/ 2¾in in diameter. Sprinkle with almonds, if using, and bake for 10–12 minutes until golden around the edges. Peel away the paper and transfer to a wire rack to cool.

4 Place a scoop of slightly softened ice cream on to one cookie and top with another, gently pressing them together. Dust with sugar and serve.

Cook's Tip

Don't be tempted to use greaseproof (waxed) paper instead of baking parchment as the cookies may stick to it.

Kids' Party Pieces

There's nothing quite like an extra-special cookie to make a kids' party go with a swing. This chapter is packed with fun ideas that kids will love, including cookie bracelets to slip around the wrist, novelty cookies that look like mini pizzas or a giant birthday cookie studded with candles to take the place of the more traditional birthday cake.

Stained Glass Windows

Baking coloured sweets inside a cookie frame creates a stunning stained glass effect, particularly if you hang the cookies in front of a window or near a lamp or wall light where the light can shine through. The transluscent cookie centre will stay brittle for a day or so before softening and finally melting, so don't be tempted to hang them up for too long.

Makes 12–14

175g/6oz/1½ cups plain
  (all-purpose) flour
2.5ml/½ tsp bicarbonate of soda
  (baking soda)
2.5ml/½ tsp ground cinnamon
75g/3oz/6 tbsp unsalted (sweet)
  butter, chilled and diced
75g/3oz/scant ½ cup caster
  (superfine) sugar
30ml/2 tbsp golden (light
  corn) syrup
1 egg yolk
150g/5oz brightly coloured, clear
  boiled sweets (hard candies)

1 Put the flour, bicarbonate of soda, cinnamon and butter into a food processor. Process until the mixture resembles breadcrumbs.

2 Add the sugar, syrup and egg yolk to the food processor, then process again until the mixture starts to cling together in a dough.

3 Turn the dough out on to a lightly floured surface and knead until smooth. Wrap in clear film (plastic wrap) and chill in the refrigerator for at least 30 minutes.

4 Preheat the oven to 180°C/350°F/Gas 4. Line two large baking sheets with baking parchment.

5 Roll out the dough thinly on a lightly floured surface. Cut into 6cm/2½in wide strips, then cut diagonally across the strips to create about 12 diamond shapes.

6 Carefully transfer the diamond shapes to the lined baking sheets, spacing them slightly apart.

7 Using a sharp knife, cut out a smaller diamond shape from the centre of each cookie and remove to leave a 1cm/½in frame.

8 Using a skewer, make a hole at one end of each cookie (large enough to thread fine ribbon).

9 Bake the cookie diamonds for about 5 minutes. Meanwhile, lightly crush the sweets (still in their wrappers) by tapping them gently with the end of a rolling pin.

10 Remove the cookies from the oven and quickly fill the centre of each one with about two crushed sweets of the same colour.

11 Return the cookies to the oven for a further 5 minutes until the sweets have melted. Remove from the oven and use a skewer to re-mark the skewer holes if they have shrunk during baking.

12 If the sweets haven't spread to fill the cookie centre during baking, while still hot, carefully spread the melted sweets with the tip of a skewer.

13 Leave the cookies on the baking parchment until the melted sweets have hardened. Once the centres are hard, gently peel away the paper from the cookies.

14 Thread fine ribbon of different lengths through the holes in the cookies, then hang as decorations around the home.

Cook's Tip
Make sure you re-mark the skewer holes while the cookies are still hot as they'll probably break if you try to make the holes once they've cooled.

Gold Medals

These cookies are great for kids' parties. You can present each child with a huge cookie medal when they sit down at the table, or hand them out to winners of party games. Alternatively, they make great going-home gifts when children leave.

Makes 10

50g/2oz/¼ cup unsalted (sweet) butter, at room temperature, diced
115g/4oz/generous ½ cup caster (superfine) sugar
1 egg
150g/5oz/1¼ cups self-raising (self-rising) flour
1.5ml/¼ tsp bicarbonate of soda (baking soda)

For the decoration

1 egg white
200g/7oz/1¾ cups icing (confectioners') sugar
small brightly coloured sweets (candies)

1 Preheat the oven to 180°C/350°F/Gas 4. Grease two baking sheets with a little butter.

2 In a bowl, beat together the butter and sugar until smooth and creamy, then beat in the egg. Add the flour and bicarbonate of soda and mix well to combine.

3 Place large spoonfuls of the mixture on the baking sheets, spacing them well apart to allow room for spreading. Bake for about 15 minutes, or until pale golden and slightly risen.

4 Using a skewer, make quite a large hole in the cookie, 1cm/½in from the edge. Transfer to a wire rack and leave to cool.

5 To make the icing, beat the egg white in a bowl using a wooden spoon. Gradually beat in the icing sugar to make a thick paste that just holds its shape. Spoon the icing into a small plastic bag and snip off the merest tip.

6 Write icing messages in the centre of the cookies. Secure a circle of sweets around the edge of each cookie with a little of the icing, then leave to set.

7 Once the icing has hardened, carefully thread each cookie with a piece of ribbon.

Party Bracelets

These tiny cookies are threaded on to fine ribbon along with an assortment of brightly coloured sweets that have a ready-made hole in the middle. Make the cookies a day or two in advance and simply thread together with the sweets on the day of the party.

Makes 10

50g/2oz/¼ cup unsalted (sweet) butter, at room temperature, diced
115g/4oz/generous ½ cup caster (superfine) sugar
5ml/1 tsp vanilla essence (extract)
pink or green food colouring
1 egg
200g/7oz/1¾ cups self-raising (self-rising) flour

For the decoration

2 large bags of boiled sweets (hard candies) with holes in the centre
narrow pastel-coloured ribbon, for threading

1 Preheat the oven to 180°C/350°F/ Gas 4. Grease two baking sheets.

2 In a bowl, beat together the butter, sugar and vanilla essence until pale and creamy. Add a dash of pink or green food colouring, then beat in the egg. Add the flour and mix well to form a dough.

3 Turn the dough on to a lightly floured surface and roll out under the palms of your hands into two long, thin sausage shapes, each about 40cm/16in long.

4 Cut each roll across into 5mm/¼in lengths and space them slightly apart on the baking sheets. Place the baking sheets in the refrigerator for about 30 minutes.

5 Bake the cookies for about 8 minutes until slightly risen and beginning to colour. Remove from the oven and, using a skewer, immediately make holes for the ribbon to be threaded through. (You may find it easier to bake one sheet of cookies at a time.) Transfer the cookies to a wire rack to cool.

6 Thread the cookies on to 55cm/ 22in lengths of narrow ribbon, alternating with the sweets. (You should end up with about seven cookies on each ribbon.) Tie the ends of the ribbons together in bows to finish.

Cook's Tip
When you make the holes in the cookies, you will need to work quickly. If the cookies start to harden before you have time to make holes in all of them, pop the remaining cookies back in the oven very briefly to re-soften.

Train Cookies

These simple party biscuits are so easy yet incredibly effective, particularly if you let them trail across the party table. The quantity makes enough for two trains, but double it if required.

Makes 10
*150g/5oz/1¼ cups plain
(all-purpose) flour
90g/3½oz/7 tbsp unsalted (sweet) butter,
chilled, diced
50g/2oz/½ cup golden icing
(confectioners') sugar
1 egg yolk
5ml/1 tsp vanilla essence (extract)*

For the decoration
*40g/1½oz/3 tbsp butter, softened
75g/3oz/¾ cup golden icing
(confectioners') sugar
blue food colouring
large bag of liquorice allsorts*

1 Put the flour and butter in a food processor. Process until the mixture resembles fine breadcrumbs. Add the sugar, egg yolk and vanilla; blend to a smooth dough. Wrap in clear film (plastic wrap) and chill for 30 minutes.

2 Preheat the oven to 200°C/400°F/Gas 6. Grease a large baking sheet. Roll out the dough and cut 7.5 × 4cm/3 × 1½in rectangles, re-rolling the scraps to make more cookies. Cut two 3 × 2cm/1¼ × ¾in rectangles and secure to the top of the larger rectangles for the engines.

3 Place on the baking sheet and bake for about 10 minutes until pale golden around the edges. Leave for 2 minutes on the baking sheet, then transfer to a wire rack to cool completely.

4 To decorate the biscuits, put the butter and icing sugar in a bowl with a dash of blue food colouring and beat until smooth and creamy. Chop plenty of the liquorice pieces into small dice.

Cook's Tip
If you don't want to use liquorice, try other colourful sweets (candies) or even chocolate. Round chocolates make good wheels and chopped chocolate or polka dots make good "cargo".

5 Spread a little buttercream along one long side of all the biscuits except the engines and press the chopped sweets into the buttercream. Halve some square sweets and secure to the engines for windows and another piece on the front of the engine for the funnel. Secure two wheels on all the biscuits. Arrange the biscuits in a trail across the table.

Flake "99s"

You don't need a special cutter to make these party biscuits. They're shaped using an ordinary round cutter to which you add a V-shaped cone when cutting them out – quite simple once you've made one or two. Children will find these fun biscuits irresistible.

Makes 15

150g/5oz/1¼ cups self-raising
  (self-rising) flour
90g/3½oz/7 tbsp unsalted (sweet)
  butter, diced
50g/2oz/¼ cup light muscovado
  (brown) sugar
1 egg yolk
5ml/1 tsp vanilla essence (extract)

For the decoration

75g/3oz/6 tbsp unsalted (sweet) butter,
  softened
5ml/1 tsp vanilla essence (extract)
115g/4oz/1 cup icing (confectioners')
  sugar
2 chocolate flakes

1 Put the flour and butter in a food processor and process until the mixture resembles fine breadcrumbs. Add the sugar, egg yolk and vanilla and blend to a smooth dough. Wrap in clear film (plastic wrap) and chill for 30 minutes.

2 Preheat the oven to 200°C/ 400°F/Gas 6. Grease a large baking sheet. Roll the dough out thinly on a floured surface. Lay a 5cm/2in round biscuit (cookie) cutter on the dough. Using a ruler mark a point 5cm/2in away from the edge of the cutter, then cut two lines from either side of the cutter to the point, to make cornet shapes. Cut around the rest of the cutter and transfer the cornet shape to the baking sheet. Make 14 more in the same way, re-rolling the trimmings to make the full quantity.

3 Using a sharp knife, make shallow cuts 5mm/¼in apart across the cone area of each cookie, then make more cuts diagonally across the first to create a "wafer" effect. Be careful not to cut all the way through the biscuit.

4 Bake for 8–10 minutes until pale golden. Leave for 2 minutes then transfer to a wire rack to cool.

5 For the buttercream, beat together the butter, vanilla and icing sugar until smooth. Add 5ml/1 tsp hot water and beat again until the mixture is very light and airy. Place in a piping (pastry) bag fitted with a large plain nozzle. Pipe swirls on to the tops of the biscuits so that they look like swirls of ice cream.

6 Cut the flakes across into 5cm/2in lengths. Carefully cut each piece lengthways into four small lengths. Push a flake piece into each biscuit.

Cook's Tip

The biscuits and buttercream can be made ahead, but assemble them on the day they're served as the cream will gradually soften the biscuits.

Name Cookies

You could decorate these cookies for children coming to a party, either in vibrant, bright colours or in more delicate pastels. It can be a fun idea to prop a name cookie up against the glass at each place setting around the tea table and let the children find their own seats.

Makes 20

200g/7oz/scant 1 cup unsalted (sweet) butter, chilled and diced
300g/10oz/2½ cups plain (all-purpose) flour
finely grated rind of 1 orange
90g/3½oz/scant 1 cup icing (confectioners') sugar
2 egg yolks

For the decoration

1 egg white
200g/7oz/1¾ cups icing sugar
2 different food colourings
jelly beans or silver balls

1 Put the butter, flour and orange rind in a food processor and process until the mixture resembles fine breadcrumbs. Add the icing sugar and egg yolks and blend until smooth. Wrap in clear film (plastic wrap) and chill for 30 minutes.

2 Preheat the oven to 200°C/400°F/ Gas 6. Grease two baking sheets.

3 Roll out the dough on a floured surface and cut out cookies in a variety of shapes, such as squares, hearts and rounds. Make sure each cookie is at least 7.5cm/3in across.

4 Transfer the cookies to the baking sheets, spacing them slightly apart, and bake for 10–12 minutes until pale golden around the edges.

5 Leave the cookies on the baking sheet for about 2 minutes to firm up, then transfer to a wire rack to cool completely.

6 To make the icing, put the egg white and icing sugar in a bowl and beat together until smooth, and the icing only just holds its shape.

7 Divide the icing between two bowls, then beat a few drops of food colouring into each bowl to make two different colours.

8 Spoon the two different icings into separate small plastic bags and gently squeeze into one corner.

Variation

If you prefer, add food colouring to only one of the bowls of icing, leaving the second bowl of icing white. This can look very pretty, particularly if you choose a pastel colour for the second bowl of icing and decorate with silver balls.

9 Cut off the merest tip from each bag so the icing can be piped in a very thin line, then write the names or initials of party guests on the cookies. Pipe decorative borders around the edges of the cookies using both colours of icing. Use either straight lines, flutes, dots of icing or squiggled lines of piping to decorate.

10 Chop the jelly beans, if using, into small pieces. Secure the jelly beans or the silver balls on to the icing on the cookies to finish. Leave the cookies to set for at least 1 hour.

Giant Birthday Cookie

This enormous cookie is one for cookie-lovers of any age. Complete with candles, it makes the perfect party centrepiece. To personalize the cookie, write the recipient's name on top in icing.

Makes one 28cm/11in cookie
175g/6oz/¾ cup unsalted
  (sweet) butter, at room
  temperature, diced
125g/4¼oz/⅔ cup light muscovado
  (brown) sugar
1 egg yolk
175g/6oz/1½ cups plain
  (all-purpose) flour
5ml/1 tsp bicarbonate of soda
  (baking soda)
finely grated rind of 1 orange
  or lemon
75g/3oz/scant 1 cup rolled oats

For the decoration
125g/4¼oz/generous ½ cup
  cream cheese
225g/8oz/2 cups icing
  (confectioners') sugar
5–10ml/1–2 tsp lemon juice
birthday candles
white and milk chocolate-coated
  raisins or peanuts
cocoa powder, for dusting
gold or silver balls, for sprinkling

1 Preheat the oven to 190°C/375°F/ Gas 5. Grease a 28cm/11in metal flan tin (tart pan) and place on a large baking sheet.

2 Put the diced butter and the sugar in a large bowl and beat together until pale and creamy.

3 Add the egg yolk to the butter and sugar mixture and stir well to mix. Add the flour, bicarbonate of soda, grated orange or lemon rind and rolled oats and stir thoroughly until evenly combined.

4 Turn the mixture into the tin and flatten with a wet wooden spoon.

5 Bake for 15–20 minutes until risen and golden. Leave to cool in the tin. (If any of the mixture has seeped under the ring during baking, trim it off with a knife while still warm.)

6 Carefully slide the cookie from the tin on to a large, flat serving plate or board.

7 To decorate, beat the cream cheese in a bowl, then add the icing sugar and 5ml/1 tsp of the lemon juice. Beat until smooth and peaking, adding more juice if required.

8 Spoon the mixture into a piping (pastry) bag and pipe swirls around the edge of the cookie. Press the candles into the frosting. Sprinkle with chocolate raisins or peanuts and dust with cocoa powder. Finish by sprinkling with gold or silver balls.

Mini Party Pizzas

These cute little cookie confections look amazingly realistic and older children will love them. They're fun to make and are simply a basic cookie topped with icing, marzipan and dark cherries.

Makes 16

90g/3½oz/7 tbsp unsalted (sweet)
   butter, at room temperature, diced
90g/3½oz/½ cup golden caster
   (superfine) sugar
15ml/1 tbsp golden (light corn) syrup
175g/6oz/1½ cups self-raising
   (self-rising) flour

For the topping

150g/5oz/1¼ cups icing
   (confectioners') sugar
20–25ml/4–5 tsp lemon juice
red food colouring
90g/3½oz yellow marzipan,
   grated (shredded)
8 dark glacé (candied) cherries, halved
a small piece of angelica, finely chopped

1 Preheat the oven to 180°C/350°F/ Gas 4. Grease two baking sheets.

2 In a bowl, beat together the butter and sugar until creamy. Beat in the syrup, then add the flour and mix to a smooth paste.

3 Turn the mixture on to a lightly floured surface and cut into 16 even-size pieces. Roll each piece into a ball, then space well apart on the baking sheets, slightly flattening each one.

4 Bake for about 12 minutes, or until pale golden. Leave on the baking sheets for 3 minutes, then transfer to a wire rack to cool.

5 To make the topping, put the icing sugar in a bowl and stir in enough lemon juice to make a fairly thick, spreadable paste. Beat in enough food colouring to make the paste a deep red colour.

Cook's Tip

Make sure you use a red food colouring rather than cochineal, which will colour the icing pink. Red food colouring is more readily available in paste form.

6 Spread the icing to within 5mm/ ¼in of the edges of the cookies. Sprinkle with the shredded marzipan and place a halved cherry in the centre. Arrange a few pieces of chopped angelica on top so that the cookies resemble little cheese and tomato pizzas.

Silly Faces

These funny little characters can be made using almost any type of cookie mix, as long as the baked cookies are quite big and not too craggy. Silly faces are great fun for kids to decorate as they can really go to town, experimenting with different hairstyles and features.

5 Bake for 10–12 minutes until turning golden around the edges. Transfer to a wire rack to cool.

6 To decorate, beat together the butter and icing sugar in a bowl until smooth and creamy.

7 Using a small palette knife (metal spatula) spread a little buttercream along the top edge of each cookie, then secure the strawberry, apple or liquorice strands. Either snip the strands to make straight hair, or twist the strands to make curly hair.

8 Use a dot of buttercream to secure a glacé cherry to the middle of each cookie for a nose. Pipe eyes and mouths using the writer icing, then add halved sweets, attached with buttercream, for the centres of the eyes.

Makes 14

115g/4oz/ ½ cup unsalted (sweet) butter, at room temperature, diced
115g/4oz/generous ½ cup golden caster (superfine) sugar
1 egg
115g/4oz/scant ⅓ cup golden (light corn) syrup
400g/14oz/3½ cups self-raising (self-rising) flour

For the decoration

75g/3oz/6 tbsp unsalted (sweet) butter, at room temperature, diced
150g/5oz/1¼ cups icing (confectioners') sugar
strawberry, apple or liquorice strands
glacé (candied) cherries, halved
red and black writer icing
small multi-coloured sweets (candies)

1 Put the butter and sugar in a large bowl and beat together until pale and creamy. Beat in the egg and golden syrup, then add the flour and mix together to make a thick paste.

2 Turn the mixture on to a lightly floured surface and knead until smooth. Wrap in clear film (plastic wrap) and chill for 30 minutes.

3 Preheat the oven to 180°C/350°F/ Gas 4. Grease two baking sheets.

4 Roll out the chilled dough on a lightly floured surface and cut out rounds using a 9cm/3½in cookie cutter. Transfer the rounds to the baking sheets, re-rolling the trimmings to make more cookies.

Gingerbread House Cookies

For a party of young children, these gingerbread house cookies provide plenty of entertainment. You could incorporate a house decorating session as one of the party games, allowing the children to design their own house and take it home after the party.

Makes 10

115g/4oz/½ cup unsalted (sweet)
   butter, at room temperature, diced
115g/4oz/generous ½ cup light
   muscovado (brown) sugar
1 egg
115g/4oz/scant ⅓ cup black treacle
   (molasses) or golden (light corn) syrup
400g/14oz/3½ cups self-raising
   (self-rising) flour
5ml/1tsp ground ginger (optional)

For the decoration

1 tube white decorating icing
1 tube pastel-coloured decorating icing
selection of small multi-coloured sweets
   (candies), sugar flowers and silver balls

1 Put the butter and sugar in a large bowl and beat together until pale and creamy. Beat in the egg and treacle or syrup, then add the flour and ginger, if using. Mix together to make a thick paste.

2 Turn the mixture on to a lightly floured surface and knead until smooth. Wrap in clear film (plastic wrap) and chill for 30 minutes.

3 Preheat the oven to 180°C/350°F/ Gas 4. Grease three baking sheets. On a piece of cardboard, draw an 11 x 8cm/4¼ x 3¼in rectangle. Add a pitched roof. Cut out the shape to use as a template.

4 Roll out the dough on a lightly floured surface. (It might be easier to roll out half the quantity of dough at a time.)

5 Using the template, cut out house shapes. Transfer to the baking sheets and re-roll the trimmings to make more. Bake for 12–15 minutes until risen and golden. Transfer the cookies to a wire rack to cool.

6 Use the icing in the tubes to pipe roof tiles, window and door frames and other decorative touches. Secure sweets and decorations to finish, cutting them into smaller pieces if preferred.

Jelly Bean Cones

Chocolate-dipped cookie cones filled with jelly beans make great treats for kids of all ages. The filled cones look very pretty arranged in glasses or other small containers to keep them upright. This way they can double as a tasty treat and a delightful table decoration.

Makes 10

3 egg whites

90g/3½oz/½ cup caster (superfine) sugar

25g/1oz/2 tbsp unsalted (sweet) butter, melted

40g/1½oz/⅓ cup plain (all-purpose) flour

30ml/2 tbsp single (light) cream

90g/3½oz plain (semisweet) chocolate

jelly beans or other small sweets (candies)

1 Preheat the oven to 190°C/375°F/ Gas 5. Line two baking sheets with baking parchment and lightly grease.

2 Put the egg whites and sugar in a bowl and whisk lightly with a fork until the egg whites are broken up. Add the melted butter, flour and cream and stir well to make a smooth batter.

3 Using a 15ml/1 tbsp measure, place a rounded tablespoon of the mixture on one side of a baking sheet. Spread to a 9cm/3½in round with the back of the spoon. Spoon more mixture on to the other side of the baking sheet and spread out to make another round.

4 Bake for about 8–10 minutes until the edges are deep golden. Meanwhile, spoon two more rounds of cookie mixture on to the second baking sheet.

5 Remove the first batch of cookies from the oven and replace with the second batch. Peel away the paper from the baked cookies and roll them into cone shapes. Leave to set. Continue in this way until you have made 10 cones.

6 Break the chocolate into a heatproof bowl set over a pan of simmering water and stir until melted. Dip the wide ends of the cookies in the chocolate and prop them inside narrow glasses to set, then fill with jelly beans or sweets.

Secret Message Cookies

These fortune cookies are light and wafery, and what they lack in substance, they certainly make up for in their fun capacity. These are great for older kids who can prepare birthday messages, jokes or predictions to tuck into the cookies as soon as they're baked.

Makes 18

3 egg whites
50g/2oz/ ½ cup icing
   (confectioners') sugar
40g/1½oz/3 tbsp unsalted (sweet)
   butter, melted
50g/2oz/ ½ cup plain (all-purpose) flour

1 Preheat the oven to 200°C/400°F/ Gas 6. Line two baking sheets with baking parchment and grease. Cut a piece of paper into 18 small strips, measuring 6 × 2cm/2½ × ¾in. Write a message on each one.

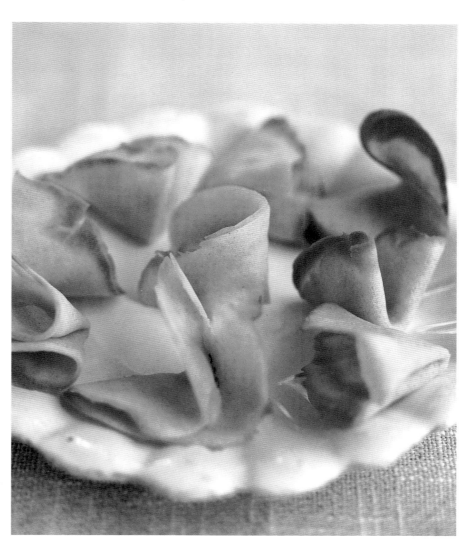

2 Lightly whisk the egg whites and icing sugar until the whites are broken up. Add the melted butter and flour and beat until smooth.

3 Using a 10ml/2 tsp measure, spoon a little of the paste on to one baking sheet and spread to a 7.5cm/3in round with the back of a spoon. Add two more spoonfuls of mixture to the baking sheet and shape in the same way.

4 Bake for 6 minutes until the cookies are golden. Meanwhile, prepare three more cookies on the second baking sheet.

5 Remove the first batch of cookies from the oven and replace with the second batch.

6 Working quickly, peel a hot cookie from the paper and fold it in half, tucking a message inside the fold. Rest the cookie over the rim of a glass or bowl and, very gently, fold again. (It probably won't fold over completely.) Fold the remaining two cookies in the same way.

7 Continue to bake and shape the remaining cookies in the same way until all the batter and messages have been used.

Cook's Tips
• *The secret to success is to spread the batter as thinly as possible on the paper. This will give a really crisp, light result.*
• *Don't be tempted to bake more than three cookies at once or they'll harden before you can shape them.*

Celebration Cookies

Food and festivals go together – from China to America and from January to December, you cannot have a celebration without cooking something special to eat. Of course, you don't have to wait for Diwali to enjoy Neuris, Hanukkah to feast on Rugelach or Easter to bake a batch of Simnel Cookies. Making any of the cookies in this chapter will turn an ordinary day into a special occasion and an international celebration.

Spicy Hearts and Stars

These soft, sweet cookies have a wonderfully chewy texture and a deliciously warm, fragrant flavour. Serve with coffee at the end of a festive meal, or make them as a gift on a special occasion.

Makes about 25

115g/4oz/½ cup unsalted (sweet) butter, softened

115g/4oz/generous ½ cup light muscovado (brown) sugar

1 egg

50g/2oz/1½ tbsp golden (light corn) syrup

50g/2oz/1½ tbsp black treacle (molasses)

400g/14oz/3½ cups self-raising (self-rising) flour

10ml/2 tsp ground ginger

For the toppings

200g/7oz plain (semisweet) or milk chocolate

150g/5oz/1¼ cups icing (confectioners') sugar, sifted

1 Beat together the butter and sugar until creamy. Beat in the egg, syrup and treacle together. Sift in the flour and ginger and mix to form a firm dough. Chill for 20 minutes. Meanwhile, preheat the oven to 180°C/350°F/Gas 4 and line two large baking sheets with a layer of baking parchment.

2 Roll out the dough on a lightly floured surface to just under 1cm/½in thick and use biscuit (cookie) cutters to stamp out heart and star shapes. Place, spaced slightly apart, on the prepared baking sheets and bake for about 10 minutes, or until risen. Cool on a wire rack.

3 To make the toppings, melt the chocolate in a microwave or in a heatproof bowl set over a pan of barely simmering water. Use the melted chocolate to coat the heart-shaped cookies. Put the icing sugar into a bowl and mix with enough warm water to make a coating consistency, then use this to glaze the star-shaped cookies.

Kourabiedes

Lightly spiced and delicately flavoured with orange flower water and almonds, these crisp little crescents are perfect for parties and festive occasions such as christenings and weddings.

Makes about 20

115g/4oz/½ cup unsalted (sweet)
   butter, softened
pinch of ground nutmeg
10ml/2 tsp orange flower water
50g/2oz/½ cup icing (confectioners')
   sugar, plus extra for dusting
90g/3½oz/¾ cup plain
   (all-purpose) flour
115g/4oz/1 cup ground almonds
25g/1oz/¼ cup whole almonds, toasted
   and chopped

1 Preheat the oven to 160°C/325°F/ Gas 3. Line two large baking sheets with baking parchment. Beat the butter in a large bowl until soft and creamy.

2 Beat in the nutmeg and orange flower water. Add the icing sugar and beat until fluffy.

3 Add the flour, ground and chopped almonds and mix well, then use your hands to bring the mixture together to form a dough, being careful not to overwork it.

4 Shape pieces of dough into sausages about 7.5cm/3in long. Curve each one into a crescent shape and place, spaced well apart, on the prepared baking sheets. Bake for about 15 minutes, or until firm but still pale in colour. Cool for about 5 minutes, then dust with a little icing sugar.

Christmas Tree Angels

Why not make these charming edible decorations to brighten your Yuletide? However, don't hang them on the tree until Christmas Eve or they'll all be gone by Christmas Day.

Makes 20–30

90g/3½oz/scant ½ cup demerara
  (raw) sugar
200g/7oz/scant1 cup golden
  (light corn) syrup
5ml/1 tsp ground ginger
5ml/1 tsp ground cinnamon
1.5ml/¼ tsp ground cloves
115g/4oz/½ cup unsalted (sweet) butter,
  cut into pieces
10ml/2 tsp bicarbonate of soda
  (baking soda)
1 egg, beaten
500g/1¼lb/4½ cups plain (all-purpose)
  flour, sifted

For the decoration

1 egg white
175–225g/6–8oz/1½–2 cups icing
  (confectioners') sugar, sifted
silver and gold balls
fine ribbon

1 Preheat the oven to 160°C/325°F/ Gas 3. Line two large baking sheets with baking parchment. Put the sugar, syrup, ginger, cinnamon and cloves into a heavy pan and bring to the boil over a low heat, stirring constantly. Once the mixture has boiled, remove the pan from the heat.

2 Put the pieces of butter in a large heatproof bowl and pour over the hot sugar and syrup mixture. Add the bicarbonate of soda and stir well until the butter has completely melted. Beat the egg into the mixture, then stir in the flour. Mix thoroughly and then knead to form a smooth dough.

3 Divide the dough into four pieces and roll out, one at a time, between sheets of baking parchment, to a thickness of about 3mm/⅛in. Keep the unrolled dough in a polythene bag until needed to prevent it from drying out. Stamp out festive shapes, such as Christmas trees, using biscuit (cookie) cutters, or make angels, as follows.

4 To make simple angels, stamp out rounds of dough of any size you like, using a plain cutter. Don't make them too big or they might be too heavy to hang on the Christmas tree. As shown in the photograph, cut off two segments from either side of the round to give a body and two wings. Place the wings, rounded side facing down, behind the body and press lightly together with your fingers.

5 Roll a small piece of dough for the head, place at the top of the body and flatten with your fingers. Using a skewer, make a wide hole in the cookies through which ribbon can be threaded when they are cooked. Place on the baking sheets. Bake the cookies for 10–15 minutes until golden brown. Transfer to a wire rack to cool.

6 To make the decoration, beat the egg white with a fork. Whisk in icing sugar until you have an icing of soft-peak consistency.

7 Put the icing in a piping (pastry) bag fitted with a plain writing nozzle and decorate the cookies with simple designs. Add silver and gold balls before the icing has set. Finally, thread fine ribbon through the holes in the cookies.

Speculaas

These Dutch cookies are made from a spicy dough wrapped around a wonderfully rich marzipan filling. They are eaten in Holland around the Feast of St Nicholas on 6 December.

Makes about 35

175g/6oz/1½ cups ground hazelnuts
175g/6oz/1½ cups ground almonds
175g/6oz/scant 1 cup caster
 (superfine) sugar
175g/6oz/1½ cups icing
 (confectioners') sugar
1 egg, beaten
10–15ml/2–3 tsp lemon juice
250g/9oz/2¼ cups self-raising
 (self-rising) flour
5ml/1 tsp mixed (apple pie) spice
75g/3oz/⅓ cup light muscovado
 (brown) sugar
115g/4oz/½ cup unsalted (sweet) butter,
 at room temperature, diced
2 eggs
15ml/1 tbsp milk
15ml/1 tbsp caster (superfine) sugar
about 35 blanched almond halves

1 For the filling, put the ground hazelnuts, almonds, caster sugar, icing sugar, beaten egg and 10ml/2 tsp lemon juice in a bowl and mix to a firm paste, adding more lemon juice if needed. Divide the mixture in half and roll each piece into a sausage shape about 25cm/10in long. Wrap in clear film (plastic wrap) and chill in the refrigerator.

2 To make the dough, sift the flour and mixed spice into a large mixing bowl then stir in the muscovado sugar. Add the butter and rub in well with your fingertips.

3 Beat one of the eggs, add to the mixture and mix together to form a dough. Knead lightly, then wrap in clear film and chill in the refrigerator for 15 minutes. Meanwhile, preheat the oven to 180°C/350°F/Gas 4 and line a large baking sheet with baking parchment.

4 Roll out the pastry on a lightly floured surface to a 30cm/12in square and cut in half to make two equal rectangles. Beat the remaining egg and brush some all over the pastry rectangles.

5 Place a roll of filling on each piece of pastry and roll the pastry to enclose the filling. Place, join side down, on the baking sheet.

6 Beat the remains of the egg with the milk and caster sugar and brush over the rolls. Press almond halves along the top. Bake for 35 minutes until golden brown. Leave to cool before cutting diagonally into slices.

Sweet Hearts

These cookies are for Valentine's Day or an anniversary, but you could use different-shaped cutters in the same way to make cookies for other occasions – stars and bells for Christmas, perhaps, or fluted "flowers" for a special birthday or Mother's Day present.

Makes 12–14
50g/2oz/¼ cup unsalted (sweet) butter, softened
75g/3oz/scant ½ cup caster (superfine) sugar
1 egg yolk
150g/5oz/1¼ cups plain (all-purpose) flour
25g/1oz dark (bittersweet) chocolate, melted and cooled
25–50g/1–2oz dark (bittersweet) chocolate, to decorate

1 Preheat the oven to 180°C/350°F/ Gas 4. Line two baking sheets with baking parchment. Put the butter, sugar and egg yolk in a mixing bowl and beat well. Stir in the flour and then knead until smooth.

2 Divide the dough in half, then knead the melted chocolate into one half until it is evenly coloured.

3 Roll out the chocolate dough between two sheets of baking parchment, to a thickness of about 3mm/⅛in. Then roll out the plain dough in the same way.

4 Cut out hearts from both doughs using a 7.5cm/3in biscuit (cookie) cutter. Place the hearts on the prepared baking sheets.

5 Using a smaller heart-shaped cutter, stamp out the centres from all the hearts. Place a light-coloured heart in the centre of a larger chocolate heart and vice versa.

6 Bake the cookies for about 10 minutes, or until just beginning to turn brown. Remove from the oven and leave to cool.

7 To decorate, melt the chocolate in a microwave or in a heatproof bowl set over a pan of hot water. Put into a disposable piping (pastry) bag. Leave the chocolate to cool slightly.

8 Snip the end off the piping bag and carefully pipe dots directly onto the outer part of the large chocolate hearts (with the plain centres). Then pipe zigzags on the pale part of the large plain hearts (with the chocolate centres). Put the cookies aside in a cool place and leave until they are set.

Variation
For a tasty variation, make chocolate and orange hearts by kneading 10ml/2 tsp very finely grated orange rind into the plain dough.

Italian Glazed Lemon Rings

These delicately flavoured, pretty cookies look almost too good to eat. The icing is flavoured with Italian liqueur, so they are strictly for adult parties.

Makes about 16

200g/7oz/1¾ cups self-raising
    (self-rising) flour
50g/2oz/¼ cup unsalted (sweet)
    butter, at room temperature, diced
25ml/1½ tbsp milk
50g/2oz/¼ cup caster (superfine) sugar
finely grated rind of ½ lemon
1 egg, beaten

For the topping

150g/5oz/1¼ cups icing (confectioners')
    sugar, sifted
30ml/2 tbsp Limoncello liqueur
15ml/1 tbsp chopped candied angelica

Variation

If you are baking for children, use lemon syrup instead of liqueur.

1 Preheat the oven to 180°C/ 350°F/Gas 4. Line two large baking sheets with baking parchment. Put the flour into a bowl and rub in the butter. Put the milk, sugar and lemon rind in a small pan and stir over a low heat until the sugar has dissolved. Add to the flour mixture, together with the egg, and mix well. Knead lightly until smooth.

2 Roll walnut-size pieces of dough into strands 15cm/6in long. Twist two strands together, and join the ends to make a circle. Place on the prepared baking sheets and bake for 15–20 minutes, or until golden.

3 To make the topping, stir the icing sugar and liqueur together. Dip the top of each cookie into the topping and sprinkle with angelica.

Persian Rice Flour Cookies

These prettily decorated cookies are traditionally served on special occasions with black tea. However, they taste as good with coffee or even a glass of chilled dry white wine.

Makes about 22

75g/3oz/⅔ cup icing (confectioners')
   sugar, sifted
225g/8oz/1 cup unsalted (sweet)
   butter, softened
300g/10oz/2½ cups rice flour
75g/3oz/⅔ cup self-raising
   (self-rising) flour
1 egg yolk
15ml/1 tbsp rose water

For the topping

150g/5oz/1¼ cups icing (confectioners')
   sugar, sifted
rose water
pink food colouring
crystallized rose petals or violets
   or pink sugar balls or
   sugar vermicelli

1 Mix together the sugar, butter, flours, egg yolk and rose water and gather into a ball. Wrap and chill. Meanwhile, preheat the oven to 160°C/325°F/Gas 3. Line two baking sheets with baking parchment.

2 Shape the mixture into balls. Place well apart on the prepared baking sheets and flatten each one slightly.

3 Bake for 15–20 minutes until firm but still quite pale in colour. Leave to cool completely on the baking sheets.

4 To make the topping, put the icing sugar into a bowl and add just enough rose water to mix to a thick, flowing consistency. Add just a light touch of pink food colouring to make a very pale shade.

5 Drizzle the icing in random squiggles and circles over all the cookies. Place a few crystallized rose petals or violets or pink sugar balls on top, or sprinkle with a little sugar vermicelli. Leave to set completely before serving the cookies.

Fourth of July Blueberry Softbakes

These are simply wonderful when eaten still warm from the oven. However, they are also good if allowed to cool and then packed for a traditional Independence Day picnic.

Makes 10

150g/5oz/1¼ cups plain
   (all-purpose) flour

7.5ml/1½ tsp baking powder

5ml/1 tsp ground cinnamon

50g/2oz/¼ cup unsalted (sweet) butter,
   at room temperature, diced

50g/2oz/¼ cup demerara (raw) sugar,
   plus extra for sprinkling

120ml/4fl oz/½ cup sour cream

90g/3½oz/1 cup fresh blueberries

50g/2oz/½ cup semi-dried cranberries

Variation

For Hallowe'en or Thanksgiving, substitute fresh cranberries for the blueberries and chopped preserved stem ginger for the semi-dried cranberries.

1 Preheat the oven to 190°C/375°F/ Gas 5. Line two baking sheets with baking parchment. Sift together the flour, baking powder and cinnamon into a large mixing bowl. Add the diced butter and rub in with your fingers until the mixture resembles fine breadcrumbs. Stir in the demerara sugar.

2 Add the sour cream, blueberries and cranberries and stir until just combined. Spoon ten mounds of the mixture, spaced well apart, on to the prepared baking sheets. Sprinkle with the extra demerara sugar and bake for about 20 minutes, or until golden and firm in the centre. Serve warm.

Simnel Cookies

Enjoy these mini variations on the sweet, marzipan-covered simnel cake that is traditionally eaten at Easter and, originally, Mothering Sunday in Britain. Children will enjoy decorating them.

Makes about 18

175g/6oz/¾ cup unsalted (sweet) butter, at room temperature, diced
115g/4oz/generous ½ cup caster (superfine) sugar
finely grated rind of 1 lemon
2 egg yolks
225g/8oz/2 cups plain (all-purpose) flour
50g/2oz/¼ cup currants

For the topping

400g/14oz/¾ cup marzipan
200g/7oz/1¾ cups icing (confectioners') sugar, sifted
2–3 shades of food colouring
mini sugar-coated chocolate Easter eggs

1 Preheat the oven to 180°C/350°F/ Gas 4. Put the butter, sugar and lemon rind in a bowl and cream with a wooden spoon or electric mixer until light and fluffy. Beat in the egg yolks, then stir in the flour and currants and mix to a firm dough. If it is a little soft, chill in the refrigerator until firm.

2 Roll the dough out on a sheet of baking parchment to just under 5mm/¼in thickness. Using a 9cm/ 3½in fluted cutter, stamp out rounds and place, spaced slightly apart, on two non-stick baking sheets.

3 To make the topping, roll out the marzipan to just under 5mm/¼in thickness and use a 6cm/2½in plain or fluted cutter to stamp out the same number of rounds as there are cookies. Place a marzipan round on top of each cookie and press down very gently to fix the marzipan to the cookie dough.

4 Bake the cookies for about 12 minutes, or until just golden. Remove from the oven and leave to cool on the baking sheets.

5 Put the icing sugar in a bowl and add just enough water to mix to a smooth, soft, spreadable consistency. Divide the icing among two or three bowls and add a few drops of different food colouring to each one. Stir until evenly mixed.

6 Divide the cooled cookies into three batches and spread each batch with icing of a different colour. While the icing is still wet, gently press a few sugar-coated eggs on top of each cookie and leave to set.

Rugelach

Jewish cookies, traditionally served during the eight-day festival of Hanukkah, these little crescents have a spicy fruit-and-nut filling. They can be enjoyed at any time of the year.

3 Divide the dough into four. Take one piece and leave the rest in the refrigerator, as it is important to keep the dough as cold as possible because it is very sticky and therefore difficult to roll out. Sprinkle a sheet of baking parchment with flour and quickly roll out the dough to a round as thin as possible. Cut into six wedges; sprinkle with a quarter of the filling.

4 Starting at the wide end, roll each triangle up towards the point. Curve each roll into a crescent and place, the pointed side down, on the prepared baking sheets. Repeat with the remaining dough and filling.

5 Brush with beaten egg and bake for about 15–20 minutes, or until golden brown. Transfer to a wire rack and leave to cool.

Makes about 24

115g/4oz/½ cup unsalted (sweet) butter, chilled and diced
115g/4oz/½ cup cream cheese
120ml/4fl oz/½ cup sour cream
250g/9oz/2¼ cups plain (all-purpose) flour
beaten egg, to glaze

For the filling

50g/2oz/¼ cup caster (superfine) sugar
10ml/2 tsp ground cinnamon
60ml/4 tbsp raisins, chopped
60ml/4 tbsp ready-to-eat dried apricots, chopped
75g/3oz/¾ cup walnuts, finely chopped

1 To make the dough, put the butter, cream cheese and sour cream into a food processor and process until just creamy and combined. Add the flour and process briefly, using the pulse button, until the mixture just comes together, taking care not to overmix. Remove, wrap in clear film (plastic wrap) and chill for at least 6 hours.

2 Preheat the oven to 180°C/350°F/ Gas 4. Line two large baking sheets with baking parchment. To make the filling, put all the filling ingredients in a bowl and mix until thoroughly combined.

Oznei Haman

These little cookies, shaped like tricorns – three-cornered hats – are eaten at the Jewish feast called Purim, which celebrates the Jews' deliverance from the scheming Haman.

Makes about 20

115g/4oz/½ cup unsalted (sweet) butter, at room temperature, diced
115g/4oz/generous ½ cup caster (superfine) sugar
2.5ml/½ tsp vanilla essence (extract)
3 egg yolks
250g/9oz/2¼ cups plain (all-purpose) flour
beaten egg to seal and glaze

For the filling

40g/1½oz/3 tbsp poppy seeds
15ml/1 tbsp clear honey
25g/1oz/2 tbsp caster (superfine) sugar
finely grated rind of 1 lemon
15ml/1 tbsp lemon juice
40g/1½oz/⅓ cup ground almonds
1 small (US medium) egg, beaten
25g/1oz/scant ¼ cup raisins

1 Beat the butter with the sugar until light and creamy. Beat in the vanilla and egg yolks. Sift over the flour, stir in, then work into a dough with your hands. Knead until smooth. Wrap in clear film (plastic wrap) and chill.

2 For the filling, put the poppy seeds, honey, sugar, lemon rind and juice into a pan with 60ml/4 tbsp water and bring to the boil, stirring. Remove from the heat and beat in the almonds, egg and raisins. Cool.

3 Preheat the oven to 180°C/350°F/Gas 4. Line two large baking sheets with baking parchment. Roll out the dough on a lightly floured surface to 3mm/⅛in thickness. Using a plain round 7.5cm/3in cutter, stamp out rounds. Place a heaped teaspoon of filling on each round. Brush the edges with beaten egg, then bring the sides to the centre to form a tricorne shape. Seal the edges well together and place on the prepared baking sheets, spaced slightly apart.

4 Brush with beaten egg and bake for 20–30 minutes, or until golden brown. Transfer to a wire rack and leave to cool.

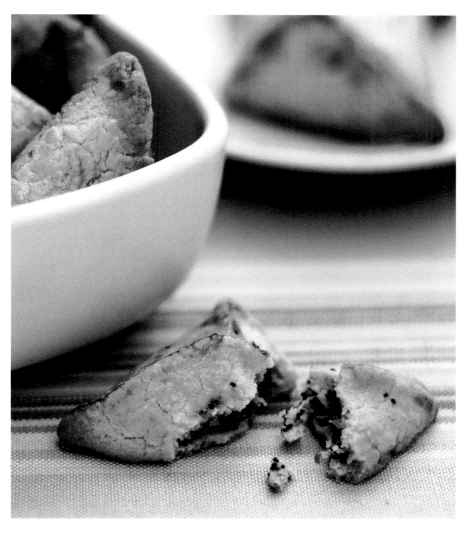

Chinese Fortune Cookies

Whether you're a rabbit or a dragon, a snake or a tiger, these charming cookies are sure to delight and are a wonderful way to celebrate the Chinese New Year with family and friends.

Makes about 35

2 egg whites

50g/2oz/½ cup icing (confectioner's)
   sugar, sifted, plus extra for dusting

5ml/1 tsp almond or vanilla
   essence (extract)

25g/1oz/2 tbsp unsalted (sweet)
   butter, melted

50g/2oz/½ cup plain (all-purpose) flour

25g/1oz/⅓ cup desiccated (dry
   unsweetened shredded) coconut,
   lightly toasted

tiny strips of paper with "good luck",
   "health, wealth and happiness" and
   other appropriate messages typed or
   written on them, to decorate

1 Preheat the oven to 190°C/375°F/ Gas 5. Prepare two or three sheets of baking parchment (they can be used more than once) by cutting them to the size of a baking sheet. Draw two or three circles of about 7.5cm/3in diameter, with a little distance between them, on each sheet of parchment. Place one of these sheets of parchment on the baking sheet and set aside.

2 Put the egg whites into a clean, grease-free bowl and whisk until foamy and white. Whisk in the icing sugar, a little at a time. Beat in the almond or vanilla essence and the butter. Stir in the flour and mix lightly until smooth.

Cook's Tip
You need to work quickly to shape the cookies. Placing the hot cookies on the rim of wine glasses sets them with a curve in the centre.

3 Place a teaspoonful of mixture into the centre of each marked circle on the prepared parchment and spread out evenly to fit the circle. Sprinkle with a little coconut. Bake one sheet at a time (as you will only have enough time to shape one sheetful of cookies before they set) for about 5 minutes, or until very lightly brown on the edges.

4 Remove the cookies from the oven, immediately loosely fold in half and place on the rim of a glass. Leave until firm, then transfer to a wire rack. Continue baking one sheet of cookies at a time.

5 Tuck the messages into the side of each cookie. Dust very lightly with icing sugar before serving.

Neuris

These melt-in-the-mouth sweet and spicy samosas are traditionally eaten during the **Hindu festival of Diwali** and are also given as little gifts to friends and family at this time.

Makes 12

75g/3oz/1 cup desiccated (dry unsweetened shredded) coconut
50g/2oz/¼ cup light muscovado (brown) sugar
25g/1oz/¼ cup cashew nuts, chopped
50g/2oz/⅓ cup seedless raisins
250ml/8fl oz/1 cup evaporated (unsweetened condensed) milk
large pinch grated nutmeg
2.5ml/½ tsp ground cinnamon
12 sheets filo pastry, about 28 x 18cm/ 11 x 7in each
sunflower oil, for brushing

For the topping

15ml/1 tbsp evaporated (unsweetened condensed) milk
15ml/1 tbsp caster (superfine) sugar
desiccated coconut

1 To make the filling, put the coconut, muscovado sugar, cashews, raisins and evaporated milk into a small pan. Bring to the boil, stirring occasionally. Reduce the heat to very low and cook for about 10 minutes, stirring, until the milk has been absorbed. Stir in the nutmeg and cinnamon, then set aside to cool.

2 Preheat the oven to 180°C/350°F/Gas 4. Line two baking sheets with baking parchment.

3 Brush one sheet of filo pastry with a little sunflower oil. Fold the sheet in half lengthways, then brush with more oil and fold widthways. Brush the edges of the folded pastry with water.

4 Place a spoonful of the cooled filling on one half of the folded pastry sheet. Fold the other half of the sheet over the filling, then press together the edges to seal. Trim off the rough edges and place on the baking sheet. Continue making neuris in this way until all the pastry and filling has been used up.

5 To make the topping, put the evaporated milk and sugar into a small pan and heat gently, stirring constantly until the sugar has completely dissolved.

6 Brush the topping over the neuris and sprinkle them with the coconut. Bake for about 20 minutes, until crisp and golden brown. Transfer to a wire rack and leave to cool before serving.

Wholesome Bites

When anyone is trying to lose weight or eat a healthier diet, the first items to be scrapped are almost always cookies, but this doesn't have to be the case. The recipes in this chapter are nutritious and delicious, packed with fruit, fibre and flavour. Many are low in fat and use natural sweeteners rather than refined sugars. You don't even have to sacrifice "chocolate" cookies. They are the perfect pick-me-up for adults and ideal for after-school snacks.

Low-fat Orange Oaties

These are so delicious that it is difficult to believe that they are healthy too. As they are packed with flavour and wonderfully crunchy, the whole family will love them.

Makes about 16

175g/6oz/¾ cup clear honey
120ml/4fl oz/½ cup orange juice
90g/3½oz/1 cup rolled oats,
   lightly toasted
115g/4oz/1 cup plain (all-purpose) flour
115g/4oz/generous ½ cup golden caster
   (superfine) sugar
finely grated rind of 1 orange
5ml/1 tsp bicarbonate of soda
   (baking soda)

1 Preheat the oven to 180°C/350°F/ Gas 4. Line two baking sheets with baking parchment.

2 Put the honey and orange juice in a small pan and simmer over a low heat for 8–10 minutes, stirring occasionally, until the mixture is thick and syrupy.

3 Put the oats, flour, sugar and orange rind into a bowl. Mix the bicarbonate of soda with 15ml/ 1 tbsp boiling water and add to the flour mixture, together with the honey and orange syrup. Mix well with a wooden spoon.

4 Place spoonfuls of the mixture on to the prepared baking sheets, spaced slightly apart, and bake for 10–12 minutes, or until golden brown. Leave to cool on the sheets for 5 minutes before transferring to a wire rack to cool completely.

Luxury Muesli Cookies

It is best to use a "luxury" muesli for this recipe, preferably one with 50 per cent mixed cereal and 50 per cent fruit, nuts and seeds. These buttery, crunchy cookies are ideal for a snack at any time.

Makes about 20

115g/4oz/½ cup unsalted (sweet) butter
45ml/3 tbsp golden (light corn) syrup
115g/4oz/generous ½ cup demerara
  (raw) sugar
175g/6oz/1½ cups "luxury" muesli (granola)
90g/3½oz/¾ cup self-raising (self-rising) flour
5ml/1 tsp ground cinnamon

1 Preheat the oven to 160°C/325°F/ Gas 3. Line two or three baking sheets with baking parchment.

Variation

Tropical muesli containing coconut and dried tropical fruits makes an interesting alternative to regular luxury muesli.

2 Put the butter, syrup and sugar in a large pan and heat gently. Stir constantly until the butter has completely melted. Remove the pan from the heat then stir in the muesli, flour and cinnamon and mix together well. Set aside to cool slightly.

3 Place spoonfuls of the mixture, slightly apart, on the baking sheets. Bake for 15 minutes until the cookies are just beginning to brown around the edges. Leave to cool for a few minutes on the baking sheets, then carefully transfer to a wire rack to cool completely.

Ker-runch Cookies

An unusual coating of bran flakes covers these small cookies – a painless way of making sure that you have plenty of fibre in your diet. They are fun to make too.

Makes about 18
175g/6oz/¾ cup vegetable margarine
175g/6oz/¾ cup light muscovado
  (brown) sugar
1 egg
175g/6oz/1½ cups self-raising
  (self-rising) wholemeal
  (whole-wheat) flour
115g/4oz/generous 1 cup rolled oats
115g/4oz/⅔ cup mixed dried fruit
50g/2oz/2 cups bran flakes
  breakfast cereal

1 Preheat the oven to 160°C/325°F/ Gas 3. Line two baking sheets with baking parchment. Put the margarine and sugar in a bowl and beat until pale and creamy.

2 Add the egg to the margarine mixture and beat in until thoroughly combined. Stir in the flour, oats and fruit. Roll into walnut-size balls between the palms of your hands. Spread out the bran flakes on a shallow plate and roll the balls in them to coat.

3 Place on the prepared baking sheets and flatten each one gently with your hand.

4 Bake for about 20 minutes until firm and golden brown. Remove from the baking sheets while still hot as these cookies firm up very quickly. Place on a wire rack to cool.

Iced Carob Cookies

If you are unable to eat chocolate but still crave it, these heavenly cookies, with their creamy topping, provide the answer to your prayers.

Makes 12–16

115g/4oz/½ cup butter

10ml/2 tsp carob powder

115g/4oz/1 cup wholemeal
  (whole-wheat) flour

5ml/1 tsp baking powder

75g/3oz/⅓ cup muscovado
  (molasses) sugar

50g/2oz/generous ½ cup rolled oats

For the topping

50g/2oz carob bar, coarsely chopped

45ml/3 tbsp double (heavy) cream

15ml/1 tbsp chopped ready-to-eat
  dried apricots

Cook's Tip

Carob is derived from the carob bean, which has a nutritious, flavoursome pulp.

1 Preheat the oven to 190°C/375°F/ Gas 5. Line the base and sides of an 18cm/7in square shallow cake tin (pan) with baking parchment. Put the butter in a large pan and add the carob powder. Stir over a low heat until the mixture is smooth and combined. Stir in the remaining ingredients and mix well.

2 Press the mixture into the prepared tin and bake for about 20–25 minutes until just set. Mark into squares or bars while still hot. Leave to cool in the tin.

3 To make the topping, stir the carob and cream in a small pan over a low heat. Spread over the cookies and sprinkle the apricots on top.

Carob and Cherry Cookies

Simplicity itself to make, these little cookies are given a chocolate-like flavour by the addition of carob and are deliciously crisp and crunchy.

Makes about 20

90g/3½oz/7 tbsp unsalted (sweet) butter,
   at room temperature, diced
75g/3oz/scant ½ cup caster
   (superfine) sugar
75g/3oz/⅓ cup light muscovado
   (brown) sugar
1 egg
150g/5oz/1¼ cups self-raising
   (self-rising) flour
25g/1oz/2 tbsp
   carob powder
50g/2oz/¼ cup glacé (candied)
   cherries, quartered
50g/2oz carob bar, chopped

1 Preheat the oven to 180°C/350°F/ Gas 4. Line two large baking sheets with baking parchment. Put the unsalted butter, caster sugar, muscovado sugar and the egg in a large mixing bowl and beat well together until the mixture is smooth and creamy.

2 Add the flour, carob powder, cherries and chopped carob bar to the mixture and mix well with a wooden spoon until thoroughly combined, making sure the carob powder is completely blended in.

3 Shape the mixture into walnut-size balls and place, spaced slightly apart to allow for spreading, on the prepared baking sheets.

4 Bake for about 15 minutes. Leave on the baking sheets for 5 minutes before transferring to a wire rack to cool completely.

Variations
• *If you aren't on a diet, use unsweetened cocoa powder and a bar of chocolate instead of the carob.*
• *Use raisins instead of cherries if you like.*

Granola Bar Cookies

A gloriously dense fruity, nutty and oaty mixture, packed with goodness and delicious too, these bars are an ideal snack and perfect to pack for a school lunch.

Makes 12

175g/6oz/¾ cup unsalted (sweet)
   butter, diced
150g/5oz/⅔ cup clear honey
250g/9oz/generous 1 cup demerara
   (raw) sugar
350g/12oz/3 cups jumbo oats
5ml/1 tsp ground cinnamon
75g/3oz/¾ cup pecan nut halves
75g/3oz/generous ½ cup raisins
75g/3oz/¾ cup ready-to-eat dried
   papaya, chopped
75g/3oz/¾ cup ready-to-eat dried
   apricots, chopped
50g/2oz/scant ½ cup pumpkin seeds
50g/2oz/scant ½ cup sunflower seeds
50g/2oz/2 tbsp sesame seeds
50g/2oz/½ cup ground almonds

1 Preheat the oven to 190°C/375°F/ Gas 5. Line a 23cm/9in square cake tin (pan) with baking parchment. Put the butter and honey in a large heavy pan and heat gently until the butter has melted and the mixture is completely smooth.

2 Add the demerara sugar to the pan and heat very gently, stirring constantly, until the sugar has completely dissolved. Bring the butter mixture to the boil and continue to boil for 1–2 minutes, stirring the mixture constantly until it has formed a smooth caramel sauce.

3 Add the remaining ingredients and mix together. Transfer the mixture to the tin and press down with a spoon. Bake for 15 minutes until the edges turn brown.

4 Place in the refrigerator and chill well. Turn out of the tin, peel off the parchment and cut into bars.

Fruity Breakfast Bars

Instead of buying fruit and cereal bars from the supermarket, try making this quick and easy version – they are much tastier and more nutritious than most of the commercially-made ones. They can be stored in an airtight container for up to four days.

Makes 12

270g/10oz jar apple sauce
115g/4oz/½ cup ready-to-eat dried
   apricots, chopped
115g/4oz/¾ cup raisins
50g/2oz/¼ cup demerara (raw) sugar
50g/2oz/⅓ cup sunflower seeds
25g/1oz/2 tbsp sesame seeds
25g/1oz/¼ cup pumpkin seeds
75g/3oz/scant 1 cup rolled oats
75g/3oz/⅔ cup self-raising (self-rising)
   wholemeal (whole-wheat) flour
50g/2oz/⅔ cup desiccated (dry
   unsweetened shredded) coconut
2 eggs

Cook's Tip

Allow the baking parchment to hang over the edges of the tin; this makes baked bars easier to remove.

1 Preheat the oven to 200°C/400°F/Gas 6. Grease a 20cm/8in square shallow baking tin (pan) and line with baking parchment.

2 Put the apple sauce in a large bowl with the apricots, raisins, sugar and the sunflower, sesame and pumpkin seeds and stir together with a wooden spoon until thoroughly mixed.

3 Add the oats, flour, coconut and eggs to the fruit mixture and gently stir together until evenly combined.

4 Turn the mixture into the tin and spread to the edges in an even layer. Bake for about 25 minutes or until golden and just firm to the touch.

5 Leave to cool in the tin, then lift out on to a board and cut into bars.

Chewy Flapjacks

Flapjacks are about the easiest cookies to make and, with a little guidance, can be knocked up in minutes by even the youngest cooks. This chunky, chewy version is flavoured with orange rind, but you can substitute with other fruits such as a handful of raisins, chopped prunes or apricots.

Makes 18

250g/9oz/generous 1 cup unsalted
  (sweet) butter
finely grated rind of 1 large orange
225g/8oz/⅔ cup golden (light corn) syrup
75g/3oz/⅓ cup light muscovado
  (brown) sugar
375g/13oz/3¾ cups rolled oats

1 Preheat the oven to 180°C/350°F/ Gas 4. Line the base and sides of a 28 x 20cm/11 x 8in shallow baking tin (pan) with baking parchment.

2 Put the butter, orange rind, syrup and sugar in a large pan and heat gently until the butter has melted.

3 Add the oats to the pan and stir to mix thoroughly. Tip the mixture into the tin and spread into the corners in an even layer.

4 Bake for 15–20 minutes until just beginning to colour around the edges. (The mixture will still be very soft but will harden as it cools.) Leave to cool in the tin.

5 Lift the flapjack out of the tin in one piece and cut into fingers.

Cook's Tip
Don't be tempted to overcook flapjacks; they'll turn crisp and dry and lose their lovely chewy texture.

Apricot and Pecan Flapjack

A tried-and-tested favourite made even more delicious by the addition of maple syrup, fruit and nuts. This is a real energy booster at any time of day – great for kids and adults alike.

Makes 10

150g/5oz/⅔ cup unsalted (sweet)
  butter, diced
150g/5oz/⅔ cup light muscovado
  (brown) sugar
30ml/2 tbsp maple syrup
200g/7oz/2 cups rolled oats
50g/2oz/½ cup pecan nuts, chopped
50g/2oz/¼ cup ready-to-eat dried
  apricots, chopped

Variations

• *You can substitute walnuts for the pecan nuts if you like, although the nutty flavour won't be so intense.*
• *Use different dried fruits instead of the apricots if you like. Let children choose their own.*

I Preheat the oven to 160°C/325°F/ Gas 3. Lightly grease an 18cm/7in square shallow baking tin (pan). Put the butter, sugar and maple syrup in a large heavy pan and heat gently until the butter has melted. Remove from the heat and stir in the oats, nuts and apricots until well combined.

2 Spread evenly in the prepared tin and, using a knife, score the mixture into ten bars. Bake for about 25–30 minutes, or until golden.

3 Remove from the oven and cut through the scored lines. Leave until completely cold before removing from the tin.

Spicy Fruit Slice

A double-layered sweet cookie in which the topping combines dried fruit, with grated carrot to keep it moist. An indulgent teatime treat.

Makes 12–16

90g/3½oz/7 tbsp vegetable margarine
75g/3oz/scant ½ cup caster
   (superfine) sugar
1 egg yolk
115g/4oz/1 cup plain (all-purpose) flour
30ml/2 tbsp self-raising (self-rising) flour
30ml/2 tbsp desiccated (dry unsweetened
   shredded) coconut
icing (confectioners') sugar, for dusting

For the topping

30ml/2 tbsp ready-to-eat
   prunes, chopped
30ml/2 tbsp sultanas (golden raisins)
50g/2oz/½ cup ready-to-eat dried
   pears, chopped
25g/1oz/¼ cup walnuts, chopped
75g/3oz/⅔ cup self-raising
   (self-rising) flour
5ml/1 tsp ground cinnamon
2.5ml/½ tsp ground ginger
175g/6oz/generous 1 cup grated carrots
1 egg, beaten
75ml/5 tbsp vegetable oil
2.5ml/½ tsp bicarbonate of soda
   (baking soda)
90g/3½oz/scant ½ cup dark muscovado
   (molasses) sugar

1 Preheat the oven to 180°C/350°F/ Gas 4. Line a 28 x 18cm/11 x 7in shallow baking tin (pan) with baking parchment. In a large mixing bowl beat together the margarine, sugar and egg yolk until smooth and creamy.

Cook's Tip

There is no need to peel the carrots before grating them. Just give them a good scrub to remove any dirt.

2 Stir in the plain flour, self-raising flour and coconut and mix together well. Press into the base of the prepared tin, using your fingers to spread the dough evenly. Bake for about 15 minutes, or until firm and light brown.

3 To make the topping, mix together all the ingredients and spread over the cooked base. Bake for about 35 minutes, or until firm. Cool completely in the tin before cutting into bars or squares. Dust with icing sugar.

Date Slice

Lemon-flavoured icing tops these scrumptious, low-fat bars, which are full of succulent fruit and crunchy seeds – the perfect mid-morning pick-me-up with a cup of decaf.

Makes 12–16

175g/6oz/¾ cup light muscovado (brown) sugar

175g/6oz/1 cup ready-to-eat dried dates, chopped

115g/4oz/1 cup self-raising (self-rising) flour

50g/2oz/½ cup muesli (granola)

30ml/2 tbsp sunflower seeds

15ml/1 tbsp poppy seeds

30ml/2 tbsp sultanas (golden raisins)

150ml/¼ pint/⅔ cup plain (natural) low-fat yogurt

1 egg, beaten

200g/7oz/1¾ cups icing (confectioners') sugar, sifted

lemon juice

15–30ml/1–2 tbsp pumpkin seeds

1 Preheat the oven to 180°C/350°F/ Gas 4. Line a 28 x 18cm/11 x 7in shallow baking tin (pan) with baking parchment. Mix together all the ingredients, except the icing sugar, lemon juice and pumpkin seeds.

2 Spread in the tin and bake for about 25 minutes until golden brown. Cool.

3 To make the topping, put the icing sugar in a bowl and stir in just enough lemon juice to make a spreading consistency.

4 Spread over the baked date mixture and sprinkle generously with pumpkin seeds. Leave to set before cutting into squares or bars.

Tropical Fruit Slice

Densely packed dried exotic fruits make the filling for these deliciously moist bars. They make a popular after-school snack for hungry kids, or pop one into their lunch box as a surprise.

Makes 12–16

175g/6oz/1½ cups plain
  (all-purpose) flour
90g/3½oz/generous ½ cup white
  vegetable fat (shortening)
60ml/4 tbsp apricot jam, sieved, or
  ready-made apricot glaze

For the filling

115g/4oz/½ cup unsalted (sweet)
  butter, softened
115g/4oz/generous ½ cup caster
  (superfine) sugar
1 egg, beaten
25g/1oz/¼ cup ground almonds
25g/1oz/2½ tbsp ground rice
300g/11oz/scant 2 cups ready-to-eat
  mixed dried tropical fruits, chopped

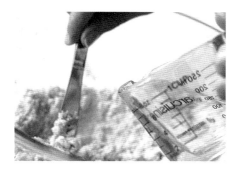

1 Preheat the oven to 180°C/350°F/ Gas 4. Lightly grease a 28 x 18cm/ 11 x 7in tin (pan). Put the flour and vegetable fat in a bowl and rub in with your fingers until the mixture resembles fine breadcrumbs. Add enough water to mix to a firm dough.

2 Roll out on a lightly floured surface and use to line the base of the prepared tin. Spread 30ml/ 2 tbsp of the jam or glaze over the dough.

3 To make the filling, cream together the butter and sugar until light and creamy. Beat in the egg, then stir in the almonds, rice and mixed fruits. Spread the mixture evenly in the tin.

4 Bake for about 35 minutes. Remove from the oven and brush with the remaining jam or glaze. Leave to cool completely in the tin before cutting into bars.

Cook's Tip

If you cannot find a ready-mixed packet of dried tropical fruits, make your own fruit mixture, choosing from the following: mangoes, apricots, guavas, dates, apples, pears, nectarines, peaches, figs and whatever else takes your fancy.

Chocolate Heaven

This has to be a favourite chapter for almost everyone – chocolate cookies are universally popular, loved by young and old alike. This is hardly surprising, with such mouthwatering recipes as Billionaire's Bars and Giant Triple Chocolate Cookies. Some, such as Rich Chocolate Cookie Slice, are astonishingly simple to make, while others, such as Mini Chocolate Marylands, take a little more time and effort, but they're certainly worth it.

Mini Chocolate Marylands

These tasty little cookies are perfect for any age group. They're easy to make and even young children can get involved with helping to press the chocolate chips into the unbaked dough.

Makes 40–45

125g/4¼oz/generous ½ cup
   unsalted (sweet) butter, at room
   temperature, diced
90g/3½oz/ ½ cup caster
   (superfine) sugar
1 egg
1 egg yolk
5ml/1 tsp vanilla essence (extract)
175g/6oz/1½ cups self-raising
   (self-rising) flour
90g/3½oz/generous ½ cup milk
90g/3½oz/generous ½ cup
   chocolate chips

1 Preheat the oven to 180°C/350°F/ Gas 4. Grease two baking sheets.

2 In a large bowl, beat together the butter and sugar until pale and creamy. Add the egg, egg yolk, vanilla essence, flour, milk and half the chocolate chips and stir well until thoroughly combined.

3 Using two teaspoons, place small mounds of the mixture on the baking sheets, spacing them slightly apart to allow room for spreading.

4 Press the remaining chocolate chips on to the mounds of cookie dough and press down gently.

5 Bake for 10–15 minutes until pale golden. Leave the cookies on the baking sheet for 2 minutes to firm up, then transfer to a wire rack to cool completely.

Cook's Tip
This recipe makes quite a large quantity. If you like, you can freeze half of the cookies for another time. Simply thaw, then return to the oven for a few minutes to re-crisp before serving.

Fruity Chocolate Cookie-cakes

The combination of spongy cookie, fruity preserve and dark chocolate makes irresistible eating for kids of all ages. As cookies go, these are a little fiddly, but that's all part of the fun.

Makes 18

90g/3½oz/½ cup caster
   (superfine) sugar
2 eggs
50g/2oz/½ cup plain (all-purpose) flour
75g/3oz/6 tbsp apricot-orange
   marmalade or apricot jam
125g/4¼oz plain (semisweet) chocolate

1 Preheat the oven to 190°C/375°F/ Gas 5. Grease 18 patty tins (muffin pans), preferably non-stick. (If you don't have that many patty tins, you'll need to bake the cookies in batches.)

2 Stand a mixing bowl in very hot water for a couple of minutes to heat through, keeping the inside of the bowl dry. Put the sugar and eggs in the bowl and whisk with a hand-held electric mixer until light and frothy and the beaters leave a ribbon trail when lifted. Sift the flour over the mixture and stir in gently using a large metal spoon.

3 Divide the mixture among the patty tins. Bake for 10 minutes until just firm and pale golden around the edges. Using a palette knife (metal spatula), lift from the tins and transfer to a wire rack to cool.

4 Press the marmalade or jam through a sieve to remove any rind or fruit pieces. Spoon a little of the smooth jam on to the centre of each cookie.

5 Break the chocolate into pieces and place in a heatproof bowl set over a pan of gently simmering water. Heat, stirring frequently, until melted and smooth.

6 Spoon a little chocolate on to the top of each cookie and spread gently to the edges with a palette knife. Once the chocolate has just started to set, very gently press it with the back of a fork to give a textured surface. Leave to set for at least 1 hour.

Rich Chocolate Cookie Slice

These rich, dark chocolate refrigerator cookies are perfect served with strong coffee, either as a mid-morning treat or even in place of dessert. They are always very popular.

Makes about 10

275g/10oz fruit and nut plain
  (semisweet) chocolate
130g/4½oz/½ cup unsalted (sweet)
  butter, diced
90g/3½oz digestive biscuits
  (graham crackers)
90g/3½oz white chocolate

1 Grease and line the base and sides of a 450g/1lb loaf tin (pan) with baking parchment. Break the fruit and nut chocolate into even-size pieces and place in a heatproof bowl along with the diced unsalted butter.

2 Set the bowl over a pan of simmering water and stir gently until melted. Cool for 20 minutes.

3 Break the digestive biscuits into small pieces with your fingers. Finely chop the white chocolate.

4 Stir the broken biscuits and white chocolate into the cooled, melted fruit and nut chocolate until combined. Turn the mixture into the prepared tin and pack down gently. Chill for 2 hours, or until set.

5 To serve, turn out the mixture and remove the lining paper. Cut into slices with a sharp knife.

Variation
You can use this simple, basic recipe for all kinds of variations. Try different kinds of chocolate, such as ginger, hazelnut, honey and almond, peanut or mocha.

Giant Triple Chocolate Cookies

Here is the ultimate cookie, packed full of chocolate and macadamia nuts. You will have to be patient when they come out of the oven, as they are too soft to move until completely cold.

Makes 12 large cookies

90g/3½oz milk chocolate

90g/3½oz white chocolate

300g/11oz dark (bittersweet) chocolate
  (minimum 70 per cent cocoa solids)

90g/3½oz/7 tbsp unsalted (sweet) butter,
  at room temperature, diced

5ml/1 tsp vanilla essence (extract)

150g/5oz/¾ cup light muscovado
  (brown) sugar

150g/5oz/1¼ cups self-raising
  (self-rising) flour

100g/3½oz/scant 1 cup macadamia
  nut halves

1 Preheat the oven to 180°C/350°F/ Gas 4. Line two baking sheets with baking parchment. Coarsely chop the milk and white chocolate and put them in a bowl.

2 Chop 200g/7oz of the dark chocolate into very large chunks, at least 2cm/¾in in size. Set aside.

3 Break up the remaining dark chocolate and place in a heatproof bowl set over a pan of barely simmering water. Stir until melted and smooth. Remove from the heat and stir in the butter, then the vanilla essence and muscovado sugar.

4 Add the flour and mix gently. Add half the dark chocolate chunks, all the milk and white chocolate and the nuts and fold together.

5 Spoon 12 mounds on to the baking sheets. Press the remaining dark chocolate chunks into the top of each cookie. Bake for about 12 minutes until just beginning to colour. Cool on the baking sheets.

Chocolate Wands

Shaping these long, wafery chocolate cookies is fun, but you need to work quickly so it might take a few attempts to get the technique just right. Only bake two cookies at a time; any more and they will become brittle before you have time to shape them into wands.

Makes 10–12

3 egg whites
90g/3½oz/½ cup caster (superfine) sugar
25g/1oz/2 tbsp unsalted (sweet) butter, melted
30ml/2 tbsp plain (all-purpose) flour
15ml/1 tbsp cocoa powder (unsweetened)
30ml/2 tbsp single (light) cream
90g/3½oz milk chocolate and multi-coloured sprinkles, to decorate

1 Preheat the oven to 180°C/350°F/ Gas 4. Line two large baking sheets with baking parchment and grease the paper well.

2 In a bowl, briefly beat together the egg whites and sugar until the whites are broken up.

3 Add the melted butter, flour, cocoa powder and cream to the egg whites and beat with a wooden spoon until smooth.

Cook's Tip
These cookies look best when the wands are really slender. Use a wooden spoon with a thin handle for shaping the cookies around. Alternatively, use a chunky pencil wrapped in kitchen foil.

4 Place 2 teaspoons of the mixture to one side of a baking sheet and spread the mixture into an oval shape, about 15cm/6in long. Spoon more mixture on to the other side of the baking sheet and shape in the same way.

5 Bake for 7–8 minutes until the edges begin to darken. Meanwhile, prepare two more cookies on the second baking sheet so you can put them in the oven while shaping the first batch into wands.

6 Leave the baked cookies on the paper for 30 seconds, then carefully lift one off and wrap it around the handle of a wooden spoon. As soon as it starts to hold its shape ease it off the spoon and shape the second cookie in the same way.

7 Continue baking and shaping the cookies in this way until all the mixture has been used up.

8 Break the chocolate into pieces and place in a heatproof bowl set over a pan of gently simmering water. Heat, stirring occasionally, until the chocolate has melted.

9 Dip the ends of the cookies in the chocolate, turning them until the ends are thickly coated.

10 Sprinkle the chocolate-coated ends of the cookies with coloured sprinkles and place on a sheet of baking parchment. Leave for about 1 hour until the chocolate has set.

Chocolate Caramel Nuggets

Inside each of these buttery cookies lies a soft-centred chocolate-coated caramel. They're at their most delicious served an hour or so after baking, so you might want to shape them in advance, then put the baking sheet of uncooked nuggets in the refrigerator until you are ready to bake them.

Makes 14

150g/5oz/1¼ cups self-raising
   (self-rising) flour
90g/3½oz/7 tbsp unsalted (sweet) butter,
   chilled and diced
50g/2oz/¼ cup golden caster
   (superfine) sugar
1 egg yolk
5ml/1 tsp vanilla essence (extract)
14 soft-centred chocolate caramels
icing (confectioners') sugar and cocoa
   powder (unsweetened), for dusting

1 Put the flour and diced butter in a food processor and process until the mixture resembles fairly fine breadcrumbs.

2 Add the sugar, egg yolk and vanilla essence to the food processor and process to a smooth dough. Wrap the dough in clear film (plastic wrap) and chill for 30 minutes.

3 Preheat the oven to 200°C/400°F/ Gas 6. Grease a large baking sheet.

4 Roll out the dough thinly on a lightly floured surface and cut out 28 rounds using a 5cm/2in cutter.

5 Place one chocolate caramel on a cookie round, then lay a second round on top. Pinch the edges of the dough together so that the chocolate caramel is completely enclosed, then place on the baking sheet. Make the remaining cookies in the same way. Bake for about 10 minutes until pale golden.

6 Transfer to a wire rack and leave to cool. Serve lightly dusted with icing sugar and cocoa powder.

Chocolate Whirls

These cookies are so easy that you don't even have to make any dough. They're made with ready-made puff pastry rolled up with a chocolate filling. They're not too sweet and are similar to Danish pastries, so you could even make them as a special treat for breakfast.

Makes about 20
75g/3oz/⅓ cup golden caster
  (superfine) sugar
40g/1½oz/6 tbsp cocoa powder
  (unsweetened)
2 eggs
500g/1lb 2oz puff pastry
25g/1oz/2 tbsp butter, softened
75g/3oz/generous ½ cup sultanas
  (golden raisins)
90g/3½oz milk chocolate

1 Preheat the oven to 220°C/425°F/ Gas 7. Grease two baking sheets.

2 Put the sugar, cocoa powder and eggs in a bowl and mix to a paste.

3 Roll out the pastry on a lightly floured surface to make a 30cm/ 12in square. Trim off any rough edges using a sharp knife.

4 Dot the pastry all over with the softened butter, then spread with the chocolate paste and sprinkle the sultanas over the top.

Cook's Tip
Use a sharp knife to cut the cookie slices from the pastry roll, and wipe the blade clean with a cloth every few slices.

5 Roll the pastry into a sausage-shape, then cut the roll into 1cm/ ½in slices. Place the slices on the baking sheets, spacing them apart.

6 Bake the cookies for 10 minutes until risen and pale golden. Transfer to a wire rack and leave to cool.

7 Break the milk chocolate into pieces and put in a heatproof bowl set over a pan of gently simmering water. Heat, stirring frequently until melted and smooth.

8 Spoon or pipe lines of melted chocolate over the cookies, taking care not to completely hide the swirls of chocolate filling.

Chocolate Cookies on Sticks

Let your imagination run riot when decorating these fun chocolate cookies. Use plenty of brightly coloured sweets or create a real chocolate feast by only using chocolate decorations. Whichever you choose, these cookies are very sweet so should be kept as a real treat for special occasions.

3 Spoon the milk chocolate into the outlines on the paper, reserving one or two spoonfuls of chocolate. Using the back of a spoon, carefully spread the chocolate to the edges to make neat shapes.

4 Press the end of a wooden ice lolly stick into each of the shapes, and spoon over a little more melted milk chocolate to cover the stick. Sprinkle the chocolate shapes with the crumbled cookies.

5 Pipe or drizzle the cookies with the melted white chocolate, then sprinkle the cookies with the coloured sweets, chocolate chips or chocolate-coated raisins, pressing them gently to make sure they stick.

6 Chill for about 1 hour until set, then carefully peel away the paper.

Makes 12

125g/4¼oz milk chocolate

75g/3oz white chocolate

50g/2oz chocolate-coated
  sweetmeal cookies, crumbled
  into chunks

a selection of small coloured sweets
  (candies), chocolate chips
  or chocolate-coated raisins

12 wooden ice lolly
  (popsicle) sticks

1 Break the milk and white chocolate into pieces and put in separate heatproof bowls. Place each bowl in turn over a pan of gently simmering water and heat, stirring frequently, until melted.

2 Meanwhile, draw six 7cm/2¾in rounds on baking parchment and six 9 x 7cm/3½ x 2¾in rectangles. Invert the paper on to a large tray.

Chocolate Thumbprint Cookies

Chunky, chocolatey and gooey all at the same time, these gorgeous cookies are filled with a spoonful of chocolate spread after baking to really add to their indulgent feel. Use your favourite chocolate spread, whether it is plain, milk, white or nut-flavoured.

Makes 16

115g/4oz/½ cup unsalted (sweet) butter, at room temperature, diced

115g/4oz/generous ½ cup light muscovado (brown) sugar

1 egg

75g/3oz/⅔ cup plain (all-purpose) flour

25g/1oz/¼ cup cocoa powder (unsweetened)

2.5ml/½ tsp bicarbonate of soda (baking soda)

115g/4oz/generous 1 cup rolled oats

75–90ml/5–6 tbsp chocolate spread

1 Preheat the oven to 180°C/350°F/ Gas 4. Grease a large baking sheet. In a bowl, beat together the butter and sugar until creamy.

2 Add the egg, flour, cocoa powder, bicarbonate of soda and rolled oats to the bowl and mix well.

3 Using your hands, roll spoonfuls of the mixture into balls. Place the balls on the baking sheet, spacing them well apart to allow room for spreading. Flatten slightly.

4 Dip a thumb in flour and press into the centre of each cookie to make an indent. Bake the cookies for 10 minutes. Leave for 2 minutes, then transfer to a wire rack to cool.

5 Spoon a little chocolate spread into the centre of each cookie.

Chocolate Box Cookies

These prettily decorated, bite-size cookies look as though they've come straight out of a box of chocolates. They're great for a special tea or for wrapping as gifts, and older children will love getting thoroughly absorbed in making and decorating them.

Makes about 50

175g/6oz/1½ cups self-raising
   (self-rising) flour
25g/1oz/¼ cup cocoa powder
   (unsweetened)
5ml/1 tsp mixed (apple pie) spice
50g/2oz/¼ cup unsalted (sweet)
   butter, at room temperature, diced
115g/4oz/generous ½ cup caster
   (superfine) sugar
1 egg
1 egg yolk

For the decoration

150g/5oz milk chocolate
150g/5oz white chocolate
100g/3¾oz plain (semisweet) chocolate
whole almonds or walnuts
cocoa powder, for dusting

1 Preheat the oven to 180°C/350°F/ Gas 4. Grease two baking sheets.

2 Put the flour, cocoa powder, spice and butter into a food processor. Process until the ingredients are thoroughly blended. Add the sugar, egg and egg yolk and mix to a smooth dough.

3 Turn the dough out on to a lightly floured surface and knead gently. Cut the dough in half and roll out each piece under the palms of your hands to form two long logs, each 33cm/13in long.

4 Cut each log into 1cm/½in slices. Place the slices on the prepared baking sheet, spacing slightly apart, and chill for at least 30 minutes.

5 Bake for 10 minutes until slightly risen. Transfer to a wire rack to cool.

6 To decorate, break the chocolate into three separate heatproof bowls. Place each bowl, in turn, over a pan of gently simmering water and stir frequently until melted.

7 Divide the cookies into six batches. Using a fork, dip one batch, a cookie at a time, into the milk chocolate to coat completely. Place on a sheet of baking parchment.

8 Taking the next batch of cookies, half-dip in milk chocolate and place on the baking parchment.

9 Continue with the next two batches of cookies and the white chocolate. Completely coat one batch, then half-coat the second.

10 Continue with the remaining cookies, completely coating one batch in the plain chocolate and half-dipping the other. Press a whole nut on to the tops of the plain chocolate-coated cookies.

11 Put the leftover white chocolate in a small plastic bag and squeeze it into one corner. Snip off the tip, then drizzle lines of chocolate over the milk chocolate-coated cookies.

12 Dust the white chocolate-coated cookies with a little cocoa powder. Store all the cookies in a cool place until ready to serve.

Cook's Tip
Once you have mastered the art of decorating the cookies, vary the combinations. Try drizzling milk or dark chocolate over the different cookies.

Chocolate Florentines

These big, flat, crunchy cookies are just like traditional florentines but use tiny seeds instead of nuts. Rolling the edges in milk or white chocolate makes them feel like a real treat.

Makes 12

50g/2oz/¼ cup unsalted (sweet) butter
50g/2oz/¼ cup caster (superfine) sugar
15ml/1 tbsp milk
25g/1oz/scant ¼ cup pumpkin seeds
40g/1½oz/generous ¼ cup
  sunflower seeds
50g/2oz/scant ½ cup raisins
25g/1oz/2 tbsp multi-coloured glacé
  (candied) cherries, chopped
30ml/2 tbsp plain (all-purpose) flour
125g/4¼oz milk or white chocolate

1 Preheat the oven to 180°C/350°F/Gas 4. Line two baking sheets with baking parchment and grease the paper well.

2 In a pan, melt the butter with the sugar, stirring, until the sugar has dissolved, then cook until bubbling. Remove the pan from the heat and stir in the milk, pumpkin and sunflower seeds, raisins, glacé cherries and flour. Mix well.

3 Spoon 6 teaspoonfuls of the mixture on to each baking sheet, spacing them well apart. Bake for 8–10 minutes until the cookies are turning dark golden. Using a palette knife (metal spatula), push back the edges of the cookies to neaten. Leave on the baking sheets for about 5 minutes to firm up, then transfer to a wire rack to cool.

4 Break up the chocolate and put in a heatproof bowl set over a pan of gently simmering water. Heat, stirring frequently, until melted. Roll the edges of the cookies in the chocolate and leave to set on a clean sheet of baking parchment for about 1 hour.

Variation
If you prefer, use plain (semisweet)
chocolate to decorate the cookies.

Triple Chocolate Sandwiches

Chocolate shortbread is a brilliant base for sandwiching or coating in lashings of melted chocolate. Kids of any age can enjoy making them as they don't need to be perfectly uniform.

Makes 15

125g/4¼oz/generous ½ cup unsalted
   (sweet) butter, chilled and diced
150g/5oz/1¼ cups plain
   (all-purpose) flour
30ml/2 tbsp cocoa powder (unsweetened)
50g/2oz/¼ cup caster (superfine) sugar
75g/3oz white chocolate
25g/1oz/2 tbsp unsalted (sweet) butter
115g/4oz milk chocolate

1 Put the butter, flour and cocoa in a food processor. Process until the mixture resembles breadcrumbs. Add the sugar and process again until the mixture forms a dough.

2 Transfer the dough to a clean surface and knead lightly. Wrap in clear film (plastic wrap) and chill for 30 minutes.

3 Preheat the oven to 200°C/400°F/Gas 6. Grease a large baking sheet.

4 Roll out the chilled dough on a floured surface to a 33 x 16cm/13 x 6¼in rectangle. Lift on to the baking sheet and trim the edges.

5 Cut the dough in half lengthways, then cut across at 2cm/¾in intervals to make 30 small bars.

6 Prick each bar with a fork and bake for 12–15 minutes until just beginning to darken around the edges. Remove from the oven and cut between the bars again while the cookies are still warm. Leave for 2 minutes, then transfer to a wire rack to cool.

7 To make the filling, break the white chocolate into a heatproof bowl. Add half the butter and set the bowl over a pan of gently simmering water and stir frequently until melted.

8 Spread a little of the filling evenly on to one of the bars. Place another bar on top and push together to sandwich the cookies. Continue in the same way with the remaining cookies and filling.

9 To make the topping, break the milk chocolate into a heatproof bowl. Add the remaining butter and set over a pan of simmering water, stirring frequently until melted. Using a teaspoon, drizzle the chocolate over the top of the cookies, then leave to set.

Marbled Caramel Chocolate Slice

The classic millionaire's slice is made even more special here with a decorative and tasty marbled chocolate topping – guaranteed to make you feel like a lottery winner.

Makes about 24

For the base

250g/9oz/2¼ cups plain
   (all-purpose) flour
75g/3oz/scant ½ cup caster
   (superfine) sugar
175g/6oz/¾ cup unsalted (sweet)
   butter, softened

For the filling

90g/3½oz/7 tbsp unsalted (sweet)
   butter, diced
90g/3½oz/scant ½ cup light muscovado
   (brown) sugar
2 x 397g/14oz cans sweetened
   condensed milk

For the topping

90g/3½oz plain (semisweet) chocolate
90g/3½oz milk chocolate
50g/2oz white chocolate

1 Preheat the oven to 180°C/350°F/ Gas 4. Line and lightly grease a 33 x 23cm/13 x 9in Swiss roll tin (jelly roll pan). Put the flour and caster sugar in a bowl and rub in the butter until the mixture resembles fine breadcrumbs. Work with your hands until the mixture forms a dough.

2 Put the dough into the prepared tin and press it out with your hand to cover the base. Then use the back of a tablespoon to smooth it evenly into the tin. Prick all over with a fork and bake for about 20 minutes, or until firm to the touch and very light brown. Set aside and leave in the tin to cool.

3 To make the filling, put the butter, muscovado sugar and condensed milk into a pan and heat gently, stirring, until the sugar has dissolved. Stirring constantly, bring to the boil. Reduce the heat and simmer the mixture very gently, stirring constantly, for about 5–10 minutes, or until it has thickened and has turned a caramel colour. Take care that the mixture does not burn on the base of the pan, as this will spoil the flavour. Remove from the heat.

4 Pour the filling mixture over the cookie base, spread evenly, then leave until cold.

5 To make the topping, melt each type of chocolate separately in a microwave or in a heatproof bowl set over a pan of hot water. Spoon lines of plain and milk chocolate over the set caramel filling.

6 Add small spoonfuls of white chocolate. Use a skewer to form a marbled effect on the topping.

Ultimate Indulgence

In case all the previous recipes haven't spoilt you for choice, here is a superb collection of mouthwatering treats that will prove totally irresistible – from blissful Tiramisu Cookies to light-as-air Praline Pavlova Cookies. There is something special to indulge everyone, whether your tastes are for the rich and creamy, fresh and fruity or dark and chocolatey. There are even breakfast cookies that cook overnight while you sleep.

Florentine Cookies

These are not your traditional Florentines but an utterly yummy cookie version with a soft crumbly base and a wonderfully sticky chewy topping.

Makes 24

115g/4oz/½ cup unsalted (sweet) butter,
   at room temperature, diced
115g/4oz/generous ½ cup caster
   (superfine) sugar
1 egg
a few drops of almond essence
   (extract) (optional)
225g/8oz/2 cups self-raising
   (self-rising) flour

For the topping

175g/6oz/1½ cups ready-to-eat dried
   apricots, chopped
50g/2oz/½ cup dried mango pieces,
   chopped
100g/3½oz/scant 1 cup flaked
   (sliced) almonds
60ml/4 tbsp plain (all-purpose) flour
50g/2oz/¼ cup unsalted (sweet) butter
50g/2oz/¼ cup golden caster
   (superfine) sugar
60ml/4 tbsp golden (light corn) syrup

1 Preheat the oven to 190°C/375°F/ Gas 5. Lightly grease two baking sheets. Cream together the butter and sugar until the mixture is light and fluffy, then beat in the egg, making sure it is well combined. Stir in the almond essence, if using, and the flour and mix to a firm yet soft dough, working it together with your hands.

Variation

For an even more self-indulgent treat, make the topping using maple, rather than golden syrup. Make sure you buy the pure syrup that has not been blended with other cheaper syrups, as it has an incomparable flavour.

2 Roll the dough out on a floured surface and, using a 7.5cm/3in plain round biscuit (cookie) cutter, stamp out 24 rounds. Place them on the prepared baking sheets, spaced slightly apart to allow for spreading.

3 To make the topping, put the apricots, mango pieces, almonds and flour in a bowl and toss gently together to mix. Put the butter, sugar and syrup in a small pan and heat gently until the butter has melted and the mixture is smooth and combined. Pour the butter mixture over the fruit and nuts and mix thoroughly.

4 Spoon the mixture on top of the cookies, spreading it right to the edges. Bake for 12–14 minutes until golden brown and crisp on top. Leave the cookies on the baking sheets for 5 minutes to firm up slightly, then transfer to a wire rack to cool completely.

Candied Peel Crumble Cookies

Crumbly, melt-in-the-mouth cookies, these incorporate candied peel, walnuts and white chocolate chips and are coated with a zingy lemon glaze.

Makes about 24

175g/6oz/¾ cup unsalted (sweet) butter,
   at room temperature, diced
90g/3½oz/½ cup caster (superfine) sugar
1 egg, beaten
finely grated rind of 1 lemon
200g/7oz/1¾ cups self-raising
   (self-rising) flour
90g/3½oz/generous ½ cup
   candied peel, chopped
75g/3oz/¾ cup chopped walnuts
50g/2oz/⅓ cup white chocolate chips

For the glaze

50g/2oz/½ cup icing (confectioners')
   sugar, sifted
15ml/1 tbsp lemon juice
thin strips of candied peel, to
   decorate (optional)

1 Preheat the oven to 180°C/350°F/ Gas 4. Grease two baking sheets or line them with baking parchment. Put the butter and sugar in a large bowl and cream together. Add the egg and beat thoroughly. Add the lemon rind and flour and stir together gently. Finally, fold the candied peel, walnuts and chocolate chips into the mixture.

2 Place tablespoonfuls of mixture, spaced slightly apart, on the baking sheets and bake for 12–15 minutes, until cooked but still pale in colour. Transfer the cookies to a wire rack.

3 For the glaze, put the icing sugar in a bowl and stir in the lemon juice. Spoon glaze over each cookie. Decorate with candied peel, if using.

Midnight Cookies

These cookies are so called because you can make them up before you go to bed and leave them to bake slowly in the switched-off oven. Hey presto – there they are in the morning, lightly crunchy on the outside and deliciously soft in the middle. A wonderfully indulgent way to start the day.

Makes 9

1 egg white
90g/3½oz/½ cup caster
 (superfine) sugar
50g/2oz/½ cup ground almonds
90g/3½oz/generous ½ cup milk
 chocolate chips
90g/3½oz/scant ½ cup glacé (candied)
 cherries, chopped
50g/2oz/⅔ cup sweetened,
 shredded coconut

1 Preheat the oven to 220°C/425°F/Gas 7. Line a baking sheet with baking parchment. Put the egg white in a large, clean, grease-free bowl and whisk until stiff peaks form.

2 Add the caster sugar to the whisked egg white, a spoonful at a time, whisking well between each addition until the sugar is fully incorporated. The mixture should be completely smooth and glossy in appearance. Use an electric mixer for speed.

3 Fold in the almonds, chocolate chips, cherries and coconut. Place 9 spoonfuls on the baking sheet. Place in the oven, close the door then turn the oven off. Leave overnight (or at least 6 hours during the day) and don't open the door. Serve the cookies for breakfast.

Banana Cream Cookies

These delicious cookies are inspired by the classic childhood dessert bananas and cream. The warm banana cookies are coated in crisp sugar-frosted cornflakes and, for the ultimate indulgence, are delicious served warm drizzled with clear honey.

Makes about 24

2 eggs

250g/9oz/1¼ cups soft light
   brown sugar

5ml/1 tsp vanilla essence (extract)

100ml/3½fl oz/scant ½ cup
   sunflower oil

90g/3½oz/scant ½ cup crème fraîche

200g/7oz/1¾ cups plain
   (all-purpose) flour

200g/7oz/1¾ cups self-raising
   (self-rising) flour

50g/2oz/2½ cups frosted cornflakes

125g/4¼oz dried small bananas,
   chopped, or 2 bananas, peeled
   and chopped

icing (confectioners') sugar, sifted,
   for dredging

1 Preheat the oven to 180°C/350°F/ Gas 4. Line two or three baking sheets with baking parchment. Put the eggs and brown sugar in a large bowl and whisk together until well blended. Stir in the vanilla essence. Add the oil and crème fraîche and stir in well. Add the flour and mix well. (The mixture will be quite runny at this stage.) Cover with clear film (plastic wrap) and chill in the refrigerator for about 30 minutes.

2 Put the frosted cornflakes in a large bowl. Remove the cookie dough from the refrigerator and stir in the bananas. Using a tablespoon, drop heaps into the flakes. Lightly toss so each cookie is well coated, then remove and place on the prepared baking sheets. Flatten very slightly with your fingertips.

3 Bake for 15–20 minutes, or until risen and golden brown and crispy. Transfer the cookies to a wire rack and dredge with sifted icing sugar. Serve while still warm.

Praline Pavlova Cookies

Crisp, melt-in-the-mouth meringue with a luxurious velvety chocolate filling is topped with nutty praline – just the thing for a special tea party or simply when you feel in need of a treat.

Makes 14

2 large (US extra large)
   egg whites
large pinch of ground cinnamon
90g/3½oz/½ cup caster
   (superfine) sugar
50g/2oz/½ cup pecan nuts,
   finely chopped

For the filling

50g/2oz/¼ cup unsalted (sweet) butter,
   at room temperature, diced
100g/3½oz/scant 1 cup icing
   (confectioners') sugar, sifted
50g/2oz plain (semisweet) chocolate

For the praline

60ml/4 tbsp caster (superfine) sugar
15g/½oz/1 tbsp finely chopped
   toasted almonds

2 Place 14 spoonfuls of meringue on the prepared baking sheets, spaced well apart. Using the back of a wetted teaspoon, make a small hollow in the top of each meringue so it looks like a little nest. Bake in the oven for 45–60 minutes until dry and just beginning to colour. Remove from the oven and set aside to cool.

4 To make the praline, put the sugar in a small non-stick frying pan. Heat gently until the sugar melts to form a clear liquid. When the mixture begins to turn brown, stir in the nuts. When the mixture is a golden brown, remove from the heat and pour immediately on to a lightly oiled or non-stick baking sheet. Leave to cool completely and then break into small pieces. Sprinkle over the meringues and serve.

Cook's Tip

These cookies should be eaten immediately once they have been assembled. To make them ahead of time, store the unfilled meringues in an airtight container and place the filling in a covered container in a cool place. Make the praline on the day itself.

Variation

Use toasted hazelnuts, instead of almonds, to make the praline.

1 Preheat the oven to 140°C/275°F/ Gas 1. Line two baking sheets with baking parchment. Put the egg whites in a bowl and whisk until stiff. Stir the cinnamon into the sugar. Add a spoonful of sugar to the egg whites and whisk well. Continue adding the sugar, a spoonful at a time, whisking well until the mixture is thick and glossy. Stir in the chopped pecan nuts.

3 To make the filling, beat together the butter and icing sugar until light and creamy. Break the chocolate into even-size pieces and place in a heatproof bowl. Set over a pan of barely simmering water and stir occasionally until melted. Remove from the heat and leave to cool slightly. Add the chocolate to the butter mixture and stir well. Divide the filling among the meringues, putting a little in each hollow.

Tiramisu Cookies

These delicate cookies taste like the wonderful Italian dessert with its flavours of coffee, chocolate, rum and rich creamy custard. Serve with coffee or cups of frothy hot chocolate.

Makes 14

50g/2oz/¼ cup butter, at room
   temperature, diced
90g/3½oz/½ cup caster
   (superfine) sugar
1 egg, beaten
50g/2oz/½ cup plain (all-purpose) flour

For the filling

150g/5oz/⅔ cup mascarpone cheese
15ml/1 tbsp dark rum
2.5ml/½ tsp instant coffee powder
15ml/1 tbsp light muscovado
   (molasses) sugar

For the topping

75g/3oz white chocolate
15ml/1 tbsp milk
30ml/2 tbsp crushed chocolate flakes

1 To make the filling, put the mascarpone cheese in a bowl. Mix together the rum and coffee powder, stirring well until the coffee has dissolved. Add the rum and coffee mixture and the sugar to the cheese and mix together well. Cover with clear film (plastic wrap) and chill until required.

2 Preheat the oven to 200°C/400°F/ Gas 6. Line two or three baking sheets with baking parchment. To make the cookies, cream together the butter and sugar in a bowl until light and fluffy. Add the beaten egg and mix well. Stir in the flour and mix thoroughly again until well combined.

3 Put the mixture into a piping (pastry) bag fitted with a 1.5cm/⅝in plain nozzle and pipe 28 small blobs on to the baking sheets, spaced slightly apart. Cook for about 6–8 minutes until firm in the centre and just beginning to brown on the edges. Remove from the oven and set aside to cool.

4 When ready to assemble, spread a little of the filling on to half the cookies and place the other halves on top. Put the chocolate and milk in a heatproof bowl and melt over a pan of hot water. Take care not to overheat. When the chocolate has melted, stir vigorously to make a smooth spreadable consistency. Spread the chocolate topping evenly over the cookies, then sprinkle with crushed chocolate flakes to finish.

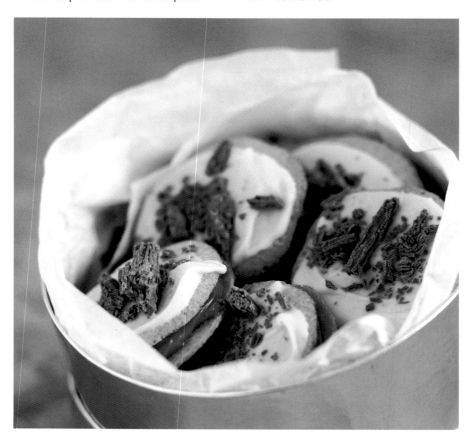

Chocolate and Prune Cookies

When freshly baked, these cookies have a deliciously gooey centre. As they cool down the mixture hardens slightly to form a firmer, fudge-like consistency. Try these with a glass of brandy.

Makes 18
150g/5oz/⅔ cup butter, at room
   temperature, diced
150g/5oz/¾ cup caster (superfine) sugar
1 egg yolk
250g/9oz/2¼ cups self-raising
   (self-rising) flour
25g/1oz/¼ cup (unsweetened)
   cocoa powder
about 90g/3½oz plain (semisweet)
   chocolate, coarsely chopped

For the topping
50g/2oz plain (semisweet) chocolate
9 ready-to-eat prunes, halved

1 Preheat the oven to 190°C/375°F/ Gas 5. Line two baking sheets with baking parchment. Cream the butter and sugar together until light and creamy. Beat in the egg yolk. Sift over the flour and cocoa powder and stir in to make a firm yet soft dough.

2 Roll out about a third of the dough on baking parchment. Using a 5cm/2in round biscuit (cookie) cutter, stamp out 18 rounds and place them on the baking sheets.

3 Sprinkle the chopped chocolate in the centre of each cookie.

4 Roll out the remaining dough in the same way as before and, using a 7.5cm/3in round biscuit cutter, stamp out 18 "lids". Carefully lay the lids over the cookie bases and press the edges well together to seal. Don't worry if the lids crack slightly when you do this.

5 Bake for about 10 minutes until the cookies have spread a little and are just firm to a light touch. Leave them on the baking sheets for about 5 minutes to firm up slightly, then, using a palette knife (metal spatula), transfer to a wire rack to cool completely.

6 For the topping, melt the chocolate in a heatproof bowl set over a pan of hot water. Dip the cut side of the prunes in the chocolate then place one on top of each cookie. Spoon any remaining chocolate over the prunes.

Ice Cream Sandwich Cookies

These are great when you get those midnight munchies – either keep the cookies in an airtight container and sandwich together each time with the softened ice cream of your choice or make the sandwiches complete with ice cream and coating and freeze until required.

Makes 12

115g/4oz/½ cup unsalted (sweet) butter, at room temperature, diced
115g/4oz/generous ½ cup caster (superfine) sugar
1 egg, beaten
200g/7oz/1¾ cups plain (all-purpose) flour
25g/1oz/¼ cup (unsweetened) cocoa powder, sieved
ice cream, to fill
toasted nuts, biscuit (cookie) crumbs, chocolate flakes or demerara (raw) sugar, to coat

1 Preheat the oven to 180°C/350°F/ Gas 4. Cream the butter and sugar together until light and fluffy, then beat in the egg. Stir in the flour and cocoa powder to make a firm dough.

2 Roll the dough out to a thickness of 6mm/¼in on baking parchment. Using a 7.5cm/3in plain round biscuit (cookie) cutter, stamp out 24 rounds and place on the prepared baking sheets. Alternatively cut into squares or rectangles of equal size. Bake the cookies for about 15 minutes. Set aside on the baking sheets to cool.

3 To make the ice cream cookies, spread 2 good spoonfuls of softened ice cream on a cookie and press a second on top. Squeeze so the filling reaches the edges.

4 Put your chosen coating on a plate and roll the cookies in it to coat the sides. Either eat straight away or wrap individually in foil and freeze. The cookies may be kept for up to 2 weeks in the freezer.

Cook's Tip

For super deluxe cookies, half-dip the ice cream cookies in melted chocolate. Shake off the excess, place on a sheet of baking parchment and freeze at once. When the chocolate has set, either eat or wrap in foil and freeze for later.

Nut Bar Cookies

If you love chocolate, condensed milk, nuts and crumb crust then these are the cookies for you. It's fortunate that they are incredibly easy to make because they are even easier to eat and are sure to become firm favourites with all the family. Children enjoy helping to make them.

Makes 16–18

250g/9oz digestive biscuits
   (graham crackers)
115g/4oz/½ cup butter, melted
150g/5oz/scant 1 cup milk
   chocolate chips
200g/7oz mixed whole nuts, such as
   pecan nuts, hazelnuts, brazil nuts,
   walnuts and almonds
200ml/7fl oz/scant 1 cup can sweetened
   condensed milk

Cook's Tip

If you prefer, use a shallow 20cm/8in cake tin (pan) instead, and cut the cookies into squares.

1 Preheat the oven to 180°C/350°F/ Gas 4. Crush the biscuits in a polythene bag with a rolling pin.

2 Put the biscuit crumbs in a bowl and stir in the melted butter. Mix well. Press the mixture evenly into the base of a 10 x 36cm/4 x 14in cake tin (pan).

3 Sprinkle the chocolate chips over the biscuit base. Arrange the nuts on top and pour the condensed milk over the top evenly.

4 Bake for 25 minutes, or until bubbling and golden. Cool in the tin, loosen from the sides, then cool completely and slice into thin bars.

Apple Crumble and Custard Slice

These luscious apple slices are easy to make using ready-made sweet pastry and custard. Just think, all the ingredients of one of the world's most popular desserts – in a cookie.

Makes 16
350g/12oz ready-made sweet pastry
1 large cooking apple, about 250g/9oz
30ml/2 tbsp caster (superfine) sugar
60ml/4 tbsp ready-made thick custard

For the crumble topping
115g/4oz/1 cup plain (all-purpose) flour
2.5ml/½ tsp ground cinnamon
60ml/4 tbsp granulated sugar
90g/3½oz/7 tbsp unsalted (sweet)
  butter, melted

I Preheat the oven to 190°C/375°F/ Gas 5. Roll out the pastry and use to line the base of a 28 × 18cm/ 11 × 7in shallow cake tin (pan). Prick the pastry with a fork, line with foil and baking beans and bake blind for about 10–15 minutes. Remove the foil and baking beans and return the pastry to the oven for a further 5 minutes until cooked and golden brown.

2 Meanwhile, peel, core and chop the apple evenly. Place in a pan with the sugar. Heat gently until the sugar dissolves, then cover with a lid and cook gently for 5–7 minutes until a thick purée is formed. Beat with a wooden spoon and set aside to cool.

3 Mix the cold apple with the custard. Spread over the pastry.

4 To make the crumble topping, put the flour, cinnamon and sugar into a bowl and pour over the melted butter. Stir thoroughly until the mixture forms small clumps. Sprinkle the crumble over the filling.

5 Return to the oven and bake for about 10–15 minutes until the crumble topping is cooked and a golden brown. Leave to cool in the tin, then slice into bars to serve.

Creamy Fig and Peach Squares

A sweet cream cheese and dried fruit filling with a hint of mint makes these cookies really special. They are ideal for quietening hunger pangs after school or work.

Makes 24
350g/12oz/3 cups plain (all-purpose) flour
200g/7oz/scant 1 cup unsalted
   (sweet) butter, diced
1 egg, beaten
caster (superfine) sugar,
   for sprinkling

For the filling
500g/1¼lb/2½ cups ricotta cheese
115g/4oz/generous ½ cup
   caster (superfine) sugar
5ml/1 tsp finely chopped fresh mint
50g/2oz/⅓ cup ready-to-eat dried
   figs, chopped
50g/2oz/⅓ cup ready-to-eat dried
   peaches, chopped

1 Preheat the oven to 190°C/375°F/ Gas 5. And then lightly grease a 33 x 23cm/13 x 9in Swiss roll tin (jelly roll pan) or shallow cake tin (pan). Put the flour and butter into a bowl. Rub in the butter until the mixture resembles fine breadcrumbs. Add the egg and enough water to mix to a firm but not sticky dough.

2 Divide the pastry into two and roll out one piece to fit the base of the prepared tin. Place in the tin and trim.

3 To make the filling, put all the ingredients in a bowl and mix together. Spread over the pastry base. Roll out the remaining pastry and place on top of the filling. Prick lightly all over with a fork then sprinkle with caster sugar.

4 Bake for about 30 minutes until light golden brown. Remove from the oven and sprinkle more caster sugar thickly over the top. Cool and cut into slices to serve.

Dessert Cookies

Mousses, sorbets, ice creams and fresh fruit salads are among the many desserts complemented by delicate, elegant or richly flavoured cookies – and, of course, there is nothing so delicious as special little nibbles served with coffee and liqueurs. The recipes in this chapter will be an inspiration for those who love to entertain, as they provide that professional finishing touch that turns a good meal into a truly memorable occasion.

Rosemary-scented Citrus Tuiles

These delicious crisp cookies are flavoured with tangy orange and lemon rind, and made beautifully fragrant with fresh rosemary – an unusual but winning combination.

Makes 18–20

50g/2oz/¼ cup unsalted (sweet)
   butter, diced
2 egg whites
115g/4oz/generous ½ cup caster
   (superfine) sugar
finely grated rind of ½ lemon
finely grated rind of ½ orange
10ml/2 tsp finely chopped fresh rosemary
50g/2oz/½ cup plain (all-purpose) flour

1 Preheat the oven to 190°C/375°F/ Gas 5. Line a baking sheet with baking parchment. Melt the butter in a pan over a low heat. Leave to cool. Whisk the egg whites until stiff, then gradually whisk in the sugar.

2 Fold in the lemon and orange rinds, rosemary and flour and then the melted butter. Place 2 large tablespoonfuls of mixture on the baking sheet. Spread each to a thin disc about 9cm/3½in in diameter. Bake for 5–6 minutes until golden.

3 Remove from the oven and lift the tuiles using a palette knife (metal spatula) and drape over a rolling pin. Transfer to a wire rack when set in a curved shape. Continue baking the rest of the mixture in the same way.

Ginger Glass Cookies

As thin, delicate and elegant as fine glass, these ginger cookies are ideal served with creamy desserts, syllabubs, sorbets and luxury ice creams.

Makes about 18
50g/2oz/¼ cup unsalted (sweet)
  butter, diced
40g/1½oz/3 tbsp liquid glucose
  (clear corn syrup)
90g/3½oz/½ cup caster
  (superfine) sugar
40g/1½oz/⅓ cup plain (all-purpose) flour
5ml/1 tsp ground ginger

1 Put the butter and liquid glucose in a heatproof bowl set over a pan of gently simmering water. Stir together until melted. Set aside.

Cook's Tip
Use unlipped baking sheets so you can roll the cookies thinly.

2 Put the sugar in a bowl and sift over the flour and ginger. Stir into the butter mixture, then beat well until combined. Cover with clear film (plastic wrap) and chill for about 25 minutes, until firm. Meanwhile, preheat the oven to 180°C/350°F/ Gas 4 and line two or three baking sheets with baking parchment.

3 Roll teaspoonfuls of the cookie mixture into balls between your hands and place them, spaced well apart to allow room for spreading, on the prepared baking sheets.

4 Place a second piece of baking parchment on top and roll the cookies as thinly as possible. Peel off the top sheet. Then stamp each cookie with a 7.5 or 9cm/3 or 3½in plain round cutter.

5 Bake for 5–6 minutes, or until golden. Leave for a few seconds on the baking sheets to firm up slightly, then either leave flat or curl over in half. Leave to cool completely.

Sablés with Caramel Glaze

These are very buttery French cookies with a dark caramel glaze. The leftover glaze can be kept in the refrigerator and used to flavour fruit salads and especially oranges, both of which are good served with sablés. Use on the day of baking for the most delicious results.

Makes about 18

200g/7oz/1¾ cups plain
    (all-purpose) flour
pinch of salt
75g/3oz/⅔ cup icing
    (confectioners') sugar
130g/4½oz/generous ½ cup unsalted
    (sweet) butter, chilled and diced
3 egg yolks
2.5ml/½ tsp vanilla essence (extract)
1 egg yolk, for glazing

For the caramel syrup

50g/2oz/¼ cup granulated sugar
20ml/4 tsp water
2.5ml/½ tsp lemon juice
50ml/2fl oz/¼ cup water

1 First make the caramel syrup. Put the sugar, 20ml/4 tsp water and lemon juice into a small pan. Place over a gentle heat and stir until no longer cloudy. Boil until bubbly and allow to become a rich golden brown. Once this colour, remove the pan immediately from the heat and plunge the base of the pan into a bowl of cold water to stop the cooking. Carefully stir in the 50ml/2fl oz/¼ cup water. Set the caramel syrup aside to cool completely.

2 Preheat the oven to 180°C/ 350°F/Gas 4. Put all the cookie ingredients, except the egg yolks and vanilla, into a food processor then process until the mixture resembles fine breadcrumbs. Add the egg yolks and vanilla and blend until the mixture just begins to come together as a firm dough. Form into a ball, wrap in clear film (plastic wrap) then chill in the refrigerator for 15 minutes.

3 Roll the dough out on baking parchment to a thickness of just under 5mm/¼in. Using a 7.5cm/3in fluted biscuit (cookie) cutter, stamp out rounds and place them on two non-stick baking sheets. (If you do not have non-stick baking sheets, line two ordinary sheets with baking parchment.)

4 In a small bowl, beat the egg yolk together with 15ml/1 tbsp of the caramel glaze. Use this to brush sparingly over the cookies. Leave this coating to dry then apply a second thin layer. Using a fork, prick the cookies, then mark in a neat checked pattern by dragging the tines of the fork over the glaze.

5 Bake for about 10–15 minutes, or until crisp and golden brown. Transfer to a wire rack to cool.

Cook's Tip
If the caramel does not dissolve evenly when the water is added, place the pan over a gentle heat and stir until it is completely dissolved.

Lace Cookies

Very pretty, delicate and crisp, these lacy cookies are ideal for serving with elegant creamy or iced desserts at the end of a dinner party. Don't be tempted to bake more than four on a sheet.

Makes about 14

75g/3oz/6 tbsp butter, diced

75g/3oz/¾ cup rolled oats

115g/4oz/generous ½ cup golden caster (superfine) sugar

1 egg, beaten

10ml/2 tsp plain (all-purpose) flour

5ml/1 tsp baking powder

2.5ml/½ tsp mixed (apple pie) spice

1 Preheat the oven to 180°C/350°F/ Gas 4. Line three or four baking sheets with baking parchment. Put the butter in a pan and set over a low heat until just melted. Remove the pan from the heat.

2 Stir the rolled oats into the melted butter. Add the remaining ingredients and mix well.

3 Place only 3 or 4 heaped teaspoonfuls of the mixture, spaced well apart, on each of the lined baking sheets.

4 Bake for about 5–7 minutes, or until a deepish golden brown all over. Leave the cookies on the baking sheets for a few minutes. Carefully cut the parchment so you can lift each cookie singly. Invert on to a wire rack and carefully remove the parchment. Leave to cool.

Florentine Bites

Very sweet and rich, these little mouthfuls are great with after-dinner coffee and liqueurs, and would also make an ideal and special gift to offer to a dinner party host.

Makes 36

200g/7oz good quality plain (semisweet) chocolate (minimum 70 per cent cocoa solids)

50g/2oz/2½ cups cornflakes

50g/2oz/scant ½ cup sultanas (golden raisins)

115g/4oz/1 cup toasted flaked (sliced) almonds

115g/4oz/½ cup glacé (candied) cherries, halved

50g/2oz/⅓ cup cut mixed (candied) peel

200ml/7fl oz/scant 1 cup can sweetened condensed milk

1 Preheat the oven to 180°C/350°F/ Gas 4. Line the base of a shallow 20cm/8in cake tin (pan) with baking parchment. Lightly grease the sides. Melt the chocolate in a heatproof bowl set over a pan of hot water. Spread evenly over the base of the tin. Put in the refrigerator to set.

2 Meanwhile, put the cornflakes, sultanas, almonds, cherries and mixed peel in a large bowl. Pour over the condensed milk and toss the mixture gently, using a fork.

3 Spread the mixture evenly over the chocolate base and bake for 12–15 minutes until golden brown. Cool in the tin, then chill for 20 minutes. Cut into tiny squares.

Almond and Vanilla Cookies with Praline Coating

These short-textured almond cookies, filled with vanilla cream and coated in praline, are just the thing to have with an espresso – a sweet *bonne bouche* to counter the strong coffee.

Makes 17–18

150g/5oz/1¼ cups plain
  (all-purpose) flour
75g/3oz/¾ cup ground almonds
75g/3oz/6 tbsp unsalted (sweet) butter,
  at room temperature, diced
1 egg yolk
5ml/1 tsp vanilla essence (extract)
icing (confectioners') sugar, sifted,
  for dusting

For the praline

25g/1oz/¼ cup whole blanched almonds
50g/2oz/¼ cup caster (superfine) sugar

For the filling

150g/5oz/1¼ cups icing (confectioners')
  sugar, sifted
75g/3oz/6 tbsp unsalted (sweet) butter,
  at room temperature, diced
5ml/1 tsp vanilla essence (extract)

1 First make the praline. Lightly oil a baking sheet and place the almonds on it, fairly close together. Melt the sugar in a small non-stick pan over a very low heat. Continue heating until it turns dark golden brown and pour immediately over the almonds. Set aside to cool. Crush the praline finely in a food processor.

2 Preheat the oven to 160°C/325°F/ Gas 3. Line three baking sheets with baking parchment.

3 Put the flour, ground almonds and butter in a bowl. Rub together until the mixture starts to cling together. Add the egg and vanilla and work together using your hands to make a soft but not sticky dough. Roll out to a thickness of about 5mm/¼in on baking parchment. Using a 5cm/2in round biscuit (cookie) cutter, stamp out rounds and place them on the prepared baking sheets.

4 Bake the cookies for about 15–20 minutes, or until light golden brown. Leave on the baking sheets for 5 minutes to firm up slightly, then transfer to a wire rack to cool.

5 To make the filling, beat together the icing sugar, butter and vanilla until light and creamy. Use this mixture to sandwich the cookies in pairs. Be generous with the filling, spreading right to the edges. Press the cookies gently so the filling oozes out of the sides and, using your finger, smooth around the sides of the cookie.

6 Put the praline on a plate and roll the edges of each cookie in the praline until thickly coated. Dust the tops of the cookies with icing sugar.

Cook's Tip

These cookies should be made on the day of serving or the filling will cause them to become soggy and unpleasant.

Tea Finger Cookies

The unusual ingredient in these cookies is Lady Grey tea – similar to Earl Grey but with the addition of Seville orange and lemon peel – which imparts a subtle flavour.

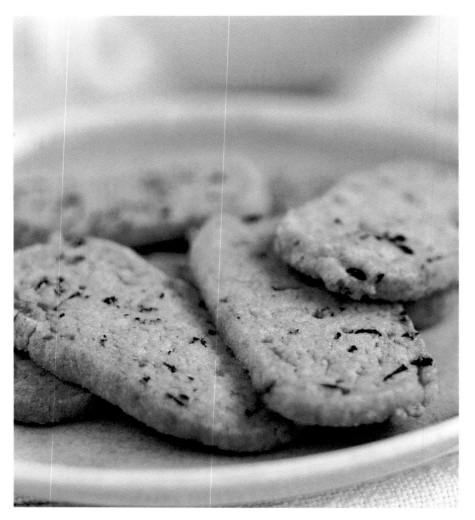

3 Using your hands, roll the dough on a lightly floured surface into a long cylinder, about 23cm/9in long.

4 Gently press down on the top of the dough cylinder with the palm of your hand to flatten slightly. Wrap the dough in clear film (plastic wrap) and chill for about 1 hour until the dough is firm enough to slice.

5 Using a sharp knife, cut the dough cylinder widthways into 5mm/¼in slices and place, slightly apart, on the prepared baking sheets.

6 Sprinkle the cookies with a little demerara sugar, then bake for 10–15 minutes until lightly browned. Using a palette knife (metal spatula), transfer the cookies to a wire rack and leave to cool.

Makes about 36

150g/5oz/10 tbsp unsalted (sweet)
  butter, at room temperature, diced
115g/4oz/generous ½ cup light
  muscovado (brown) sugar
15–30ml/1–2 tbsp Lady Grey tea leaves
1 egg, beaten
200g/7oz/1¾ cups plain
  (all-purpose) flour
demerara (raw) sugar, for sprinkling

1 Preheat the oven to 190°C/375°F/ Gas 5. Line two or three baking sheets with baking parchment.

2 Beat the butter and sugar until light and creamy. Stir in the Lady Grey tea leaves until well combined. Beat in the egg, then carefully fold in the flour.

Variation

You could use other exotic types of tea for making these cookies. Try Earl Grey, flavoured with bergamot, or aromatic flower or fruit teas, such as jasmine, rose congou or pouchong, chrysanthemum, passion fruit or strawberry.

Butterfly Cookies

Melt-in-the-mouth puff pastry interleaved with sugar, nuts and cinnamon produces a slightly outrageous-looking cookie that teams well with ice creams and fruit salads.

Makes about 12

500g/1¼lb packet ready-made
    puff pastry
1 egg, beaten
115g/4oz/generous ½ cup
    granulated sugar
25g/1oz/¼ cup chopped mixed nuts
5ml/1 tsp ground cinnamon

1 Preheat the oven to 200°C/400°F/ Gas 6. Roll out the pastry on a lightly floured surface to a rectangle measuring 50 × 17cm/20 × 6½in. Cut widthways into four pieces. Brush each piece with beaten egg.

Cook's Tip

If using frozen puff pastry, thaw it first, but keep it chilled. Handle the dough lightly so it doesn't toughen.

2 Mix together 75g/3oz/6 tbsp of the sugar, the nuts and cinnamon in a bowl. Sprinkle this mixture evenly over three of the pieces of pastry. Place the pieces one on top of the other, ending with the uncoated piece, placing this one egg side down on the top. Press lightly together with the rolling pin.

3 Cut the stack of pastry sheets widthways into 5mm/¼in slices. Carefully place one strip on a non-stick baking sheet and place the next strip over it at an angle. Place a third strip on top at another angle so that it looks like a butterfly. Don't worry if the strips separate slightly when you are transferring them to the baking sheet.

4 Using your fingers, press the centre very flat. Sprinkle with a little of the reserved sugar. Continue in this way to make more cookies until all the pastry is used up.

5 Bake the cookies for about 10–15 minutes, or until golden brown all over. Leave to cool completely on the baking sheet before serving with your dessert.

Chocolate and Pistachio Wedges

These cookies are rich and grainy textured, with a bitter chocolate flavour. They go extremely well with vanilla ice cream and are especially delicious with bananas and custard.

Makes 16

200g/7oz/scant 1 cup unsalted (sweet) butter, at room temperature, diced
90g/3½oz/½ cup golden caster (superfine) sugar
250g/9oz/2¼ cups plain (all-purpose) flour
50g/2oz/½ cup (unsweetened) cocoa powder
25g/1oz/¼ cup shelled pistachio nuts, finely chopped
(unsweetened) cocoa powder, for dusting

1 Preheat the oven to 180°C/350°F/Gas 4 and line a shallow 23cm/9in round sandwich tin (pan) with baking parchment.

2 Beat the butter and sugar until light and creamy. Sift the flour and cocoa powder, then add the flour mixture to the butter and work in with your hands until the mixture is smooth. Knead until soft and pliable then press into the prepared tin.

3 Using the back of a tablespoon, spread the mixture evenly in the tin. Sprinkle the pistachio nuts over the top and press in gently. Prick with a fork, then mark into 16 segments using a round-bladed knife.

4 Bake for about 15–20 minutes. Do not allow to brown at all or the cookies will taste bitter.

5 Remove the tin from the oven and dust the cookies with cocoa powder. Cut through the marked sections with a round-bladed knife and leave to cool completely before removing from the tin.

Dark Chocolate Fingers

With their understated elegance and distinctly grown-up flavour, these deliciously decadent chocolate fingers are ideal for serving with after-dinner coffee and liqueurs.

Makes about 26

115g/4oz/1 cup plain (all-purpose) flour
2.5ml/½ tsp baking powder
30ml/2 tbsp (unsweetened)
   cocoa powder
50g/2oz/¼ cup unsalted (sweet)
   butter, softened
50g/2oz/¼ cup caster (superfine) sugar
20ml/4 tsp golden (light corn) syrup
150g/5oz dark (bittersweet) chocolate
chocolate-flavour mini flakes,
   for sprinkling

1 Preheat the oven to 160°C/325°F/ Gas 3. Line two baking sheets with baking parchment. Put the flour, baking powder, cocoa powder, butter, sugar and syrup in a large mixing bowl.

2 Work the ingredients together with your hands to combine and form into a dough.

3 Roll the dough out between sheets of baking parchment to an 18 x 24cm/7 x 9½in rectangle. Remove the top sheet. Cut in half lengthways, then into bars 2cm/¾in wide. Place on the baking sheets.

4 Bake for about 15 minutes, taking care not to allow the bars to brown or they will taste bitter. Transfer to a wire rack to cool.

5 Melt the chocolate in a heatproof bowl set over a pan of hot water. Half-dip the cookies, place on baking parchment, sprinkle with chocolate flakes, then leave to set.

Mini Fudge Bites

These cute little cookies have the flavour of butterscotch and fudge and are topped with chopped pecan nuts for a delicious crunch – just the right size for a special little treat.

Makes 30

200g/7oz/1¾ cups self-raising
    (self-rising) flour
115g/4oz/½ cup butter, at room
    temperature, diced
115g/4oz/generous ½ cup dark
    muscovado (molasses) sugar
75g/3oz vanilla cream fudge, diced
1 egg, beaten
25g/1oz/¼ cup pecan nut halves,
    sliced widthways

1 Preheat the oven to 190°C/375°F/ Gas 5. Line two or three baking sheets with baking parchment. Put the flour in a bowl and rub in the butter until the mixture resembles fine breadcrumbs.

2 Add the muscovado sugar and diced vanilla cream fudge to the flour mixture and stir well until combined. Add the beaten egg and mix in well. Bring the dough together with your hands, then knead gently on a lightly floured surface. It will be soft yet firm.

3 Roll the dough into two cylinders, 23cm/9in long. Cut into 1cm/½in slices and place on the baking sheets. Sprinkle over the pecan nuts and press in lightly. Bake for about 12 minutes until browned at the edges. Transfer to a wire rack to cool.

Chocolate Truffle Cookies

Deeply decadent, chocolatey truffle cookies are given a wicked twist by the addition of cherry brandy – the perfect way to end dinner.

Makes 18

50g/2oz/½ cup plain
  (all-purpose) flour
25g/1oz/¼ cup (unsweetened)
  cocoa powder
2.5ml/½ tsp baking powder
90g/3½oz/½ cup caster
  (superfine) sugar
25g/1oz/2 tbsp butter, diced
1 egg, beaten
5ml/1 tsp cherry brandy or fresh
  orange juice
50g/2oz/½ cup icing
  (confectioners') sugar

1 Preheat the oven to 200°C/400°F/
Gas 6. Line two baking sheets with
baking parchment.

2 Sift the flour, cocoa and baking
powder into a bowl and stir in
the sugar. Rub in the butter until the
mixture resembles breadcrumbs. Mix
together the beaten egg and cherry
brandy or orange juice and stir into
the flour mixture. Cover with clear
film (plastic wrap) and chill in the
refrigerator for 30 minutes.

3 Put the icing sugar into a bowl.
Shape walnut-size pieces of dough
roughly into a ball and drop into the
icing sugar. Toss until thickly coated
then place on the baking sheets.

4 Bake for about 10 minutes, or
until just set. Transfer to a wire rack
to cool completely.

Brownies and Bars

Cookies with attitude, brownies and bars make filling snacks, lunchtime treats, perfect picnic fare and a marvellous morale and energy boost at any time of day. There are probably more variations on the basic brownie than on any other cookie in the world and when you try some of the recipes here, you will understand why. As for bars and slices, the sky's the limit – crisp and nutty, chewy and succulent, sweet and fruity. You choose.

Chocolate Cheesecake Brownies

A very dense chocolate brownie mixture is swirled with creamy cheese to give a marbled effect. Cut into tiny squares for little mouthfuls of absolute heaven.

Makes 16

For the cheesecake mixture

1 egg

225g/8oz/1 cup full-fat
   cream cheese

50g/2oz/¼ cup caster
   (superfine) sugar

5ml/1 tsp vanilla essence (extract)

For the brownie mixture

115g/4oz dark (bittersweet)
   chocolate (minimum 70 per cent
   cocoa solids)

115g/4oz/½ cup unsalted
   (sweet) butter

150g/5oz/¾ cup light muscovado
   (brown) sugar

2 eggs, beaten

50g/2oz/½ cup plain
   (all-purpose) flour

1 Preheat the oven to 160°C/325°F/Gas 3. Line the base and sides of a 20cm/8in cake tin (pan) with baking parchment.

2 To make the cheesecake mixture, beat the egg in a mixing bowl, then add the cream cheese, caster sugar and vanilla essence. Beat together until smooth and creamy.

3 To make the brownie mixture, melt the chocolate and butter together in the microwave or in a heatproof bowl set over a pan of gently simmering water. When the mixture is melted, remove from the heat, stir well, then add the sugar. Add the eggs, a little at a time, and beat well. Gently stir in the flour.

4 Spread two-thirds of the brownie mixture over the base of the tin. Spread the cheesecake mixture on top, then spoon on the remaining brownie mixture in heaps. Using a skewer, swirl the mixtures together.

5 Bake for 30–35 minutes, or until just set in the centre. Leave to cool in the tin, then cut into squares.

Butterscotch Brownies

These gorgeous treats are made with brown sugar, white chocolate chips and walnuts. Who could possibly have the will power to resist? You might want to make two batches at a time.

Makes 12

450g/1lb white chocolate chips

75g/3oz/6 tbsp unsalted (sweet) butter

3 eggs

*175g/6oz/¾ cup light muscovado
   (brown) sugar*

*175g/6oz/1½ cups self-raising
   (self-rising) flour*

175g/6oz/1½ cups walnuts, chopped

5ml/1 tsp vanilla essence (extract)

1 Preheat the oven to 190°C/ 375°F/Gas 5. Line the base of a 28 x 18cm/11 x 7in shallow tin (pan) with baking parchment. Lightly grease the sides. Melt 90g/3½oz of the chocolate chips with the butter in a bowl set over a pan of hot water. Leave to cool slightly.

2 Put the eggs and light muscovado sugar into a large bowl and whisk well, then whisk in the melted chocolate mixture.

3 Sift in the flour into the bowl and gently fold in along with the chopped walnuts, vanilla essence and the remaining chocolate chips. Be careful not to overmix.

4 Spread the mixture out in the prepared tin and bake for about 30 minutes, or until risen and golden brown. The centre should be firm to the touch but will be slightly soft until it cools down.

5 Leave to cool in the tin, then cut into twelve bars when the brownie is completely cool.

White Chocolate Brownies

These irresistible brownies are packed full of creamy white chocolate and juicy dried fruit. They are best served cut into very small portions as they are incredibly rich – but also because kids seem to find something utterly irresistible about tiny, bite-size cookies.

Makes 18

75g/3oz/6 tbsp unsalted (sweet)
   butter, diced
400g/14oz white chocolate, chopped
3 eggs
90g/3½oz/½ cup golden caster
   (superfine) sugar
10ml/2 tsp vanilla essence (extract)
90g/3½oz/¾ cup sultanas
   (golden raisins)
coarsely grated rind of 1 lemon, plus
   15ml/1 tbsp juice
200g/7oz/1¾ cups plain
   (all-purpose) flour

1 Preheat the oven to 190°C/375°F/ Gas 5. Grease and line a 28 × 20cm/ 11 × 8in shallow baking tin (pan) with baking parchment.

2 Put the butter and 300g/11oz of the chocolate in a bowl and melt over a pan of gently simmering water, stirring frequently.

3 Remove the bowl from the heat and beat in the eggs and sugar, then add the vanilla essence, sultanas, lemon rind and juice, flour and the remaining chocolate.

4 Tip the mixture into the tin and spread into the corners. Bake for about 20 minutes until slightly risen and the surface is only just turning golden. The centre should still be slightly soft. Leave to cool in the tin.

5 Cut the brownies into small squares and remove from the tin.

Fudge-nut Bars

Although your kids will be desperate to tuck into these fudgy treats, it's well worth chilling them for a few hours before slicing so that they can be cut into neat pieces. You can use any kind of nut, from mild-flavoured almonds, peanuts or macadamia nuts to slightly stronger pecans or hazelnuts.

Makes 16

150g/5oz/10 tbsp unsalted (sweet) butter,
  chilled and diced
250g/9oz/2¼ cups plain
  (all-purpose) flour
75g/3oz/scant ½ cup caster
  (superfine) sugar

For the topping

150g/5oz milk chocolate, broken
  into pieces
40g/1½oz/3 tbsp unsalted butter
405g/14¼oz can sweetened
  condensed milk
50g/2oz/½ cup chopped nuts

1 Preheat the oven to 160°C/ 325°F/ Gas 3. Grease a 28 × 18cm/ 11 × 7in shallow baking tin (pan).

2 Put the butter and flour in a food processor and process until the mixture resembles breadcrumbs. Add the sugar and blend again until the mixture starts to cling together.

3 Tip the mixture into the baking tin and spread out with the back of a wooden spoon to fill the base in an even layer. Bake for 35–40 minutes until the surface is very lightly coloured.

4 To make the topping, put the chocolate in a heavy pan with the butter and condensed milk. Heat gently until the chocolate and butter have melted, then increase the heat and cook, stirring, for 3–5 minutes until the mixture starts to thicken.

5 Add the chopped nuts to the pan and pour the mixture over the cookie base, spreading it in an even layer. Leave to cool, then chill for at least 2 hours until firm. Serve cut into bars.

Rainbow Gingerbread Squares

These gingerbread squares have a more spongy texture than traditional gingerbread cookies and look stunning decorated with vibrantly coloured sprinkles. Ground and preserved stem ginger gives a really spicy flavour, but can easily be left out for younger children.

Makes 16

225g/8oz/2 cups plain
  (all-purpose) flour
5ml/1 tsp baking powder
10ml/2 tsp ground ginger
2 pieces preserved stem ginger from
  a jar, finely chopped
90g/3½oz/¾ cup raisins
50g/2oz/¼ cup glacé (candied)
  cherries, chopped
115g/4oz/½ cup unsalted (sweet)
  butter, diced
115g/4oz/⅓ cup golden (light
  corn) syrup
30ml/2 tbsp black treacle (molasses)
75g/3oz/⅓ cup dark muscovado
  (molasses) sugar
2 eggs, beaten

For the decoration

200g/7oz/1¾ cups icing
  (confectioners') sugar
50g/2oz/¼ cup unsalted (sweet) butter,
  at room temperature, diced
multi-coloured sprinkles

1 Preheat the oven to 160°C/325°F/ Gas 3. Grease a 20cm/8in square shallow baking or cake tin (pan) and line with baking parchment.

2 Sift the flour, baking powder and ground ginger into a bowl. Add the stem ginger, raisins and cherries and stir together well.

3 Put the butter, syrup, treacle and muscovado sugar in a small pan and heat gently until the butter melts. Pour the mixture into the dry ingredients. Add the eggs and stir well until evenly combined.

4 Tip the mixture into the baking tin and spread in an even layer, using the back of a wooden spoon. Bake for about 55 minutes, or until risen and firm in the centre. Leave to cool in the tin.

5 To make the topping, put the icing sugar and butter in a bowl with 20ml/4 tsp hot water and beat together until smooth and creamy.

6 Turn the gingerbread out of the baking tin on to a board. Using a large, sharp knife, carefully cut the gingerbread into 16 squares.

7 Using a teaspoon, drizzle a thick line of icing around the top edge of each gingerbread square. Don't worry if it falls down the sides. (If the icing is too stiff and doesn't come off the spoon easily, stir a little more hot water into the icing: about 5ml/1 tsp.)

8 Scatter the coloured sprinkles over the icing to finish and leave to set before serving.

Sticky Treacle Slices

This three-layered treat of buttery cookie base, covered with a sticky dried fruit filling, followed by an oaty flapjack-style topping, is utterly delicious and unbelievably easy to make.

Makes 14

175g/6oz/1½ cups plain
  (all-purpose) flour
90g/3½oz/7 tbsp unsalted (sweet)
  butter, diced
50g/2oz/¼ cup caster (superfine) sugar
250g/9oz/generous 1 cup mixed dried
  fruit, such as prunes, apricots, peaches,
  pears and apples
300ml/½ pint/1¼ cups apple or
  orange juice
225g/8oz/⅔ cup golden (light
  corn) syrup
finely grated rind of 1 small orange,
  plus 45ml/3 tbsp juice
90g/3½oz/1 cup rolled oats

1 Preheat the oven to 180°C/350°F/ Gas 4. Grease a 28 x 18cm/11 x 7in shallow baking tin (pan).

2 Put the flour and butter in a food processor and process until the mixture begins to resemble fine breadcrumbs. Add the sugar and mix until the dough starts to cling together in a ball.

3 Tip the mixture into the baking tin and press down in an even layer with the back of a fork. Bake for about 15 minutes until the surface is just beginning to colour.

4 Meanwhile, prepare the filling. Remove the stones (pits) from any of the dried fruits, if not already done. Chop the fruit fairly finely and put in a pan with the fruit juice. Bring to the boil, reduce the heat and cover with a lid. Simmer gently for about 15 minutes, or until all the juice has been absorbed.

5 Leaving the base in the tin, tip the dried fruit filling on top and spread out in an even layer with the back of a spoon.

6 Put the golden syrup in a bowl with the orange rind and juice and oats and mix together. Spoon the mixture over the fruits, spreading it out evenly. Return to the oven for 25 minutes. Leave to cool in the tin for several hours before cutting into squares or bars.

Jewelled Shortbread Fingers

These shortbread fingers are made using a classic, buttery shortbread base, drizzled with icing and decorated with sparkling, crushed sweets and glistening gold or silver balls.

Makes 14

90g/3½oz/7 tbsp unsalted (sweet)
  butter, diced
175g/6oz/1½ cups plain
  (all-purpose) flour
50g/2oz/¼ cup caster (superfine) sugar

To decorate

150g/5oz/1¼ cups icing
  (confectioners') sugar
10–15ml/2–3 tsp lemon juice
coloured boiled sweets (hard candies)
gold or silver balls

1 Preheat the oven to 160°C/325°F/ Gas 3. Grease an 18cm/7in square shallow baking tin (pan).

2 Put the butter and flour in a food processor and process until the mixture resembles breadcrumbs. Add the sugar and process until the ingredients cling together.

3 Put the dough in the baking tin and press down in an even layer using the back of a spoon. Bake for 35 minutes, or until just beginning to colour. Leave to cool in the tin.

4 To make the topping, put the icing sugar in a bowl and add enough lemon juice to make a thick paste that only just holds its shape.

5 Tap the boiled sweets (in their wrappers) gently with a rolling pin to break them into small pieces. Unwrap the sweets and mix them together in a bowl.

Cook's Tip
Use a serrated knife and a sawing action to cut the shortbread into neat fingers.

6 Turn out the shortbread base on to a board. Cut in half, then across into fingers. Drizzle with the icing, then sprinkle with the sweets and gold or silver balls. Leave to set.

Marshmallow Toasties

These soft cookie squares topped with a layer of strawberry jam and melted marshmallow make a sweet, sticky treat for kids of all ages. When you're toasting the marshmallows, watch them very closely because once they start to colour, they brown extremely quickly.

Makes 12

130g/4½oz/generous ½ cup unsalted
    (sweet) butter, at room temperature,
    diced
75g/3oz/scant ½ cup caster
    (superfine) sugar
finely grated rind of 1 lemon
10ml/2 tsp vanilla essence (extract)
75g/3oz/¾ cup ground almonds
1 egg
115g/4oz/1 cup self-raising
    (self-rising) flour
150g/5oz/½ cup strawberry jam
200g/7oz pink and white marshmallows
icing (confectioners') sugar, for dusting

1 Preheat the oven to 180°C/350°F/ Gas 4. Grease the base and sides of a 23cm/9in square baking tin (pan) and line with baking parchment.

2 Put the butter, sugar and lemon rind in a bowl and beat until creamy. Beat in the vanilla essence, ground almonds and egg, then add the flour and stir well.

3 Turn the mixture into the tin and spread in an even layer. Bake for 20 minutes until pale golden and just firm. Leave to cool in the tin for 10 minutes.

4 Spread the cookie base with jam. Using scissors, cut the marshmallows in half, then arrange them, cut sides down, in an even layer over the jam. Preheat the grill (broiler) to medium.

5 Put the tin under the grill for about 2 minutes until the marshmallows are melted and pale golden. Remove from the heat and gently press down each marshmallow with the back of a spoon to create an even layer of melted marshmallow. Return to the grill for a further minute until the surface is very toasted. Leave to cool.

6 To serve, dust lightly with icing sugar, cut into 12 squares or bars and remove from the tin.

Fruity Lemon Drizzle Bars

These tangy iced, spongy bars are great for popping in lunch boxes or for kids to snack on after school. This fruit and lemon mixture is lovely but you can easily experiment with other combinations, such as orange and dried apricots or lime and dried pineapples.

Makes 16

250g/9oz ready-made sweet
    shortcrust pastry
90g/3¼oz/¾ cup self-raising
    (self-rising) flour
75g/3oz/¾ cup fine or
    medium oatmeal
5ml/1 tsp baking powder
130g/4½oz/generous ½ cup light
    muscovado (brown) sugar
2 eggs
150g/5oz/10 tbsp unsalted
    (sweet) butter, at room
    temperature, diced
finely grated rind of 1 lemon
90g/3½oz/¾ cup sultanas
    (golden raisins)
150g/5oz/1¼ cups icing
    (confectioners') sugar
15–30ml/3–4 tsp lemon juice

1 Preheat the oven to 190°C/375°F/ Gas 5 and place a baking sheet in the oven to heat through. Generously grease a 28 × 18cm/ 11 × 7in shallow baking tin (pan).

2 Roll out the pastry thinly on a lightly floured, clean surface. Use to line the base of the baking tin, pressing the pastry up the sides. (Don't worry about rough edges.)

3 Put the flour, oatmeal, baking powder, sugar, eggs, butter and lemon rind in a mixing bowl. Beat with a hand-held electric whisk for about 2 minutes until pale and creamy. Stir in the sultanas.

4 Tip the filling into the pastry case and spread evenly into the corners using the back of a spoon.

5 Place the tin on the heated baking sheet in the oven and bake for about 30 minutes until pale golden and the surface feels firm to the touch.

6 Put the icing sugar in a small bowl with enough lemon juice to mix to a thin paste, about the consistency of pouring (half-and-half) cream.

7 Using a teaspoon, drizzle the icing diagonally across the warm cake in thin lines. Leave to cool in the tin.

8 When the icing has set, use a sharp knife to cut the cake in half lengthways. Cut each half across into 8 even-size bars.

Luscious Lemon Bars

A crisp cookie base is covered with a tangy lemon topping. The bars make a delightful addition to the tea table on a warm summer's day in the garden.

Makes 12
150g/5oz/1¼ cups plain
   (all-purpose) flour
90g/3½oz/7 tbsp unsalted (sweet) butter,
   chilled and diced
50g/2oz/½ cup icing (confectioners')
   sugar, sifted

For the topping
2 eggs
175g/6oz/scant 1 cup caster
   (superfine) sugar
finely grated rind and juice of
   1 large lemon
15ml/1 tbsp plain (all-purpose) flour
2.5ml/½ tsp bicarbonate of soda
   (baking soda)
icing (confectioners') sugar, for dusting

3 To make the topping, whisk the eggs in a bowl until frothy. Add the caster sugar, a little at a time, whisking well between each addition. Whisk in the lemon rind and juice, flour and soda. Pour over the cookie base. Bake for 20–25 minutes, until set and golden.

4 Leave to cool slightly. Cut into twelve bars and dust lightly with icing sugar. Leave to cool completely.

1 Preheat the oven to 180°C/350°F/Gas 4. Line the base of a 20cm/8in square shallow cake tin (pan) with baking parchment and lightly grease the sides of the tin.

2 Process the flour, butter and icing sugar in a food processor until the mixture comes together as a firm dough. Press evenly into the base of the tin and spread smoothly using the back of a tablespoon. Bake for 12–15 minutes until lightly golden. Cool in the tin.

Sticky Marmalade Squares

These baked treats have a plain lower layer supporting a scrumptious nutty upper layer flavoured with orange and chunky marmalade. Cut into squares or bars – whichever you prefer.

Makes 24

350g/12oz/3 cups plain
  (all-purpose) flour
200g/7oz/scant 1 cup unsalted (sweet)
  butter, diced
150g/5oz/⅔ cup light muscovado
  (molasses) sugar
2.5ml/½ tsp bicarbonate of soda
  (baking soda)
1 egg, beaten
120ml/4fl oz/½ cup single
  (light) cream
50g/2oz/½ cup pecan nuts, chopped
50g/2oz/⅓ cup mixed (candied) peel
90ml/6 tbsp chunky marmalade
15–30ml/1–2 tbsp orange juice

1 Preheat the oven to 190°C/ 375°F/Gas 5. Line the base of a 28 x 18cm/11 x 7in tin (pan) with baking parchment.

2 Put the flour in a bowl and rub in the butter. Stir in the sugar and then spread half the mixture over the base of the prepared tin. Press down firmly. Bake for 10–15 minutes until lightly browned. Leave to cool.

3 To make the filling, put the remaining flour mixture into a bowl. Stir in the soda. Mix in the egg and cream, pecan nuts, peel and half the marmalade.

4 Pour the mixture over the cooled base, return to the oven and bake for 20–25 minutes, or until the filling is just firm and golden brown.

5 Put the remaining marmalade into a small pan and heat gently. Add just enough orange juice to make a spreadable glaze. Brush the glaze over the baked cookie mixture while it is still warm. Leave to cool before cutting into bars or squares.

Variation
These bars would be just as delicious made with lemon, lime, grapefruit or mixed fruit marmalade instead of orange. However, do not substitute a sharper juice, such as lemon, for the orange juice as this would spoil the flavour.

Walnut and Honey Bars

A sweet, custard-like filling brimming with nuts sits on a crisp pastry base. These scrumptious bars are pure heaven to bite into.

Makes 12–14

175g/6oz/1½ cups plain
  (all-purpose) flour
30ml/2 tbsp icing (confectioners')
  sugar, sifted
115g/4oz/½ cup unsalted (sweet)
  butter, diced

For the filling

300g/11oz/scant 3 cups walnut halves
2 eggs, beaten
50g/2oz/¼ cup unsalted (sweet)
  butter, melted
50g/2oz/¼ cup light muscovado
  (brown) sugar
90ml/6 tbsp dark clear honey
30ml/2 tbsp single (light) cream

1 Preheat the oven to 190°C/375°F/
Gas 5. Lightly grease a 28 x 18cm/
11 x 7in shallow tin (pan).

2 Put the flour, icing sugar and butter in a food processor and process until the mixture forms crumbs. Using the pulse button, add 15–30ml/1–2 tbsp water – enough to make a firm dough.

3 Roll the dough out on baking parchment and line the base and sides of the tin. Trim and fold the top edge inwards.

4 Prick the base, line with foil and baking beans and bake blind for 10 minutes. Remove the foil and beans. Return the base to the oven for about 5 minutes, until cooked but not browned. Reduce the temperature to 180°C/350°F/Gas 4.

5 For the filling, sprinkle the walnuts over the base. Whisk the remaining ingredients together. Pour over the walnuts and bake for 25 minutes.

Mincemeat Wedges

The flour used in these wedge-shaped cookies gives a nutty flavour that combines well with the mincemeat. These are great for winter tea parties around a blazing fire.

Makes 12

225g/8oz/2 cups self-raising (self-rising)
  wholemeal (whole-wheat) flour
75g/3oz/6 tbsp unsalted (sweet)
  butter, diced
75g/3oz/⅓ cup demerara (raw) sugar
1 egg, beaten
115g/4oz/⅓ cup good-quality mincemeat
about 60ml/4 tbsp milk
crushed brown or white café (sugar)
  cubes or a mixture, for sprinkling

Cook's Tip

If you can't find self-raising (self-rising)
flour, add 10ml/2 tsp baking powder to
the plain wholemeal (whole-wheat) flour.

1 Preheat the oven to 200°C/400°F/
Gas 6. Line the base of a 20cm/8in
round sandwich tin (layer pan) and
lightly grease the sides. Put the
flour in a bowl, add the diced butter
and rub in with your fingertips
just until the mixture resembles
coarse breadcrumbs.

2 Stir in the demerara sugar, egg
and mincemeat. Add enough milk to
mix to a soft dough. Spread evenly
in the prepared tin and sprinkle
generously with the crushed sugar.
Bake for about 20 minutes until firm
and golden. Cool in the tin, then cut
into wedges to serve.

Almond, Orange and Carrot Bars

An out-of-this-world cookie version of the ever-popular carrot cake, these flavoursome, moist bars are best eaten fresh or stored in the refrigerator after making.

Makes 16

75g/3oz/6 tbsp unsalted (sweet)
  butter, softened
50g/2oz/¼ cup caster (superfine) sugar
150g/5oz/1¼ cups plain
  (all-purpose) flour
finely grated rind of 1 orange

For the filling

90g/3½oz/7 tbsp unsalted (sweet)
  butter, diced
75g/3oz/scant ½ cup caster
  (superfine) sugar
2 eggs
2.5ml/½ tsp almond essence (extract)
175g/6oz/1½ cups ground almonds
1 cooked carrot, coarsely grated

For the topping

175g/6oz/¾ cup cream cheese
30–45ml/2–3 tbsp chopped walnuts

1 Preheat the oven to 190°C/375°F/ Gas 5. Lightly grease a 28 × 18cm/ 11 × 7in shallow baking tin (pan). Put the butter, caster sugar, flour and orange rind into a bowl and rub together until the mixture resembles coarse breadcrumbs. Add water, a teaspoon at a time, to mix to a firm but not sticky dough. Roll out on a lightly floured surface and use to line the base of the tin.

2 To make the filling, cream the butter and sugar together. Beat in the eggs and almond essence. Stir in the ground almonds and the grated carrot. Spread the mixture over the dough base and bake for about 25 minutes until firm in the centre and golden brown. Leave to cool in the tin.

3 To make the topping, beat the cream cheese until smooth and spread it over the cooled, cooked filling. Swirl with a small palette knife (metal spatula) and sprinkle with the chopped walnuts. Cut into bars with a sharp knife.

Hazelnut and Raspberry Bars

The hazelnuts are ground and used to make a superb sweet pastry which is then baked with a layer of raspberry jam in the middle and sprinkled with flaked almonds.

Makes 30

250g/9oz/2¼ cups hazelnuts
300g/10oz/2½ cups plain
  (all-purpose) flour
5ml/1 tsp mixed (apple pie) spice
2.5ml/½ tsp ground cinnamon
150g/5oz/1¼ cups golden icing
  (confectioners') sugar
15ml/1 tbsp grated lemon rind
300g/10oz/1¼ cups unsalted (sweet)
  butter, softened
3 egg yolks
350g/12oz/1¼ cups seedless
  raspberry jam

For the topping

1 egg, beaten
15ml/1 tbsp clear honey
50g/2oz/½ cup flaked (sliced) almonds

1 Grind the hazelnuts in a food processor and then put in a bowl. Sift in the flour, spices and icing sugar. Add the lemon rind and mix well, then add the butter and the egg yolks and, using your hands, knead until a smooth dough is formed. Wrap in clear film (plastic wrap) and chill for 30 minutes. Meanwhile, preheat the oven to 200°C/400°F/Gas 6 and lightly grease a 33 x 23cm/13 x 9in Swiss roll tin (jelly roll pan).

2 Roll out half the dough to fit the base of the prepared tin and place in the tin. Spread the jam all over the dough base. Roll out the remaining dough and place on top of the jam.

3 To make the topping, beat the egg and honey together and brush over the dough. Sprinkle the almonds evenly over the top.

4 Bake for 10 minutes, then lower the oven temperature to 180°C/350°F/Gas 4 and bake for another 20–30 minutes until golden brown. Cool then cut into bars.

Cook's Tip
Don't use ready-ground hazelnuts for these bars as they lose their flavour very quickly.

No-bake Cookies

The recipes in this chapter require even less time and effort than travelling to the supermarket to buy a packet of cookies – and they taste a lot better too. Not just no-bake, some are even no-cook, making them great for kids to prepare as well. None of them requires anything more demanding than melting some chocolate, but you may have to be patient to allow the cookies enough time to set in the refrigerator before sampling them.

Nutty Marshmallow and Chocolate Squares

Unashamedly sweet, with chocolate, marshmallows, cherries, nuts and coconut, this recipe is a favourite with children of all ages, and sweet-toothed adults too.

Makes 9

200g/7oz digestive biscuits
   (graham crackers)
90g/3½oz plain (semisweet) chocolate
200g/7oz mini coloured marshmallows
150g/5oz/1¼ cups chopped walnuts
90g/3½oz/scant ½ cup glacé (candied)
   cherries, halved
50g/2oz/⅔ cup sweetened desiccated
   (dry shredded) coconut
350g/12oz milk chocolate

1 Put the digestive biscuits in a polythene bag and, using a rolling pin, crush them until they are fairly small. Place them in a bowl. Melt the plain chocolate in the microwave or in a heatproof bowl set over a pan of hot water. Pour the melted plain chocolate over the broken biscuits and stir well. Spread the mixture in the base of a 20cm/8in square shallow cake tin (pan).

2 Put the marshmallows, walnuts, cherries and coconut in a large bowl. Melt the milk chocolate in the microwave or in a heatproof bowl set over a pan of hot water.

3 Pour the melted milk chocolate over the marshmallow and nut mixture and toss gently together until almost everything is coated. Spread the mixture over the chocolate base, but leave in chunky lumps – do not spread flat.

4 Chill until set, then cut into squares or bars.

Variation
Other nuts can be used instead of the walnuts – the choice is yours.

Almond-scented Chocolate Cherry Wedges

These cookies are a chocoholic's dream, and use the very best quality chocolate. Erratically shaped, they are packed with crunchy cookies, juicy raisins and munchy nuts.

Makes about 15

50g/2oz ratafia biscuits (almond macaroons) or small amaretti

90g/3½oz shortcake biscuits (cookies)

150g/5oz/1 cup jumbo raisins

50g/2oz/¼ cup undyed glacé (candied) cherries, quartered

450g/1lb dark (bittersweet) chocolate (minimum 70 per cent cocoa solids)

90g/3½oz/scant ½ cup unsalted (sweet) butter, diced

30ml/2 tbsp amaretto liqueur (optional)

25g/1oz/¼ cup toasted flaked (sliced) almonds

1 Line a baking sheet with baking parchment. Put the ratafia biscuits or amaretti in a large bowl. Leave half whole and break the remainder into coarse pieces. Break each of the shortcake biscuits into three or four jagged pieces and add to the bowl. Add the raisins and cherries and toss lightly together.

Cook's Tip

If you cannot find undyed glacé cherries in the supermarket, look for them in your local delicatessen instead.

2 Melt the chocolate and butter with the liqueur, if using, in the microwave or in a heatproof bowl set over a pan of hot water. When the chocolate has melted, remove from the heat and stir the mixture until combined and smooth. Set aside to cool slightly.

3 Pour the chocolate over the biscuit mixture and toss lightly together until everything is coated in chocolate. Spread out over the prepared baking sheet. Sprinkle over the almonds and push them in at angles so they stick well to the chocolate-coated biscuits.

4 When the mixture is completely cold and set, cut or break into crazy shapes, as you wish, such as long thin triangles, short stumpy squares or irregular shapes.

Chocolate Crispy Cookies

These little chocolate-coated cornflake cakes are always a hit with kids. They couldn't be easier to make – and are great for young aspiring cooks who want to get involved in the kitchen. The only problem is giving the mixture time to set before they've been gobbled up by hungry helpers.

4 Remove the bowl from the heat and tip in the cornflakes. Mix well until the cornflakes are thoroughly coated in the chocolate mixture.

5 Place a 6.5cm/2½in round cutter on the paper and put a spoonful of the chocolate mixture in the centre. Pack down firmly with the back of the spoon to make a thick cookie.

6 Gently ease away the cutter, using the spoon to help keep the mixure in place. Continue making cookies in this way until all the mixture has been used up. Chill for 1 hour.

7 Put a little icing sugar in a small bowl. Lift each cookie from the paper and roll the edges in the icing sugar to finish.

Makes 10

90g/3½oz milk chocolate
15ml/1 tbsp golden (light corn) syrup
90g/3½oz/4½ cups cornflakes
icing (confectioners') sugar, for dusting

1 Line a large baking sheet with baking parchment.

2 Break the chocolate into a heatproof bowl and add the syrup. Rest the bowl over a pan of gently simmering water and leave until melted, stirring frequently.

3 Put the cornflakes in a plastic bag and, using a rolling pin, lightly crush the cornflakes, breaking them into fairly small pieces.

Chocolate Nut Slice

Children of all ages will love this combination of broken cookies, chocolate and nuts. Although the unsliced bar looks small, it's very rich so is best sliced very thinly. If you have any other plain cookies in the cupboard, you can use them instead of the rich tea, with equally good results.

Makes 10 slices

225g/8oz milk chocolate

40g/1½oz/3 tbsp unsalted (sweet) butter, diced

75g/3oz rich tea biscuits (plain cookies)

50g/2oz/½ cup flaked (sliced) almonds

75g/3oz plain (semisweet) or white chocolate, roughly chopped

icing (confectioners') sugar, for dusting

I Break the milk chocolate into pieces and place in a heatproof bowl with the butter. Rest the bowl over a pan of simmering water and stir frequently until melted.

2 Meanwhile, dampen a 450g/1lb loaf tin (pan) and line the base and sides with clear film (plastic wrap). Don't worry about smoothing out the creases in the film.

3 When the chocolate has melted, remove it from the heat and leave for 5 minutes until slightly cooled.

4 Break the biscuits into small pieces, then stir into the melted chocolate with the almonds. Add the chopped chocolate to the bowl and fold in quickly and lightly.

5 Turn the mixture into the tin and pack down with a fork. Tap the base of the tin gently on the work surface. Chill for 2 hours until set.

6 To serve, turn the chocolate loaf on to a board and peel away the clear film. Dust lightly with icing sugar and slice thinly.

Chocolate Birds' Nests

These delightful crispy chocolate nests make a perfect Easter teatime treat and are a real favourite with kids. They're so quick and easy to make and young children can have great fun shaping the chocolate mixture inside the paper cases and tucking the pastel-coloured eggs inside.

Makes 12

200g/7oz milk chocolate

25g/1oz/2 tbsp unsalted (sweet) butter, diced

90g/3½oz Shredded Wheat cereal

36 small pastel-coloured, sugar-coated chocolate eggs

Cook's Tip

Bags of sugar-coated chocolate eggs are widely available in supermarkets at Easter time. However, if you have trouble finding them out of season, try an old-fashioned sweet store. Often they have large jars of this type of sweet (candy), which they sell all year round.

1 Line the sections of a tartlet tray (muffin pan) with 12 decorative paper cake cases.

2 Break the milk chocolate into pieces and put in a bowl with the butter. Rest the bowl over a pan of gently simmering water and stir frequently until melted. Remove the bowl from the heat and leave to cool for a few minutes.

3 Using your fingers, crumble the Shredded Wheat into the melted chocolate. Stir well until the cereal is completely coated in chocolate.

4 Divide the mixture among the paper cases, pressing it down gently with the back of a spoon and make a slight indentation in the centre. Tuck three eggs into each nest and leave to set for about 2 hours.

White Chocolate Snowballs

These little spherical cookies are particularly popular during the Christmas season. They're simple to make, yet utterly delicious and bursting with creamy, buttery flavours. If you like, make them in advance of a special tea as they will keep well in the refrigerator for a few days.

Makes 16

200g/7oz white chocolate
25g/1oz/2 tbsp butter, diced
90g/3½oz/generous 1 cup desiccated
   (dry unsweetened shredded) coconut
90g/3½oz syrup sponge or
   Madeira cake
icing (confectioners') sugar, for dusting

1 Break the chocolate into pieces and put in a heatproof bowl with the butter. Rest the bowl over a pan of gently simmering water and stir frequently until melted. Remove the bowl from the heat and set aside for a few minutes.

2 Meanwhile, put 50g/2oz/⅔ cup of the coconut on a plate and set aside. Crumble the cake and add to the melted chocolate with the remaining coconut. Mix well to form a chunky paste.

3 Take spoonfuls of the mixture and roll into balls, about 2.5cm/ 1in in diameter, and immediately roll them in the reserved coconut. Place the balls on greaseproof (waxed) paper and leave to set.

4 To serve, dust the snowballs with plenty of icing sugar.

Cook's Tip
You'll need to shape the mixture into balls as soon as you've mixed in the coconut and cake; the mixture sets very quickly and you won't be able to shape it once it hardens.

Ice Mountain

To create an alternative shape to rounds and squares, this refrigerator cookie is set in the corner of a cake tin, giving it a "pyramid" shape for slicing into triangles.

Makes 12

75g/3oz malted milk biscuits (cookies)
90g/3½oz milk chocolate
75g/3oz white chocolate mint sticks
250g/9oz white chocolate
60ml/4 tbsp double (heavy) cream
several clear mints (hard mint candies),
   to decorate

1 Break the biscuits into small pieces, chop the milk chocolate into small dice and break the chocolate mint sticks into short lengths. Keep these ingredients separate.

2 Reserve 50g/2oz of the white chocolate. Break up the remainder and put in a small heatproof bowl with the cream. Set the bowl over a pan of gently simmering water and leave until melted, stirring the chocolate frequently. Remove the bowl from the heat and scrape the melted chocolate into a clean bowl.

Cook's Tip

It is important to avoid overheating white chocolate when you are melting it. It is less robust than other types of chocolate as it contains no cocoa solids. Do make sure that the base of the bowl is not touching the surface of the water.

3 Cut out a 23cm/9in square piece of baking parchment. Grease one side and 5cm/2in of the base of an 18cm/7in square cake tin (pan). Fold the paper in half and fit the crease line into the greased corner of the tin so the side and part of the base and ends are lined. Make sure the ends are greased under the lining paper too.

4 Stir the biscuits into the white chocolate mixture followed by the chocolate mint sticks. Add the milk chocolate, stir quickly to combine then turn the mixture into the lined section of the tin. Hold the tin at an angle, then smooth the surface of the chocolate level. Place in the refrigerator, propping the tin up with another container to maintain the angle to form the pyramid shape. Leave for about 2 hours, until set.

5 Remove the cake from the tin, place on a flat plate and peel off the paper. In their wrappers, crush the mints with a rolling pin. Melt the reserved white chocolate in a heatproof bowl set over a pan of hot water.

6 Spread the white chocolate over the top sloping side of the pyramid, sprinkle with the crushed mints and press in lightly.

Pink Piggies

These are what you could call rainy day cookies. They are fun to make and thoroughly absorbing when the family is stuck indoors. You might want to make up icings in other colours and experiment with your own animal variations. Children's books are a great source of inspiration.

Makes 10

90g/3½oz/scant 1 cup icing
(confectioners') sugar, plus extra
for dusting
50g/2oz/¼ cup unsalted (sweet)
butter, at room temperature, diced
10 rich tea (plain cookies) or digestive
biscuits (graham crackers)
200g/7oz white ready-to-roll icing
pink food colouring
small, pink soft sweets (candies)
tube of black writer icing

1 To make the buttercream, put the icing sugar and butter in a bowl and beat with a hand-held electric whisk until smooth, pale and creamy.

2 Using a small palette knife (metal spatula) spread the rich tea or digestive biscuits almost to the edges with the buttercream.

3 Reserve 25g/1oz of the ready-to-roll icing and add a few drops of the pink food colouring to the remainder. Knead on a clean work surface that has been lightly dusted with icing sugar until the pink colouring is evenly distributed.

4 Reserve about 25g/1oz of the pink icing. If necessary, lightly dust your work surface with more icing sugar and roll out the remaining pink icing very thinly.

5 Using a cookie cutter that is just slightly smaller than the rich tea or digestive biscuits, cut out rounds of pink icing. Lay a round over each biscuit and press it down gently on to the buttercream.

6 Halve five of the pink sweets and press into an oval shape. Make two small holes in each one with a wooden skewer or cocktail stick (toothpick) to make a nose.

7 Using a little of the buttercream, attach a halved sweet to the centre of each cookie.

8 Using the black writer icing, pipe two small dots of icing above the nose to resemble eyes, then pipe a small, curved mouth.

9 Thinly roll out the reserved pink icing and the reserved white icing. Dampen the white icing with a little water and press the pink icing gently on top. Using a small sharp knife, cut out triangles for ears.

10 Dampen one edge of the ears with a little water and secure, pink side up, to the cookies. Gently curl the ears out at the ends.

Cook's Tip
If you cannot get black writer icing, use any dark food colouring such as black, blue or brown and paint on the features with a fine brush.

Apricot and Coconut Kisses

These tangy, fruity treats make a colourful addition to the tea table. Although they are easy to make and can be mixed and shaped in a matter of a few minutes, remember to allow plenty of time for the apricots to soak, and also for the kisses to chill before serving.

Makes 12

130g/4½oz/generous ½ cup ready-to-eat
  dried apricots
100ml/3½fl oz/scant ½ cup orange juice
40g/1½oz/3 tbsp unsalted (sweet)
  butter, at room temperature, diced
75g/3oz/¾ cup icing (confectioners')
  sugar, plus extra for dusting
90g/3½oz/generous 1 cup desiccated
  (dry unsweetened shredded) coconut,
  lightly toasted
2 glacé (candied) cherries, cut
  into wedges

1 Finely chop the dried apricots, then tip them into a bowl. Pour in the orange juice and leave to soak for about 1 hour until all the juice has been absorbed.

2 In a large bowl, beat together the butter and sugar with a wooden spoon until pale and creamy.

3 Gradually add the soaked apricots to the creamed butter and sugar mixture, beating well after each addition, then stir in the toasted coconut.

4 Line a small baking tray with greaseproof (waxed) paper.

5 Place teaspoonfuls of the coconut mixture on to the paper, piling them up into little pyramid shapes. Gently press the mixture together with your fingers to form neat shapes.

6 Top each kiss with a tiny wedge of cherry, gently pressing it into the mixture. Chill the kisses for about 1 hour until firm, then serve lightly dusted with a little icing sugar.

Cook's Tip
It is essential that all the orange juice has been absorbed by the apricots before adding them to the butter mixture, otherwise the kisses will be too moist to set properly.

Sweet Peanut Wafers

Delicate wafers filled with a sweet, peanut-flavoured buttercream make a fun, no-bake recipe that kids of any age can help with. Just remember to chill the wafer sandwiches after they have been assembled, otherwise they will be almost impossible to cut.

Makes 12

65g/2½oz/4 tbsp unsalted (sweet) butter, at room temperature, diced
65g/2½oz/generous ½ cup icing (confectioners') sugar
115g/4oz/½ cup crunchy peanut butter
12 fan-shaped wafers
50g/2oz plain (semisweet) chocolate

1 Put the butter and sugar in a bowl and beat with a hand-held electric whisk until very light and creamy. Beat in the peanut butter.

2 Using a small palette knife (metal spatula), spread a thick layer of the mixture on to a wafer and spread to the edges.

3 Place another wafer on top of the peanut buttercream and press it down very gently. Spread the top wafer with more buttercream, then place another wafer on top and press down gently.

4 Use the remaining buttercream and wafers to assemble three more fans in the same way. Spread any remaining buttercream around the sides of the fans. Chill for at least 30 minutes until firm.

5 Using a serrated knife, carefully slice each fan into three equal wedges and arrange in a single layer on a small tray.

6 Break the chocolate into pieces and put in a heatproof bowl placed over a pan of gently simmering water. Stir frequently until melted.

7 Remove the bowl from the heat and leave to stand for a few minutes to cool slightly.

8 Drizzle lines of chocolate over the wafers, then leave to set in a cool place for at least 1 hour.

Cookies for Special Diets

Food intolerances, allergies and health problems need not deprive you of the pleasures of baking and eating home-made cookies. You will be amazed by the range of low-fat, dairy-free, reduced-sugar or gluten-free sweet treats you can make – and what's more, they're so scrumptious, the whole family will be clamouring for them. Whether layered slices or fabulous brownies, the cookies in this chapter are special in every way.

Very Low-fat Brownies

If you ever need proof that you can still enjoy sweet treats even when you are on a low-fat diet, here it is. These brownies are not just tasty, but also very quick and easy to make.

Makes 16

100g/3½oz/scant 1 cup plain
   (all-purpose) flour
2.5ml/½ tsp baking powder
45ml/3 tbsp (unsweetened) cocoa
   powder
200g/7oz/1 cup caster (superfine) sugar
100ml/3½fl oz/scant ½ cup natural
   (plain) low-fat yogurt
2 eggs, beaten
5ml/1 tsp vanilla essence (extract)
25ml/1½ tbsp vegetable oil

1 Preheat the oven to 180°C/350°F/ Gas 4. Line a 20cm/8in square cake tin (pan) with baking parchment.

2 Sift the flour, baking powder and cocoa powder into a bowl. Stir in the caster sugar, then beat in the yogurt, eggs, vanilla and vegetable oil until thoroughly combined. Put the mixture into the prepared tin.

3 Bake for about 25 minutes until just firm to the touch. Leave in the tin until cooled completely.

4 Using a sharp knife, cut into 16 squares, then remove from the tin using a spatula.

Carob Chip Shorties

Perfect for anyone on a gluten-free or cow's-milk-free diet, these lovely cookies are best eaten freshly made, preferably while still slightly warm from the oven.

Makes 12

175g/6oz/1½ cups gluten-free flour
25g/1oz/2 tbsp soft light brown sugar
75g/3oz/6 tbsp vegetable margarine
50g/2oz/⅓ cup carob chips
15–25ml/1–1½ tbsp clear honey, warmed
demerara (raw) or caster (superfine) sugar, for sprinkling

1 Preheat the oven to 160°C/325°F/ Gas 3. Line two baking sheets with baking parchment.

Cook's Tip
Gluten-free flour can be bought at most health-food stores.

2 Put the flour and brown sugar in a mixing bowl and rub in the margarine. Add the carob chips, then stir in just enough honey to bring the mixture together but not make it sticky. Roll the dough out between two sheets of baking parchment to about 8mm/⅓in.

3 Stamp out rounds using a plain 5cm/2in round biscuit (cookie) cutter. Place on the baking sheets. Prick each cookie once with a fork and sprinkle with sugar.

4 Bake for about 15–20 minutes, or until firm. Cool on a wire rack.

Rocky Road Wedges

Free from gluten and wheat, these crumbly chocolate wedges contain home-made popcorn in place of broken cookies, which are the classic ingredient in no-bake cookies such as this. This recipe uses an orange-flavoured chocolate bar, but any gluten-free chocolate can be used.

Makes 8

15ml/1 tbsp vegetable oil
25g/1oz/2½ tbsp popping corn
150g/5oz orange-flavoured plain
   (semisweet) chocolate
25g/1oz/2 tbsp unsalted (sweet)
   butter, diced
75g/3oz soft vanilla fudge, diced
icing (confectioners') sugar, for dusting

Cook's Tip

When buying products such as chocolate or fudge, always check the label to make sure they are gluten-free.

1 Heat the oil in a heavy pan. Add the popping corn, cover with a lid and heat, shaking the pan once or twice, until the popping noises die down. (It is important not to lift the lid until the popping stops.)

2 Remove the pan from the heat and leave for about 30 seconds before removing the lid. Be careful, as there may be quite a lot of steam trapped inside. Transfer the popcorn to a bowl and leave to cool for about 5 minutes.

3 Meanwhile, line the base of an 18cm/7in sandwich tin (pan).

4 Once cooled, tip the corn into a plastic bag and tap with a rolling pin to break up into small pieces.

5 Break the chocolate into a heatproof bowl. Add the butter and rest the bowl over a pan of gently simmering water. Stir frequently until melted. Remove the bowl from the heat and leave to cool for 2 minutes.

6 Stir the popcorn and fudge into the chocolate until well coated, then turn the mixture into the tin and press down firmly in an even layer. Leave to set for about 30 minutes.

7 Turn the cookie out on to a board and cut into eight wedges. Serve lightly dusted with sugar.

Meringue Squiggles

Free from gluten, wheat and cow's milk, these wiggly wands are great for children's parties. They are fun to shape and eat, and kids of all ages love making and decorating them. Be sure to check that the multi-coloured sprinkles are free from gluten and cow's milk.

Makes 14–16

2 egg whites
90g/3½oz/½ cup caster
 (superfine) sugar
45ml/3 tbsp icing (confectioners') sugar
multi-coloured sugar sprinkles,
 to decorate

1 Preheat the oven to 150°C/300°F/ Gas 2. Line a large baking sheet with baking parchment.

2 Put the egg whites in a large, clean bowl and whisk with a hand-held electric whisk until they form firm peaks.

3 Add a spoonful of caster sugar to the whisked egg whites and whisk for about 15 seconds to combine. Add another spoonful and whisk again. Continue in this way until all the sugar has been added.

4 Spoon the meringue mixture into a large piping (pastry) bag fitted with a large plain nozzle. Alternatively, spoon the mixture into a plastic bag, gently push it into one corner and snip off the tip so that the meringue can be pushed out in a 2cm/¾in-thick line.

5 Pipe wavy lines of meringue, about 13cm/5in long, on to the baking sheet and bake for about 1 hour until dry and crisp.

6 Carefully peel the meringues off the baking parchment and transfer to a wire rack to cool.

7 Put the icing sugar in a small bowl and mix in a few drops of water to make a smooth paste.

8 Using a fine pastry brush, brush the tops of the meringues with a little of the sugar paste, then scatter over the multi-coloured sugar sprinkles to decorate.

Cashew Nut Button Cookies

These light little cookies, flavoured with ground cashew nuts, are coated in toasted hazelnuts. They are suitable for people on gluten-free and cow's-milk-free diets.

Makes about 20

1 egg white

25g/1oz/2 tbsp caster
   (superfine) sugar

150g/5oz/1¼ cups unroasted cashew
   nuts, ground

50g/2oz/⅓ cup dates,
   finely chopped

5ml/1 tsp finely grated
   orange rind

30ml/2 tbsp pure maple or
   maple-flavoured syrup

90g/3½oz/scant 1 cup toasted
   hazelnuts, chopped

1 Preheat the oven to 190°C/375°F/ Gas 5. Line two baking sheets with baking parchment.

2 In a bowl, whisk the egg white until stiff. Whisk in the sugar. Stir in the cashews, dates, orange rind and syrup. Mix well. Put the chopped hazelnuts in a small bowl.

3 Drop small spoonfuls of the cookie mixture into the hazelnuts and toss until well coated.

4 Place on the prepared baking sheets and bake for about 10 minutes until lightly browned. Leave to cool on the baking sheets.

Fruit and Millet Treacle Cookies

These little cookies are quick to make, and will no doubt disappear just as quickly when they come out of the oven. They are gluten- and cow's milk-free.

Makes about 25–30

90g/3½oz/7 tbsp vegetable
   margarine
150g/5oz/⅔ cup light muscovado
   (brown) sugar
30ml/2 tbsp black treacle (molasses)
1 egg
150g/5oz/1¼ cups gluten-free flour
50g/2oz/½ cup millet flakes
50g/2oz/½ cup almonds, chopped
200g/7oz/generous 1 cup luxury
   mixed dried fruit

Cook's Tip
Make sure that you use millet flakes for these cookies rather than millet grains. The grains will swell too much during cooking and spoil the cookies.

1 Preheat the oven to 190°C/375°F/ Gas 5. Line two large baking sheets with baking parchment.

2 Put the margarine, muscovado sugar, treacle and egg in a large bowl and beat together until well combined. (The mixture should be light and fluffy.)

3 Stir in the flour and millet flakes, the almonds and dried fruit. Put tablespoonfuls of the mixture on to the prepared baking sheets.

4 Bake for about 15 minutes until brown. Leave on the baking sheets for a few minutes, then transfer to a wire rack to cool completely.

Big Macs

These giant macaroons are crisp on the outside, chewy in the middle and naturally free from gluten and cow's milk. Ground almonds can be a great alternative to the wheat flour used in most cookies, and macaroons don't need butter for their deliciously moist, rich taste.

Makes 9

2 egg whites
5ml/1 tsp almond essence (extract)
115g/4oz/1 cup ground almonds
130g/4½oz/generous 1 cup light
   muscovado (brown) sugar

Cook's Tips

• *These macaroons will store well in an airtight container; do not store in the refrigerator because they'll turn soft and lose their lovely crisp and chewy texture.*
• *To make a macaroon with a milder flavour, use caster (superfine) sugar in place of the light muscovado sugar.*

1 Preheat the oven to 180°C/350°F/ Gas 4. Line a large baking sheet with baking parchment. Put the egg whites in a large, clean bowl and whisk until they form stiff peaks.

2 Add the almond essence to the egg whites and whisk to combine. Sprinkle over the ground almonds and sugar and gently fold in using a large metal spoon.

3 Place nine spoonfuls of the mixture, spacing them well apart, on to the baking sheet and flatten slightly. Bake for 15 minutes until risen, deep golden and beginning to turn crisp.

4 Leave the macaroons on the baking sheets for 5 minutes, then transfer to a wire rack to cool.

Shortbread Ring Cookies

Decorated with colourful chopped sweets, these little gluten- and dairy-free cookies are great for younger kids. They make delicious lunchbox fillers or snacks during the day. Don't forget to check the ingredients on the jellied fruit sweets as some varieties could contain gluten.

Makes 8–10

150g/5oz/1¼ cups gluten-free flour
90g/3½oz/½ cup rice flour
finely grated rind of 1 lemon
75g/3oz/6 tbsp dairy-free margarine
50g/2oz/¼ cup caster (superfine) sugar
1 egg yolk
10ml/2 tsp water

For the topping

90g/3½oz/scant 1 cup icing
  (confectioners') sugar
50g/2oz/½ cup dairy-free margarine
small jellied fruit sweets (candies)

1 Put the gluten-free flour, rice flour, lemon rind and margarine in a food processor and process briefly to combine. Add the sugar, egg yolk and water and mix to a dough.

2 Turn the dough on to a lightly floured surface and knead. Wrap in clear film (plastic wrap) and chill for about 30 minutes.

3 Preheat the oven to 180°C/350°F/Gas 4. Grease a baking sheet.

4 Roll out the dough on a lightly floured surface to a thickness of about 5mm/¼in.

5 Using a 6.5cm/2½in plain or fluted cutter, cut out rounds and place on the baking sheet. Using a 4cm/1½in round cutter, cut out and remove the centre of each round.

6 Bake for about 20 minutes until beginning to turn pale golden. Leave on the baking sheet for 2 minutes, then transfer to a wire rack to cool.

7 To make the topping, put the icing sugar and margarine in a bowl and beat together until creamy.

8 Pipe or spoon the topping on to the ring cookies. Chop the jellied sweets into small pieces with a pair of scissors and gently press them into the cream to decorate.

Cornflake Caramel Slice

A wickedly decadent caramel layer nestles between the gluten-free base and the crispy cornflake topping. These cookies are simply irresistible – and fun to make too.

Makes 12
175g/6oz/¾ cup butter
150g/5oz/¾ cup caster (superfine) sugar
300g/10oz/2½ cups gluten-free flour
1 egg, beaten

For the topping
30ml/2 tbsp golden (light
 corn) syrup
397g/14oz can sweetened
 condensed milk
50g/2oz/¼ cup butter
90ml/6 tbsp sour cream
about 40g/1½oz/2 cups cornflakes
icing (confectioners') sugar (optional)

1 Preheat the oven to 190°C/375°F/Gas 5. And proceed to line a 28 × 18cm/11 × 7in shallow cake tin (pan) with baking parchment.

2 Melt the butter in a pan, then remove from the heat. Put the sugar and flour in a bowl. Add the beaten egg and melted butter and mix well. Press the mixture evenly into the base of the prepared tin.

3 Bake for about 20 minutes until golden brown. Leave the base to cool completely in the tin.

4 For the topping, heat the syrup, condensed milk and butter over a low heat for 10–15 minutes, stirring occasionally, until the mixture is thick and turns a caramel colour.

5 Remove from the heat and stir in the sour cream. Spread over the base. Sprinkle over the cornflakes and leave to set. Sprinkle with icing sugar, if using, and cut into bars.

Double Chocolate Slices

These delicious gluten-free cookies have a smooth chocolate base, topped with a mint-flavoured cream and drizzles of melted chocolate. Perfect for a teatime treat – or at any time of day.

Makes 12

200g/7oz/1¾ cups gluten-free flour
25g/1oz/2 tbsp (unsweetened)
   cocoa powder
150g/5oz/⅔ cup unsalted (sweet) butter,
   cut into small pieces
75g/3oz/¾ cup icing
   (confectioners') sugar

For the topping

75g/3oz white chocolate mint crisps
50g/2oz/¼ cup unsalted (sweet)
   butter, softened
90g/3½oz/scant 1 cup icing
   (confectioners') sugar
50g/2oz milk chocolate

1 Preheat the oven to 180°C/350°F/ Gas 4. Grease an 18cm/7in square shallow baking tin (pan) and line with a strip of baking parchment that comes up over two opposite sides. This will make it easier to remove the cookie base from the tin after baking.

4 To make topping, put the chocolate mint crisps in a polythene bag and tap firmly with a rolling pin until they are crushed. Beat the butter and sugar together until creamy, then beat in the crushed chocolate mint crisps. Spread the mixture evenly over the cookie base.

2 Put the flour and cocoa powder into a food processor and add the pieces of butter. Process briefly until the mixture resembles fine breadcrumbs. Add the icing sugar and mix briefly again to form a smooth soft dough.

3 Turn the flour mixture into the prepared tin and gently press out to the edges with your fingers to make an even layer. Bake for 25 minutes, then remove from the oven and leave the base to cool completely in the tin.

5 Melt the milk chocolate in a small heatproof bowl set over a pan of hot water. Lift the cookie base out of the tin; remove the paper. Using a teaspoon, drizzle the melted chocolate over the topping. Leave to set, then cut into squares.

Savoury Crackers

Cheese and biscuits is a classic combination, but there are many other occasions when a savoury crunch is just what is needed. Crackers go well with home-made soup and salads for a light lunch and make delicious snacks when you want something with a little bite to it. This superb collection of tasty recipes offers something for all occasions, from sophisticated Wheat Thins to rustic Herby Seeded Oatcakes.

Wheat Thins

These classic wheat biscuits are especially delicious with rich-tasting creamy cheeses, and also make a quick snack simply spread with butter when you are in a hurry.

Makes 18

175g/6oz/1½ cups fine stoneground
   wholemeal (whole-wheat) flour
pinch of salt
5ml/1 tsp baking powder
50g/2oz/½ cup coarse oatmeal
40g/1½oz/3 tbsp granulated sugar
115g/4oz/½ cup unsalted (sweet) butter,
   chilled and diced

Cook's Tip

These cookies are perfect for serving with a cheeseboard and look very pretty cut into different shapes. You could make star-shaped cookies for Christmas, or heart-shaped ones for Valentine's Day.

1 Preheat the oven to 190°C/375°F/ Gas 5. Put all the ingredients into a food processor and process until the mixture starts to clump. Tip out on to a floured surface, gather the dough together with your hands and roll out.

2 Stamp out 18 rounds with a 7.5cm/3in round biscuit (cookie) cutter. Place on an ungreased baking sheet. Bake for 12 minutes until just beginning to colour at the edges. Leave to cool slightly, then transfer to a wire rack to cool completely.

Poppy Seed and Sea Salt Crackers

These attractive little crackers are ideal to use as the base of drinks party canapés, or they can be served plain as tasty nibbles in their own right.

Makes 20

115g/4oz/1 cup plain (all-purpose) flour
1.5ml/¼ tsp salt
5ml/1 tsp caster (superfine) sugar
15g/½oz/1 tbsp butter
15ml/1 tbsp poppy seeds
about 90ml/6 tbsp single (light) cream

For the topping

a little milk
sea salt flakes

Variation

You can use black or white poppy seeds – or a mixture of the two – for these crackers, or substitute sesame, caraway or celery seeds, if you like.

1 Preheat the oven to 150°C/ 300°F/Gas 2. Put the flour, salt and sugar in a bowl and rub in the butter. Stir in the poppy seeds. Add enough cream to mix to a stiff dough. Roll out on a lightly floured surface to a 20 x 25cm/8 x 10in rectangle. Cut into 20 squares.

2 Place the dough squares on an ungreased baking sheet and brush sparingly with milk. Sprinkle a few sea salt flakes over each cracker.

3 Bake in the oven for 30 minutes until crisp but still pale. Transfer to a wire rack to cool.

Herby Seeded Oatcakes

The addition of thyme and sunflower seeds to this traditional recipe makes these oatcakes an especially good accompaniment to cheese – try them spread with goat's cheese or ripe Brie.

Makes 32

175g/6oz/1½ cups plain wholemeal
   (whole-wheat) flour
175g/6oz/1½ cups fine oatmeal
5ml/1 tsp salt
1.5ml/¼ tsp bicarbonate of soda
   (baking soda)
75g/3oz/6 tbsp white vegetable fat
15ml/1 tbsp fresh thyme leaves, chopped
30ml/2 tbsp sunflower seeds
rolled oats, for sprinkling

1 Preheat the oven to 150°C/300°F/ Gas 2. Sprinkle two ungreased, non-stick baking sheets with rolled oats and set aside.

2 Put the flour, oats, salt and soda in a bowl and rub in the fat until the mixture resembles fine breadcrumbs. Stir in the thyme.

3 Add just enough cold water (about 90–105ml/6–7 tbsp) to the dry ingredients to mix to a stiff but not sticky dough.

4 Gently knead the dough on a lightly floured surface until smooth, then cut roughly in half and roll out one piece on a lightly floured surface to make a 23–25cm/ 9–10in round.

4 Sprinkle sunflower seeds over the dough and press them in with the rolling pin. Cut into triangles and arrange on one of the baking sheets. Repeat with the remaining dough. Bake for 45–60 minutes until crisp but not brown. Cool on wire racks.

Rye and Caraway Seed Sticks

Wonderful with cocktails or pre-dinner drinks and a great addition to the cheese board, these long sticks are made with rye flour and have crunchy caraway seeds inside and out.

Makes 18–20

90g/3½oz/¾ cup plain (all-purpose) flour

75g/3oz/⅔ cup rye flour

2.5ml/½ tsp salt

2.5ml/½ tsp baking powder

90g/3½oz/7 tbsp unsalted (sweet)
   butter, diced

10ml/2 tsp caraway seeds

60ml/4 tbsp boiling water

1 Preheat the oven to 180°C/350°F/ Gas 4. Put the flours, salt and baking powder in a bowl and mix together. Add the butter and rub in until the mixture resembles fine breadcrumbs. Stir in 5ml/1 tsp of the caraway seeds. Add the water and mix well to form a soft dough.

2 Divide the dough into about 18 even-size pieces and, using your fingers, gently roll each one out to a long thin stick about 25cm/10in long. Do not use any flour when rolling out the sticks unless the mixture is a little too moist and try to make the sticks as uniform as possible.

3 Place the sticks on a non-stick baking sheet. Sprinkle over the remaining caraway seeds, rolling the sticks in any spilled seeds.

4 Bake the sticks in the oven for about 20 minutes until crisp. Remove from the oven and transfer carefully to a wire rack to cool.

Malted Wheat and Mixed Seed Crackers

These large crackers have plenty of crunch and flavour provided by the selection of different seeds that are used. They taste fabulous with robust farmhouse cheeses.

Makes 12–14

250g/9oz/2¼ cups Granary
   (whole-wheat) or malted wheat flour
2.5ml/½ tsp salt
2.5ml/½ tsp baking powder
115g/4oz/½ cup butter, chilled and diced
1 egg, beaten
30ml/2 tbsp milk, plus extra for brushing
15ml/1 tbsp pumpkin seeds
15ml/1 tbsp sunflower seeds
15ml/1 tbsp sesame seeds
2.5ml/½ tsp celery salt

1 Preheat the oven to 180°C/350°F/ Gas 4. Put the flour, salt, baking powder and butter in a bowl. Rub together until well combined.

2 Add the egg and milk and mix to a stiff dough. Roll out on a floured surface to about 5mm/¼in thick.

3 Using a pastry brush, brush a little milk over the rolled dough. Sprinkle all the pumpkin, sunflower and sesame seeds over the top in an even layer, then sprinkle the celery salt over the top.

4 Very gently, roll the rolling pin back and forth over the seeds to press them into the dough.

5 Stamp out rounds using a 10cm/4in plain cookie cutter, and place on a non-stick baking sheet, spacing them slightly apart. Alternatively, use a sharp knife to trim off the rough edges of the rolled out dough, then cut the dough into equal-size squares, rectangles or triangles.

6 Bake the crackers for about 15 minutes, or until just beginning to brown. Carefully transfer the crackers to a wire rack to cool completely.

Cook's Tips
• *To make your own celery salt, grind five parts lightly toasted celery seeds with one part sea salt. Transfer to an airtight container and store in a cool, dark place.*
• *You can also use other seeds if you prefer. Try using poppy seeds in place of the sesame seeds.*

Polenta Chip Dippers

These tasty Parmesan-flavoured batons are best served warm from the oven with a spicy, tangy dip. A bowl of Thai chilli dipping sauce or a creamy, chilli-spiked guacamole are perfect.

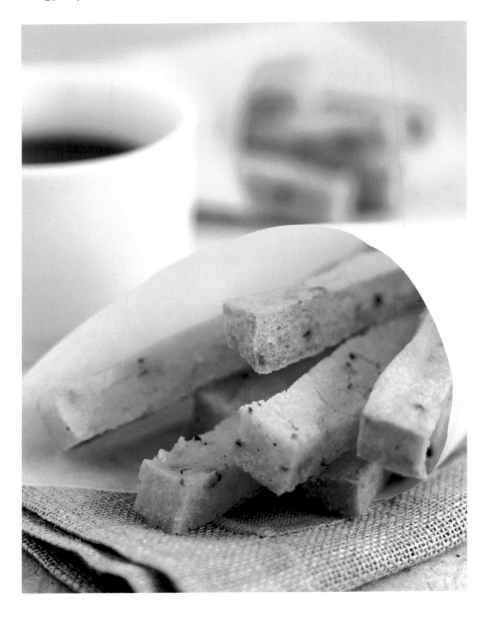

2 Remove the pan from the heat and add the cheese, butter, pepper and salt to taste. Stir well until the butter has completely melted and the mixture is smooth.

3 Pour on to a smooth surface, such as a marble slab or a baking sheet. Spread the polenta out using a palette knife (metal spatula) to a thickness of 2cm/¾in and shape into a rectangle. Leave for at least 30 minutes to become quite cold. Meanwhile preheat the oven to 200°C/400°F/Gas 6 and lightly oil two or three baking sheets with some olive oil.

4 Cut the polenta slab in half, then carefully cut into even-size strips using a sharp knife.

5 Bake the polenta chips for about 40–50 minutes until they are dark golden brown and crunchy. Turn them over from time to time during cooking. Serve warm.

Cook's Tip
The unbaked dough can be made a day ahead, then wrapped in clear film (plastic wrap) and kept in the refrigerator until ready to bake.

Makes about 80
1.5 litres/2½ pints/6¼ cups water
10ml/2 tsp salt
375g/13oz/3¼ cups instant polenta
150g/5oz/1½ cups freshly grated
   Parmesan cheese
90g/3½oz/scant ½ cup butter
10ml/2 tsp cracked black pepper
olive oil, for brushing
salt

1 Put the water in a large heavy pan and bring to the boil over a high heat. Reduce the heat, add the salt and pour in the polenta in a steady stream, stirring constantly with a wooden spoon. Cook over a low heat, stirring constantly, until the mixture thickens and starts to come away from the sides of the pan — this will take about 5 minutes.

Herb and Garlic Twists

These twists are very short and crumbly, made with garlic-flavoured dough sandwiching with fresh herbs and some chilli flakes for an extra kick. A very popular party nibble.

Makes about 20

90g/3½oz/scant ½ cup butter, at room
    temperature, diced
2 large garlic cloves, crushed
1 egg
1 egg yolk
175g/6oz/1½ cups self-raising
    (self-rising) flour
large pinch of salt
30ml/2 tbsp chopped fresh mixed
    herbs, such as basil, thyme,
    marjoram and flat
    leaf parsley
2.5–5ml/½–1 tsp dried chilli flakes
paprika or cayenne pepper,
    for sprinkling

1 Preheat the oven to 200°C/400°F/ Gas 6. Put the butter and garlic into a bowl and beat well. Add the egg and yolk and beat in thoroughly. Stir in the flour and salt and mix to a soft but not sticky dough.

2 Roll the dough out on a sheet of baking parchment to a 28cm/11in square. Using a sharp knife, cut it in half to make two rectangles.

3 Sprinkle the herbs and chilli flakes over one of the rectangles, then place the other rectangle on top. Gently roll the rolling pin over the herbs and chilli flakes to press them into the dough.

4 Using a sharp knife, cut the dough into 1cm/½in sticks. Make two twists in the centre of each one and place on a non-stick baking sheet.

5 Bake the twists for 15 minutes, or until crisp and golden brown. Leave on the baking sheet to cool slightly, then carefully transfer to a wire rack to cool completely. To serve, sprinkle with a little paprika or cayenne pepper, according to taste.

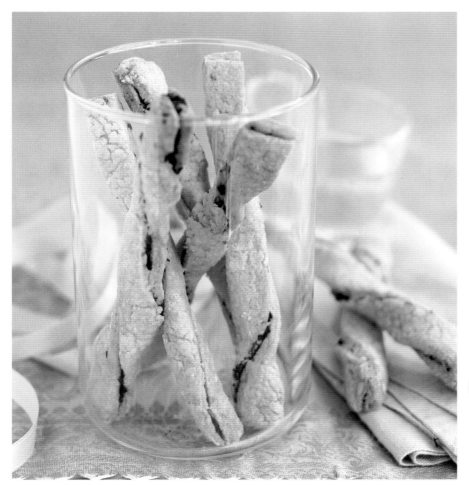

Cook's Tip

If the dough seems a little too soft to handle, wrap it in clear film (plastic wrap) and chill in the refrigerator for about 15 minutes to firm up. It will be much easier to roll it out.

Walnut Biscotti

These light crunchy cookies with toasted walnuts are flavoured with orange and coriander seeds.

Makes about 40
115g/4oz/½ cup unsalted (sweet)
  butter, diced
200g/7oz/1 cup granulated sugar
2 eggs
15ml/1 tbsp walnut or olive oil
finely grated rind of 1 large orange
350g/12oz/3 cups plain
  (all-purpose) flour
7.5ml/1½ tsp baking powder
75g/3oz/¾ cup cornmeal
115g/4oz/1 cup toasted walnuts, chopped
10ml/2 tsp coriander seeds, crushed

Cook's Tip
*To toast the nuts, spread them on a
baking sheet and place in the oven at
160°C/325°F/Gas 3 for 5–7 minutes until
just beginning to brown.*

1 Preheat the oven to 160°C/325°F/
Gas 3. Put the butter and sugar into
a bowl and beat together well. Add
the eggs, walnut or olive oil and
orange rind and mix well. Sift the
flour and baking powder over the
mixture and add the cornmeal,
walnuts and coriander seeds. Mix
thoroughly and bring together to
form a soft but not sticky dough.

2 Shape the dough into four logs,
about 18cm/7in long and 5cm/2in
in diameter. Place slightly apart on
non-stick baking sheets. Bake for
35 minutes until lightly golden.

3 Leave the logs for 10 minutes on
wire racks, then slice diagonally into
1cm/½in slices. Place on the baking
sheets and bake for 10 minutes.

Sun-dried Tomato Butter Cookies

These buttery cookies have all the flavours of classic pizza – cheese, tomato, oregano and olives.

Makes about 25

175g/6oz/1½ cups plain
    (all-purpose) flour
150g/5oz/10 tbsp unsalted (sweet)
    butter, chilled and diced
150g/5oz/1¼ cups grated mature (sharp)
    Cheddar cheese
15ml/1 tbsp sun-dried tomato paste
25g/1oz semi-dried sun-dried tomatoes,
    coarsely chopped
15ml/1 tbsp oregano
15g/½oz/2 tbsp pitted black olives, drained
15–30ml/1–2 tbsp cold water
50g/2oz sesame seeds

1 Put all the ingredients, except the water and sesame seeds, into a food processor. Process until the mixture forms fine crumbs.

2 Add enough water to mix to a soft dough, then shape it into a neat log about 25cm/10in long. Spread out the sesame seeds over a sheet of baking parchment or on a large plate. Roll the dough log in the seeds until the sides are thoroughly coated. Wrap in clear film (plastic wrap) and chill for about 2 hours.

3 Preheat the oven to 180°C/350°F/ Gas 4. Remove the clear film from the dough log. Using a long, sharp knife, slice the log into 5mm/¼in slices and place on non-stick baking sheets, spaced slightly apart. Bake for 15–20 minutes, or until golden brown. Transfer the cookies to a wire rack to cool.

Parmesan Tuiles

These lacy tuiles look very impressive, but they couldn't be easier to make. Believe or not, they use only a single ingredient – Parmesan cheese.

Makes 8–10

115g/4oz Parmesan cheese

1 Preheat the oven to 200°C/400°F/ Gas 6. Line two baking sheets with baking parchment. Grate the cheese using a fine grater, pulling it down slowly to make long strands.

Cook's Tip

Tuiles can be made into little cup shapes by draping over an upturned egg cup. These little cups can be filled to make tasty treats to serve with drinks. Try a little cream cheese flavoured with herbs.

2 Spread the grated cheese out in 7.5–9cm/3–3½in rounds. Do not spread the cheese too thickly; it should just cover the parchment. Bake for 5–7 minutes until bubbling and golden brown.

3 Leave on the baking sheet for about 30 seconds and then carefully transfer, using a palette knife (metal spatula) to a wire rack. Alternatively, drape over a rolling pin to make a curved shape.

Three-cheese Crumble Cookies

A delicious combination of mozzarella, Red Leicester and Parmesan cheese and the fresh taste of pesto make these cookies totally irresistible. Make mini ones to serve with drinks.

Makes 10

225g/8oz/2 cups self-raising
(self-rising) flour
50g/2oz/¼ cup butter, diced
50g/2oz mozzarella cheese, diced
50g/2oz Red Leicester cheese, diced
15ml/1 tbsp fresh pesto
1 egg
60ml/4 tbsp milk
15g/½oz/2 tbsp grated Parmesan cheese
15ml/1 tbsp mixed chopped nuts

| Preheat the oven to 200°C/400°F/ Gas 6. Put the flour in a bowl and rub in the butter until the mixture resembles fine breadcrumbs.

2 Add the diced mozzarella and Red Leicester cheeses to the bowl and stir to mix well. In a separate bowl, beat together the pesto, egg and milk, then pour into the flour and cheese mixture. Stir together quickly until well combined.

3 Using a tablespoon, place in rocky piles on non-stick baking sheets. Sprinkle over the Parmesan cheese and chopped nuts. Bake for 12–15 minutes until well risen and golden brown. Transfer to a wire rack to cool.

Fennel and Chilli Ring Cookies

Based on an Italian recipe, these cookies are made with yeast and are dry and crumbly. Try them with drinks, dips or with antipasti.

Makes about 30

500g/1lb 2oz/4½ cups type 00 flour
115g/4oz/½ cup white vegetable fat
5ml/1 tsp easy-blend (rapid-rise) yeast
15ml/1 tbsp fennel seeds
10ml/2 tsp crushed chilli flakes
15ml/1 tbsp olive oil
400–550ml/14–18fl oz/1⅔–2½ cups
   lukewarm water
olive oil, for brushing

1 Put the flour in a bowl and rub in the fat until the mixture resembles fine breadcrumbs. Add the yeast, fennel and chilli and mix well. Add the oil and enough water to make a soft but not sticky dough. Turn out on to a floured surface and knead lightly.

2 Take small pieces of dough and shape into sausages about 15cm/6in long. Shape into rings and pinch the ends together.

3 Place the rings on a non-stick baking sheet and brush lightly with olive oil. Cover with a dishtowel and set aside at room temperature for 1 hour to rise slightly.

4 Meanwhile, preheat the oven to 150°C/300°F/Gas 2. Bake the cookies for 1 hour until they are dry and only slightly browned. Leave on the baking sheet to cool completely.

Cook's Tip

Type 00 is an Italian grade of flour used for pasta. It is milled from the centre part of the endosperm so that the resulting flour is much whiter than plain (all-purpose) flour. It contains 70 per cent of the wheat grain. It is available from Italian delicatessens and some large supermarkets. If you cannot find it, try using strong white bread flour instead.

Curry Crackers

Crisp curry-flavoured crackers are very good with creamy cheese or yogurt dips and make an unusual nibble with pre-dinner drinks. Add a pinch of cayenne pepper for an extra kick.

Makes about 30

175g/6oz/1½ cups self-raising
   (self-rising) flour
pinch of salt
10ml/2 tsp garam masala
75g/3oz/6 tbsp butter, diced
5ml/1 tsp finely chopped fresh
   coriander (cilantro)
1 egg, beaten

For the topping

beaten egg
black onion seeds
garam masala

1 Preheat the oven to 200°C/400°F/ Gas 6. Put the flour, salt and garam masala into a bowl. Rub in the butter until the mixture resembles fine breadcrumbs. Stir in the coriander, add the egg and mix to a soft dough.

Cook's Tip

Garam masala is a mixture of Indian spices, that usually contains a blend of cinnamon, cloves, peppercorns, cardamom seeds and cumin seeds. You can buy it ready-made or make your own.

2 Turn out on to a lightly floured surface and knead gently until smooth. Roll out to a thickness of about 3mm/⅛in.

3 Using a fluted biscuit (cookie) wheel, knife or pizza wheel, cut the dough into neat rectangles measuring about 7.5 x 2.5cm/3 x 1in. Brush with a little beaten egg and sprinkle each cracker with a few black onion seeds. Place on non-stick baking sheets and bake in the oven for about 12 minutes until the crackers are light golden brown all over.

4 Remove from the oven and transfer to a wire rack using a palette knife (metal spatula). Put a little garam masala in a saucer and, using a dry pastry brush, dust each cracker with a little of the spice mixture. Leave to cool before serving.

index

A

alcohol flavouring, 17
all-in-one method, 27
almonds:
  almond, orange and carrot
    bars, 208
  almond-scented chocolate cherry
    wedges, 213
  almond and vanilla cookies with
    praline coating, 184
  Big Macs, 232
  chocolate nut slice, 215
  citrus drops, 70
  kourabiedes, 117
  layered fruit and nut bar cookie, 40
  simple almond cookies, 31
  soft almond cookies, 46
alphabetinis, 89
angels, Christmas tree, 118
Anzac cookies, 7
apples:
  apple crumble and custard slice, 174
  apple and elderflower stars, 73
  toffee apple and oat crunchies, 72
apricots:
  apricot and coconut kisses, 222
  apricot and pecan flapjacks, 140

B

baking cookies, 48–49
  baking problems, 61
banana cream cookies, 167

bar cookies, 40–43, 46
  baking, 49
  see also individual bar cookies
baskets, making, 30
Bath Olivers, 7
Big Macs, 232
bird's nests, chocolate, 216
birthday cookie, giant, 108
blueberries:
  Fourth of July blueberry
    softbakes, 124
brandy snaps, 29
  filling, 59
  making baskets with, 30
breakfast bars, fruity, 138
brownies, 42–43
  butterscotch brownies, 195
  chocolate cheesecake
    brownies, 194
  classic chocolate brownies, 42
  very low-fat brownies, 226
  white chocolate brownies, 196
butter, 10
butter cookies, 68
  sun-dried tomato butter
    cookies, 247
  Swiss butter cookies, 24
buttercream filling, 58
butterfly cookies, 187
butter gems, 88
butterscotch brownies, 195

C

candied peel crumble cookies, 165
cappuccino swirls, 79
caramel:
  chocolate caramel nuggets, 152
  cornflake caramel slice, 234
  marbled caramel chocolate
    slice, 160
  sablés with caramel glaze, 180
caraway seeds:
  rye and caraway seed sticks, 241
carob:
  carob and cherry cookies, 136
  carob chip shorties, 227
  iced carob cookies, 135
carrot:
  almond, orange and carrot
    bars, 208
cashew nut button cookies, 230
cheese:
  parmesan tuiles, 249
  polenta chip dippers, 244
  sesame cheese twists, 47
  three-cheese crumble cookies, 249
cheesecake:
  chocolate cheesecake
    brownies, 194
  citrus cheesecake topping, 41
cherries, glacé:
  almond-scented chocolate cherry
    wedges, 213
  carob and cherry cookies, 136
  mini party pizzas, 109
chewy flapjacks, 139
chilli:
  fennel and chilli ring cookies, 250
Chinese fortune cookies, 128
chocolate, 16–17
  almond-scented chocolate cherry
    wedges, 213
  chocolate birds' nests, 216
  chocolate box cookies, 156
  chocolate cheesecake
    brownies, 194
  chocolate chip cookies, 7, 28

chocolate cookies on sticks, 154
chocolate crispy cookies, 214
chocolate daisies, 37
chocolate-filled cookies, 59
chocolate florentines, 158
chocolate nut slice, 215
chocolate and pistachio
 wedges, 188
chocolate and prune cookies, 171
chocolate thumbprint
 cookies, 155
chocolate topping, 41
chocolate treacle snaps, 80
chocolate truffle cookies, 191
chocolate and vanilla swirls, 35
chocolate wands, 150
chocolate whirls, 153
classic brownies, 42
dark chocolate fingers, 189
double chocolate slices, 235
fruity chocolate cookie-cakes, 147
giant triple chocolate cookies, 149
marbled caramel chocolate slice, 60
mini chocolate Marylands, 46
nutty marshmallow and chocolate
 squares, 212
rich chocolate cookie slice, 148
rocky road wedges, 228
shape and bake cookies, 81
triple chocolate sandwiches, 159
white chocolate brownies, 196
white chocolate snowballs, 217

chocolate caramel nuggets, 152
chocolate ganache filling, 58
chocolate toppings, 41
Christmas tree angels, 118
churros, Spanish, 36
citrus cheesecake topping, 41
citrus drops, 70
citrus tuiles, rosemary-scented, 178
classic chocolate brownies, 42
classic shortbread, 25
coconut:
 apricot and coconut kisses, 222
 coconut and lime macaroons, 78
 fortune cookies, 128
cornflakes:
 banana cream cookies, 167
 cornflake caramel slices, 234
crackers, curry, 251
creaming method, 24
creamy fig and peach squares, 175
crème au beurre filling, 58
crumble topping, 41
crunch creams, Greek honey, 74
curry crackers, 251
custard:
 apple crumble and custard
  slice, 174

D
dark chocolate fingers, 189
dates:
 date slice, 142
 fig and date ravioli, 77
decorating cookies:
 after baking, 52–57
 before baking, 50–51
 chocolate, 56–57
 food-colouring pens, 53
 glazes, 51, 53
 icing, 54–55
 nuts, 50–51
 stencilling, 53
 sugar, 50, 52
digestive/Graham crackers, 7
dolly cookies, 91

double chocolate slices, 235
dried fruit, 14
 fruit and millet treacle cookies, 231
 fruity breakfast bars, 138
 fruity lemon drizzle bars, 203
 layered fruit and nut bar cookies, 40
 raisin cookies, 27
 rugelach, 126
 spicy fruit slices, 141
 sticky treacle slices, 200
 tropical fruit slices, 143
drop cookies, 28–30
 baking, 48

E
eggs, 13
elderflower and apple stars, 73
equipment, 18–23

F
fennel and chilli ring cookies, 250
figs:
 creamy fig and peach squares, 175
 fig and date ravioli, 77
filigree crowns, 36
fillings, 58–59
Flake "99s", 105
flapjacks:
 apricot and pecan flapjacks, 140
 chewy flapjacks, 139
 sticky lemon flapjacks, 46

flavourings:
  alcohol, 17
  chocolate, 16–17
  salt, 17
  spices and herbs, 17
florentines, 57
  chocolate florentines, 158
  florentine bites, 183
  florentine cookies, 164
flour, 12
flower power cookies, 90
food-colouring pens, 53
fork cookies, 39
fortune cookies, 7, 30,
  Chinese fortune cookies, 128
  secret message cookies, 113
Fourth of July blueberry softbakes, 124
fruit, dried see dried fruit
fruity chocolate cookie-cakes, 147
fudge bites, mini, 190
fudge-nut bars, 197

G
garlic:
  herb and garlic twists, 245
giant birthday cookie, 108
giant triple chocolate cookies, 149
ginger:
  gingerbread family, 92
  gingerbread house cookies, 111
  ginger cookies, 76
  ginger glass cookies, 179

gingernuts, 26
  rainbow gingerbread squares, 198
glacé cherries see cherries, glacé
glacé icing, 54
glazes, 51, 53
gold medals, 102
granola bar cookies, 137
grated shortbread topping, 41
Greek honey crunch creams, 74

H
hazelnut and raspberry bars, 209
hearts:
  pink sugared hearts, 86
  spicy hearts and stars, 116
  sweet hearts, 121
herbs, 17
  herb and garlic twists, 245
  herby seeded oatcakes, 240
history of cookies, 6–7
honey:
  Greek honey crunch creams, 74
  walnut and honey bars, 206

I
ice cream:
  ice cream sandwich cookies, 172
  ice cream sandwiches, 97
iced carob cookies, 135
ice mountain, 218
icing, 54–55
  glacé icing, 54
  icing glaze, 55
  royal icing, 55
ingredients, 10–17
Italian glazed lemon rings, 122

J
jam filling, 58
  jammie bodgers, 84
  peanut butter and jelly cookies, 69
jelly bean cones, 112
jewelled shortbread fingers, 201
jumble cookies, 7

K
ker-runch cookies, 134
kourabiedes, 117

L
lace cookies, 182
langues de chats, 35
layered fruit and nut bar cookies, 40
lemon:
  fruity lemon drizzle bars, 203
  Italian glazed lemon rings, 122
  luscious lemon bars, 204
  sticky lemon flapjacks, 46
lime:
  coconut and lime macaroons, 78
low-fat orange oaties, 132
luscious lemon bars, 204
luxury muesli cookies, 133

M
macadamia nuts:
  giant triple chocolate cookies, 149
macaroons:
  coconut and lime macaroons, 78
madeleines, 38
malted wheat and mixed seed
  crackers, 242
marbled caramel chocolate slice, 160
Maria cookies, 7
marmalade:
  sticky marmalade squares, 205

marshmallows:
   marshmallow toasties, 202
   nutty marshmallow and chocolate
      squares, 212
Marylands:
   mini chocolate Marylands, 146
marzipan:
   mini party pizzas, 109
   simnel cookies, 125
   speculaas, 120
melted drop cookies, 29–30
melted method, 26
meringues:
   meringue squiggles, 229
   meringue topping, 41
methods:
   all-in-one method, 27
   creaming method, 24
   melted method, 26
   rubbing-in method, 25
   whisked method, 26
microwaves:
   melting chocolate, 56
   microwave cookies, 46–47
midnight cookies, 166
millet:
   fruit and millet treacle
      cookies, 231
mincemeat wedges, 207
mini chocolate Marylands, 146
mini fudge bites, 190
mini party pizzas, 109
moulded cookies, 38–39
muesli:
   luxury muesli cookies, 133
multi-coloured rolled cookies, 33

N

name cookies, 106
neopolitan slices, 33
neuris, 129
no-bake cookies, 45, 212–223
nuts, 15
   fudge-nut bars, 197
   Greek honey crunch creams, 74

layered fruit and nut bar
   cookie, 40
nut bar cookies, 173
shape and bake cookies, 81
as toppings, 50–51
see also individual nuts
nut caramel topping, 41

O

oats:
   apricot and pecan flapjack, 140
   chewy flapjacks, 139
   herby seeded oatcakes, 240
   low-fat orange oaties, 132
   puppy faces, 94
   sticky lemon flapjacks, 46
   toffee apple and oat crunchies, 72
orange:
   almond, orange and carrot
      bars, 208
   low-fat orange oaties, 132
   orange biscotti, 96
oyster cookies, 35
oznei Haman, 127

P

parmesan tuiles, 248
party bracelets, 103
peaches:
   creamy fig and peach
      squares, 175

peanuts:
   peanut butter and jelly cookies, 69
   peanut crunch cookies, 85
   sweet peanut wafers, 223
pecan nuts:
   apricot and pecan flapjacks, 140
   Persian rice flour cookies, 123
petit beurres, 7
pink piggies, 220
pink sugared hearts, 87
pinwheels, 33
piped cookies, 34–36
   baking, 48
pistachio nuts:
   chocolate and pistachio
      wedges, 188
polenta:
   orange biscotti, 96
   polenta chip dippers, 244
poppy seed and sea salt crackers, 239
praline:
   almond and vanilla cookies with
      praline coating, 184
   praline Pavlova cookies, 168
presentation and packaging, 62–65
pressed cookies, 37
   baking, 48
pretzels, 39
prunes:
   chocolate and prune cookies, 171
puppy faces, 94

Q

quick vanilla cookies, 44

R

rainbow gingerbread squares, 198
raisin cookies, 27
raising agents, 13
raspberries:
   hazelnut and raspberry bars, 209
refrigerator cookies, 44
   baking, 49
rice flour:
   Persian rice flour cookies, 123

rich chocolate cookie slice, 148
ring cookies, 32
rocky road wedges, 228
rolled cookies, 31–33
    baking, 49
    multi-coloured, 33
rosemary-scented citrus tuiles, 178
royal icing, 55
rubbing-in method, 25
rugelach, 126
rye and caraway seed sticks, 241

S
sablés with caramel glaze, 180
salt, 17
    sea salt and poppy seed
    crackers, 239
secret message cookies, 113
seeds:
    fruity breakfast bars, 138
    granola bar cookies, 137
    herby seeded oatcakes, 240
    malted wheat and mixed seed
    crackers, 242
    see also individual seeds
sesame cheese twists, 47
shape and bake cookies, 81
shortbread, 7, 38
    classic shortbread, 25
    jewelled shortbread fingers, 201
    shortbread ring cookies, 233
short-cut cookies, 44–47
silly faces, 110
simnel cookies, 125
simple almond cookies, 31
snickerdoodles, 7
snowballs, white chocolate, 217
soft almond cookies, 46
Spanish churros, 36
speculaas, 120
spices, 17
spicy fruit slices, 141
spicy hearts and stars, 116
stained glass windows, 100
stars, elderflower and apple, 73

stencilling, 53
sticky lemon flapjacks, 46
sticky marmalade squares, 205
sticky treacle slices, 200
storing:
    cookies, 60
    dough, 60
streusel topping, 41
sugar, 11
    decorating with, 52
    glazes, 53
    sugar-topped vanilla cookies, 71
    as topping, 50
sun-dried tomato butter
    cookies, 247
sweet hearts, 121
sweet peanut wafers, 223
Swiss butter cookies, 24
Swiss fingers, 35

T
tea finger cookies, 186
three-cheese crumble cookies, 249
thumbprint cookies, chocolate, 155
tiramisu cookies, 170
toffee apple and oat crunchies, 72
tomato:
    sun-dried tomato butter
    cookies, 247
toppings, 41
train cookies, 104
treacle:
    chocolate treacle snaps, 80
    fruit and millet treacle
    cookies, 231
    sticky treacle slices, 200
tree cookies, 95
triple chocolate cookies, giant, 149
triple chocolate sandwiches, 159
tropical fruit slice, 143
tuiles, 26–27
    making baskets with, 30
    parmesan tuiles, 248
    rosemary-scented citrus tuiles, 178
two-tone cookies, 33

V
vanilla:
    almond and vanilla cookies
    with praline coating, 184
    chocolate and vanilla
    swirls, 35
    quick vanilla cookies, 44
    sugar-topped vanilla cookies, 71
    vanilla flowers, 37
very low-fat brownies, 226
Viennese cookies, 35
Viennese piped cookies, 34
Viennese whirls, 35

W
walnuts:
    candied peel crumble
    cookies, 165
    nutty marshmallow and
    chocolate squares, 212
    rugelach, 126
    walnut biscotti, 246
    walnut and honey bars, 206
wands, chocolate, 150
wheat:
    malted wheat and mixed seed
    crackers, 242
    wheat thins, 238
whisked method, 26–27
white chocolate brownies, 196
white chocolate snowballs, 217